11/25/80

From: David, Susan,
Michelle & Melissa

ILLUSTRATED HISTORY OF
BASKETBALL

ILLUSTRATED HISTORY OF
BASKETBALL

BY LARRY FOX

GROSSET & DUNLAP
PUBLISHERS   NEW YORK

To my father

COPYRIGHT © 1974 BY LARRY FOX

ALL RIGHTS RESERVED

PUBLISHED SIMULTANEOUSLY IN CANADA

LIBRARY OF CONGRESS CATALOG CARD NUMBER: 72-90847

ISBN 0-448-11622-7

FIRST PRINTING

PRINTED IN THE UNITED STATES OF AMERICA

CONTENTS

ACKNOWLEDGMENTS

A COMPREHENSIVE WORK SUCH as this one requires assistance from so many sources that it is really quite humbling to list them. They range from college sports information directors mailing a press brochure that tells of their school's first basketball teams to members of the Hall of Fame who were happy to spend an hour or so reliving their memories. Who helped the most? I refuse to judge. They were all of great assistance, so I will list them alphabetically, with my thanks.

Clair Bee; Ernie Calverley; Ron Cantera, Harvard; Pat Culbert, Hamline University; Nick Curran, NBA; Jack Dolph; Bill Esposito, St. John's University; Ed Fabricius, Pennsylvania; Bob Gesslein, Long Island University; Al Glassey; Eddie Gottlieb; Curt Gowdy; George Halas; Bob Harrison; Jay Horwitz, NYU; Ned Irish; Joe Lapchick, Jr.; Prof. James McCormack; Thurlo McCrady, ABA; Walter McLaughlin, St. John's University; James S. Naismith; Jones Ramsey, University of Texas; Mike Recht, ABA; Adolph Rupp; Honey Russell; Al Shrier, Temple; Jay Simon, University of Kansas; Mrs. June Steitz, librarian at the Naismith Memorial Basketball Hall of Fame; Lee Williams, executive director Naismith Memorial Basketball Hall of Fame; George Wine, University of Iowa; Bill Young, University of Wyoming.

PICTURE CREDITS

Basketball Hall of Fame: 10, 12, 15, 16, 18, 20, 21, 22, 26, 28 *(left)*, 32, 38 *(right)*, 42, 45, 51, 52, 53, 62, 64, 65, 79, 80 *(right)*, 90, 115 *(top)*, 132, 156, 221, 234, 246
The Bettmann Archives: 29
Boston Celtics: 162, 172, 200, 214
Capital Bullets: 201, 202
Carolina Cougars: 230
Culver Pictures, Inc.: 21, 28 *(right)*, 37, 38 *(left)*, 39, 40, 91
DePaul University: 77
Duke University: 113
Geneva College: 34 *(left)*
Golden State Warriors: 196, 215
Eddie Gottlieb: 47, 50
Furman University: 117
Hamline University: 34 *(right)*
Harlem Globetrotters: 222, 223
Indiana Pacers: 228 *(bottom)*
Kansas City-Omaha Kings: 213
King Features: 96
Louisiana State University: 116, 147
Milwaukee Bucks: 208, 209
New York Daily News: 63, 98, 99, 100, 102, 103, 104
New York Nets: 231
Niagara University: 148
Oklahoma State University: 81
Passaic High School: 242-43

Philadelphia 76ers: 183 *(right)*
Phillips 66: 235
Phoenix Suns: 210
Rio Grande College: 119
Seattle Times: 112
Seton Hall University: 71, 72
Temple University: 114
UCLA: 133, 140, 141, 149-51
University of Cincinnati: 126
University of Houston: 143
University of Illinois: 74
University of Kansas: 115 *(bottom)*, 123
University of Kentucky: 89 *(top)*
University of Notre Dame: 152
University of Texas: 58
United Press International: 48, 55, 66, 69, 73, 76, 78, 80 *(left)*, 83, 84, 85, 87, 88, 89 *(bottom)*, 93, 121, 125 *(top)*, 128, 129, 130, 137, 154, 158, 163, 164, 165, 166, 167, 168, 174, 175, 176, 177, 178, 179, 180, 181, 182, 183 *(left)*, 185, 186, 189, 190, 191, 199, 204, 211, 212, 216, 217, 220, 228 *(top)*, 229, 238
West Virginia University: 125 *(bottom)*, 127
Wide World Photos: 70

Jacket photograph:
Julius Erving *(front)* and Artis Gilmore *(back)* by Barton Silverman

INTRODUCTION

WHEN DR. JAMES NAISMITH, the inventor of basketball, first went to a game in Madison Square Garden and saw that it was witnessed by almost twenty thousand people, he was surprised and dismayed. Surprised, because he had never realized how popular his game had become; dismayed, because all these people were watching basketball and not playing it.

Why has basketball become such a popular sport in so few years? Possibly because it's a public game for a private person. A young man can practice by himself for hours, developing many of the individual skills necessary to play the game; and competition can be carried on with any number of players, starting with two, and in the most limited areas, indoors and out. "In the playground, it has found one of its most fruitful spheres," Dr. Naismith wrote in 1914, and his words are certainly just as true today.

Since virtually no youngster in this country, of either sex, reaches maturity without having played some competitive basketball, it's no wonder the sport has such spectator appeal.

Basketball's success, however, does not obscure its problems, but seems to emphasize them. No major sport has ever known the scandals that have twice afflicted basketball—and there is no guarantee that such scandals will not recur.

Cutthroat recruiting for top players is still the rule in college basketball. And the possibility of wrongdoing is worse in this sport than in any other, including football, because the recruitment of one superstar can so easily turn a college program around. If college administrators and coaches wink at entrance requirements and classroom absences and offer under-the-table bonuses to prospects, how are they fulfilling the ideals that the game embodies? How can they advance educational goals when many worry only about keeping a player eligible and care nothing about the ends of education?

The player, even though he may have been pampered and recruited by coaches since he was a teen-ager in high school, also carries a burden. Can he say no to the fixer? Can he attend classes regularly and choose courses that will bring him his degree on schedule?

The game of basketball is a great one, combining teamwork with individual expression. Its finest tribute may be that it has survived not only its enemies but its friends, who wrongly think that "win at any cost" should have been one of Dr. Naismith's original rules.

In writing this book I have made three editorial style decisions; for the first I offer an apology to anyone who may take offense. Kareem Abdul-Jabbar, the star center of the Milwaukee Bucks, was known in his childhood, in high school, and in his early professional career as Lew Alcindor. Since he figures in this book before he legally changed his name, I refer to him as Lew Alcindor.

The second decision involves the name of the game. In the past, the name of this game was written variously as two words or hyphenated, but I have the modern, one-word spelling, basketball, throughout.

Finally, it was awkward to refer constantly to seasons by the standard two-year reference, that is, 1900–01, 1914–15, and so on. For the sake of tidiness, I have often used one calendar year to identify a season. Whenever this occurs, the date marks the year in which the season was completed, which coincides with the dates of the various professional playoffs and college tournaments.

(1)

"HUH! ANOTHER NEW GAME"

DR. LUTHER H. GULICK was a concerned man in the winter of 1891. As head of the physical training department of the International Training School of the Young Men's Christian Association in Springfield, Massachusetts, he had long fretted over the lack of interest that American men showed in gymnastics or calisthenics. How could YMCAs around the nation attract young men during the winter, when football and baseball, the All-American sports, were out of season?

The problem was particularly acute at the Training School (later Springfield College), and this finally caused Dr. Gulick to seek the development of some new indoor sports activity. The Training School, which ex-isted to produce leaders for YMCAs throughout the world, had two courses of study, one for physical education instructors, one for "Y" executive secretaries and administrators. There were no problems involving the instructors; and in season even the secretaries gladly put in their required hour a day of physical training playing football or baseball. But in the winter they rebelled against the marching drills, calisthenics, Indian-club and medicine-ball routines that their instructors had imported from Europe.

They rebelled so strongly, in fact, that some accounts called them a class of "incorrigibles," although it seems ironic that this early version of the campus "radical" was in training to

Dr. James Naismith as he appeared in 1933.

11

Dr. Luther Gulick, who invited James Naismith to invent a new indoor recreation for the winter months.

run the local YMCA. But these men, aged twenty-six to thirty and thus older than the average college student, had already forced two instructors to quit the class and made Dr. Gulick wonder just where he could turn.

Then Dr. Gulick recalled a seminar he had given on the psychology of physical education. He had mentioned the need for a new indoor activity, but the class had derided the suggestion that one could be devised. Near the end of the session, however, twenty-nine-year-old James Naismith spoke up. "Doctor," he said confidently, "we can invent a new game that will meet your needs. All we have to do is take the factors of our known games and combine them."

The suggestion was not followed up at the time, but later Dr. Gulick remembered the boast and sought out Naismith, who was now on the faculty. "Naismith," he said, "I want you to take over that class and see what you can do with it. Now would be a good time to work on that new game you said could be invented."

As he pondered Dr. Gulick's challenge, Naismith found it more difficult than he had thought. At first he tried simple games, but they were too childish for mature students. "The boys simply would not play drop the handkerchief," he reported. Indoor rugby, with its fierce tackling, proved too rough. When he tried soccer, the students stubbed their toes trying to kick the ball while wearing ordinary sneakers and broke the windows when they succeeded in getting a foot into the ball. Lacrosse was a similar disaster.

Two weeks passed and Naismith was about to admit failure when he decided to give his class one more try. He would indeed invent a totally new game. As he had suggested during the seminar, he would adapt tried principles in a new combination.

All team sports used a ball, he thought, so he would start with that. But it had to be a large ball, because a small one would require bats or rackets and other equipment. A large ball would always be in sight, too, and easier to handle.

American rugby, or football, was the most popular large-ball game around, but Naismith had seen the damage that could be wrought by roughhouse tackling, especially indoors. "But if he can't run with the ball, we don't have to tackle!" Naismith exclaimed, and as he recalled in his autobiography, he snapped his fingers at the deduction. Now, if the player can't run with the ball, he must be able to advance it in some other way. Naismith wanted no bloody noses or barked shins; so passing was in and punching or kicking the ball was out.

Once he had the ball and a method for moving it, there had to be a purpose. He would add a goal, as in lacrosse; but again he saw the possibility of injury as players fired the ball goalward at full force in close quarters. Naismith reached back in his memory. As a child in Canada he had played a game called "Duck on a Rock," in which the object was to lob small stones onto a large rock while knocking off the opponents' "ducks." Naismith decided the goal would be horizontal like the rock of his childhood game, perhaps a box on the floor. With nine men on a side, however, the defense could merely surround the goal and make it impossible to score. How to prevent this? Simple. Place the goal above the players' heads.

Only one major problem remained. How to put the ball into play? Naismith was familiar with the rugby scrimmage in which the two full teams lined up head-to-head, the ball was thrown between them, and good luck. But what if only one man from each side was used? Thus was born the center jump.

Out of this long process Naismith drew up five guiding principles for his new game:

1. There must be a ball; it should be large, light, and handled with the hands.

2. There shall be no running with the ball.

3. No man on either team shall be restricted from getting the ball at any time that it is in play.

4. Both teams are to occupy the same area, yet there is to be no personal contact.

5. The goal shall be horizontal and elevated.

Weary from this mental exercise, Naismith tumbled into bed, but was to get little rest. He "played" the first game of his new sport over and over in his thoughts through the night. When he awoke, the basic rules were set in his mind.

The next morning, when he reported to his office, he saw a football and a soccer ball lying in the corner.

The football was designed to be carried, but no player would carry the ball in his new sport, so he picked the round soccer ball. Then he went to the gym. "Mr. Stebbins," he asked the janitor, "do you have any boxes, about eighteen inches square?"

"No, but I have two old peach baskets down in the storeroom," the janitor replied. Naismith himself nailed them to the edge of the balcony above the gym floor. The height was exactly ten feet. (It is that height today.) The peach baskets were fifteen inches across. (In later years, the diameter of the basket would be set at eighteen inches, just as Naismith had requested in the beginning.)

Then Naismith went into the office, wrote up thirteen rules for his new game, and asked the secretary, Miss Lyons, to type them.

Here they are:

The ball is to be an ordinary *Association* foot ball.*

1. The ball may be thrown in any direction with one or both hands.

2. The ball may be batted in any direction with one or both hands (never with the fist).

3. A player cannot run with the ball. The player must throw it from the spot on which he catches it, allowance to be made for a man who catches the ball when running if he tries to stop.

4. The ball must be held in or between the hands, the arms or body must not be used for holding it.

5. No shouldering, holding, pushing, tripping, or striking in any way the person of an opponent shall be allowed; the first infringement of this rule by any person shall count as a foul, the second shall disqualify him until the next goal is made, or, if there was evident intent to injure the person, for the whole of the game, no substitute allowed.

6. A foul is striking at the ball with the fist, violations of Rules 3, 4, and such as described in Rule 5.

7. If either side makes three consecutive fouls, it shall count as a goal for the opponents (consecutive means without the opponents in the mean time making a foul).

8. A goal shall be made when the ball is thrown or batted *from the grounds* into the basket and stays there, providing those defending the goal do not touch or disturb the goal. If the ball rests on the edges, and an opponent moves the basket, it shall count as a goal.

9. When the ball goes out of bounds, it shall be thrown into the field and played by the person first touching it. He has a right to hold it unmolested for five seconds. In case of a dispute the umpire shall throw it straight into the field. The thrower-in is allowed five seconds, if he holds it longer it shall go to the opponent. If any side persists in delaying the game the umpire shall call a foul on that side.

10. The umpire shall be the judge of the men and shall note the fouls and notify the referee when three consecutive fouls have been made. He shall have the power to disqualify men according to Rule 5.

11. The referee shall be the judge of the ball and shall decide when the ball is in play, in bounds, to which side it belongs, and shall keep the time. He shall decide when a goal has been made, and keep account of the goals,

* That is, a soccer ball.

with any other duties that are usually performed by a referee.

12. The time shall be two fifteen minutes' halves, with five minutes' rest between.

13. The side making the most goals in that time shall be declared the winners. In case of a draw the game may, by agreement of the captains, be continued until another goal is made.

After lunch Naismith collected his newly typed copy of the rules and posted it on the bulletin board at the Armory Street YMCA gymnasium, some blocks from the campus, where physical education classes were held. (The site is now a shopping center.)

"Huh! Another new game," snorted Frank Mahan of Tennessee when he saw the peach baskets, but Naismith promised his skeptical students that this would be the last experiment. He chose up sides, named Eugene Libby of Redlands, California, and Duncan Patton of Montreal—one of the five Canadians in the class—as captains, and showed the nine men on each side their positions.

The players, in black, long-sleeved woolen jerseys and long gray trousers, many sporting full mustaches, went at it. Naturally, there was a lot of fouling as the players struggled to get the hang of the new game. (Years later, one of them, Raymond Kaighn, would

A re-creation of the first basketball games in the International YMCA Training School before it was torn down.

The gymnasium where the first game took place in December 1891.

recall, "All of the players wanted to shoot—just like today.") William R. Chase of New Bedford, Massachusetts, scored the only goal on a shot from midcourt, and Mr. Stebbins had to climb a ladder to retrieve the ball. One of the players suggested that it might be wise to cut the bottom out of the basket so the ball could drop through.

The game was an immediate success, although through the early sessions sometimes as many as half the players on each team were on the sidelines for excessive fouling. Word of the game began to spread around the campus. Before long the secretaries found themselves playing in front of an audience of fellow students. Soon a group of young lady teachers from nearby Buckingham Grade School were coming by during the lunch hour to watch Naismith's pupils, by now wearing padded football pants or wrestling togs, compete in the new game.

The girls eventually asked if they could play too, and Naismith helped them organize a team. (He also married one of them, Maude Sherman.) The girls wore long dresses and high-necked shirts for their games, because men were present. (In 1896, when Stanford and California played the first reported intercollegiate game involving coeds, they wore middy blouses, bloomers, and long black hose—but no male spectators were allowed.)

Naismith's new game was born in the early weeks of December, 1891. When his students scattered for the Christmas holidays, many of them introduced the sport to their respective home towns. (Mahan, the first skeptic, had taken Naismith's original thirteen rules from the bulletin board for a souvenir, but, when he saw how popular the game might become, he returned them to the game's inventor.)

After vacation Mahan asked Naismith what he intended to call the new game. "How about Naismith-ball?" the student suggested. "No, that would kill any game," the modest instructor replied.

"Why not basketball?" Mahan offered.

"Well, we have a basket and a ball and it seems to me that would be a good name for it," Naismith answered. And basketball it would be.

2

IN THE BEGINNING

BASKETBALL BECAME AN international sport almost immediately. In January, 1892, a month after Naismith had tacked his rules to the bulletin board, the school newspaper, the *Triangle,* distributed to Ys throughout the world, published them under the heading "A New Game." By February the Elmira (N.Y.) Reformatory had a team (presumably they played all their games at home). And by April even the *New York Times* was writing about basketball.

That winter, according to Naismith, the Carroll Institute of Washington, D.C., became the first educational institution to play the game. And Cornell made history as the first college to try basketball—and the first to ban it. Although his first team had nine on a side (because his original class had numbered eighteen), Naismith envisioned basketball as an activity "any number can play." Cornell

tried to play the game with twenty-five on a side, but the rush from one end of the floor to the other by fifty players threatened the stability of the gym, and anxious administrators barred the game before the building collapsed.

To acquaint more people with the sport, Naismith put his basketball team on the road for exhibitions with Frank Mahan as the captain. (They traveled with a group of gymnasts from the training school known as the Springfield Flying Circus.) With Naismith's strong approval they enthusiastically promoted the new game. But Naismith visualized basketball as a recreational aid rather than as a highly competitive exercise. Two years after he had invented the sport, he suggested in a pamphlet that "at a picnic the baskets can be hung on a couple of trees and the game carried on as usual." He was also aware that basketball

The first basketball team. (*Back row, left to right*) John G. Thompson, Eugene S. Libby, Edwin P. Ruggles, William R. Chase, T. Duncan Patton; (*center*) Frank Mahan, James Naismith; (*front row*) Finlay G. MacDonald, William H. Davis, Lyman W. Archibald.

had become international in scope. By 1894 he could boast that the sport had spread "from Springfield to Paris, France, in one direction and to Melbourne, Australia, in the other."

Later he would give three reasons for the game's quick acceptance: "First, there was an absolute need for such a contribution; second, it was founded on fundamental principle; third, it was produced at an international institution, which gave it a world interest."

Naismith saw basketball as a sport for the average man and woman, not for the muscled behemoth. "I had in mind the tall, agile, graceful, and expert athlete," he wrote, referring to those who could "reach, jump, and act quickly and easily." Writing about its adaptability for the ladies, Naismith noted, "It has also been found valuable for girls and women, as there are few games which they can play that are not a strain on the nervous system rather than on bodily functions.

It is peculiarly adapted for giving health without involving severe mental strain." (In 1894 Naismith clearly did not anticipate either today's high-pressure, ulcer-producing competition or the women's liberation movement.)

In his 1894 pamphlet Naismith put down some principles for playing the game: "The object of the game is to put the ball in your opponent's goal," he wrote; but he warned, "Some teams are throwing for the goal all the time . . . only throw for the goal when there is a reasonable chance for making it. If you are so attacked that you cannot make a good throw [at the basket], instead of throwing wild, pass to the other *forward* or even the center. This is team play."

As for defense, he wrote, "A most common fault of green players is to be continually running after the ball. . . . Stick to your man like glue. Cover him so effectively that the ball cannot by any manner of means be passed into his hands."

The early game was taken up by women as well as men. This scene is from the Flushing (N.Y.) High School, which produced national high school boys' champions.

You'll hear the same at any coaching clinic today.

The first public game of basketball, according to Bill Mokray in *Ronald's Encyclopedia of Basketball,* was played on March 11, 1892, between the Training School secretaries (students) and their instructors. The secretaries, members of Naismith's original class, won, 5–1. The faculty group included Dr. Gulick, Naismith, and football's immortal Amos Alonzo Stagg, who wore his old Yale uniform. Naismith became rather upset by his colleague's rough play, even though Stagg ended up with a black eye. Other sources set the first public game at February 12, 1892, between the Central YMCA and the Armory Hill Branch in Springfield. The 2–2 tie was witnessed by a hundred spectators. (It was too early to call them fans.) A month later Armory Hill won the rematch, 1–0, before 250 viewers.

In a nine-man game, the players lined up like this:

BASKET.

O

Home.

L. Wing.   R. Wing   Forwards.

Center.

L. Center.   R. Center.   Center Men.

L. Guard.   R. Guard.   Guards.

Goal Keeper.

O

BASKET.

In those early games a field goal counted one point and a team was given a point every time its opponent committed three fouls. Later, field goals counted three points for a while, then were dropped to two, with teams being awarded free shots when they were fouled. The free-throw line was originally twenty feet from the basket and in 1897 was moved to fifteen.

In 1893 provision was made for five-man teams if the game was to be played in a small gym. Nine was still the standard for league games, and any number could play in a pickup contest. In 1894 the size of the teams was set at five, seven, or nine men, depending on the size of the gym. A year later, a team was placed at five unless the opponents "mutually agreed" on another number. And in 1897 the limit was established at five with no exceptions.

The cover and title page of *Rules for Basket Ball* as set down by Naismith in 1892.

Originally the ball had to be held in the hands and could not be hugged to the body. This restriction was abolished in 1908.

The out-of-bounds play under the original rules was an invitation to mayhem. The first player to touch the ball after it went out-of-bounds was allowed to throw it in. This led to some wild tussles as all the players on both teams would make a mad dash for the free ball. They did not hesitate to go through, or over, the spectators. Often the ball would be batted up to the balcony running track, which surrounded most gymnasiums, and then the scene looked like a Keystone Cops chase as eighteen men fought to be first up the stairs. (While most of the players wedged together on the narrow staircase, some smart teams hoisted a teammate to the balcony to beat the crush.) In 1913 the current rule was instituted: the team causing the ball to go out of bounds, or last touching it, loses possession.

The dribble was not part of Naismith's original plan but it quickly developed as a protective maneuver. If a player was guarded so closely that he could not pass off, he was allowed to throw the ball into the air (higher than his head) and then recover it. That one toss evolved into a series of throws and so the dribble was born. The dribble exists in basketball literature as far back as Naismith's 1894 account, which also called for twenty-minute halves, a referee, and two umpires (the idea of three officials is being pushed today as something quite new), and it warned that "the home team shall be held responsible for the behaviour of the spectators."

Naismith once said that "you don't coach basketball, you just play it," but many of Naismith's techniques were quite professional even then. His "qualities demanded in a successful team" are still pretty good criteria:

coolness, quickness, shooting accuracy, good judgment, endurance, self-control.

In 1895 Naismith left Springfield to become physical training director of the YMCA in Denver, Colorado. (Dr. Gulick took over his pupil's role as grand guru of the game and helped guide its future growth through the YMCAs.) While in Denver Naismith earned a degree as a medical doctor, and in 1898 he was recommended to head the physical education department at the University of Kansas. When he arrived at Kansas, basketball was considered a sissy sport, but he quickly put together a team. By December of 1898 the K.U. *Weekly* could report that "it appears that the basketball mania would carry all before it." That first team played in an old skating rink, which burned down after the season. Kansas won its first home game, 31–6, over the Topeka YMCA before a crowd that was limited to fifty by a "gas line freezeup." After nine seasons Dr. Naismith retired as coach; his record showed fifty-three victories and fifty-five losses.

Except for a leave of absence to serve with the YMCA in France during World War I, Dr. Naismith remained on the Kansas faculty until he retired in 1937. He is remembered as an enthusiastic teacher with a dry sense of humor. He also retained his interest in physical education and games that would help the students stay fit. Each Thanksgiving the freshman and sophomore classes staged an "Olympic" sports competition. If the freshmen won, as they always did, they no longer had to wear their distinctive and demeaning caps. One year Dr. Naismith, who was constantly trying to enliven the "Olympics," assigned a student to collect twenty old automobile tires. They were placed on the fifty-yard line of the football field. Two teams of twenty each lined up at the forty-yard lines. The opponents paired off, and at a signal they grabbed the tires and tried to pull them across the goal line, a sort of individual tug-of-war. At five-minute periods a whistle was blown, the various distances measured, and the score tabulated. Dr. Naismith thought his "War Tug" game might develop into a spectator sport. But after fifteen minutes, with the contestants exhausted and nobody closer to the goal than the ten-yard line, the battle was called off. "The game died a natural death," recalls the student who had been assigned to collect the tires. His name was Adolph Rupp.

Who was Dr. James Naismith? What manner of man was he? The story of the birth of basketball cannot be completed without a word about this truly remarkable sportsman, educator, minister, and physician.

Naismith was born in 1861 in Almonte, Ontario, some thirty-five miles west of Ottawa, and his parents died within days of each other just before his ninth birthday. He and his brother and sister were raised by a bachelor uncle.

Times were hard for the impromptu family, and Naismith never forgot that as a youngster he had had to improvise his own ice skates. He dropped out of high school for a couple of years to work in the lumber camps, which accounts for his sturdy physique, but an uncle persuaded him to return to school, and in 1884 he enrolled at McGill University.

Naismith's goal then was to enter the ministry, which he eventually did, but one evening he happened to be watching rugby practice when the center broke his nose. He volunteered to fill in. Thus his interest in sports was born. All through college and seminary Naismith played for the McGill rugby team. This shocked some of his less worldly seminary classmates who considered sport "the tool of the devil." Once several stayed up all night to pray for his soul, and there were also a lot of strange looks from the congregation when he showed up one Sunday to preach the sermon with two black eyes.

It was while competing in sports—he also played professional lacrosse—that Naismith realized he could do more to inspire clean living among young men through athletics than from the pulpit. After he finished his theology course he enrolled at the YMCA Training School in Springfield, Massachusetts.

At Springfield he met Dr. Gulick, who was to be a lifelong influence, and also Amos Alonzo Stagg, whose stature as one of the giants of football obscures his equally major role in basketball. Stagg, an all-sports All-America at Yale, had been, like Naismith, a theology major. At their first meeting Stagg gripped Naismith's hand as if grasping a baseball. The stocky Naismith responded with a wrestling-type hold, and they became friends through a long lifetime. (Stagg later organized a football team at Springfield, which was known as Stagg's Stubby Christians, and he placed Naismith at center because he could do "the meanest things in the most gentlemanly manner.")

The real man behind the Naismith Legend, though, comes through in an affectionate reminiscence. In a letter one of his sons, James S. Naismith, wrote:

"What kind of man was my father? Physically he was five feet nine inches tall and weighed approximately 200 pounds, had an 18-inch neck and wore a size 46 coat. At the time that he died, I still would not have wanted to engage him in physical combat. One time he said that the main thing about getting old was that you had to win your battles in a shorter length of time.

"Mentally he was very stimulating, and would go to great lengths to help you uncover many things that would affect your decisions; but he would not make your decision for you. Spiritually he was very strong in his faith (I am sure you know that he was a Presbyterian minister; I used to drive with him every Sunday out to the two small-town churches that he supplied, and thereby I acquired a lifelong aversion to chicken for dinner) and he had the feeling that a Christian should not back away from a decision simply because it was unpopular. To my knowledge he never swore, smoked or drank; however, he used to add to my pipe collection from time to time after I grew up and became a smoker.

"What was he like as a father? I think after reading the above you have some understanding of what he was like basically. A generation gap? Yes. And I am still trying to fill it in.

"We had many humorous things happen in our family, and he enjoyed them as much as his five children did. It was common for us children to sit around the table after the dishes were done until nearly midnight, discussing different ideas with him. Some would get up and leave to study, go to the movies, or leave for one reason or another, but they all would usually return before the discussion broke up. This kept up long after my older brother and sisters were married, when they returned for a visit.

"One of his classes was the physical development of the child, and when I was five days old he took me to class for the group to study; and since I was the fifth child and she was somewhat resigned to things by that time, Mother allowed it. However, when he brought me home covered with red, blue and yellow crayon markings, where he had outlined the major parts of his exhibit, that was evidently a mistake because Mother did not allow it a second time. (Of course you understand the above is purely hearsay.)

"What were his thoughts about the great game he invented? I think the main one was that you didn't need a coach. In fact, he said as much to Phog Allen one time. He enjoyed basketball. However, since he had played football for many years, I personally think he enjoyed watching football more.

"He was glad that the game he had invented was a success, but on the whole he treated it a good deal like he did his children—they were on their own. Around home we had the impression he was prouder of the fact that he

invented the first football helmet than of basketball. Actually my mother made him a helmet to his specifications, out of chamois skin, to protect his cauliflower ears.

"Did he play much basketball? To my knowledge, he never played it at all; however, some of my sisters say he played in a game or two.

"Did his children? His two boys, Jack and myself, never played basketball above the high school level. He insisted that we both be tumblers, and most of our efforts were along this line.

"Did he meet my mother through basketball? The story in our family is that Mother, along with other young ladies, dropped in to see the new game being played, and this may or may not have been their first meeting. My sisters, all three of them, could tell you very exactly, but all three of their stories would be different.

"What were my mother's thoughts about the game that basketball became? She definitely was not highly impressed, especially when Dad would bring in a visiting basketball team for lunch without letting her know beforehand."

Dr. James Naismith died at age seventy-eight in 1939, two years after he retired from the Kansas faculty. Few men have been blessed with such a vibrant, living memorial.

③

"A-BE-VO, BIVO BUM"

A-Be-vo, A-Bi-vo, A-Be-vo, Bivo Bum.
Bum get a rat trap, bigger than a cat trap.
Bum get a rat trap, bigger than a cat trap.
Bum Cannibals, cannibals, Sis! Boom! Bah!
Cambridge Young Men; Rah! Rah! Rah!
C-A-M-B-R-I-D-G-E, Cambridge!

WITH THIS STIRRING CHEER, the Cambridge(Massachusetts) YMCA basketball team was spurred to victory in 1893. As Y instructors read the rules of Naismith's new game in the *Triangle,* and as graduates of the Springfield Training School spread the gospel, the neighborhood YMCA rapidly became the center of basketball activity not just in Massachusetts, but in communities throughout the nation.

By October of 1892, less than a year after Naismith had devised his thirteen rules, the YMCA *Bulletin* of Philadelphia was reporting that "basketball is a new feature" of its program. Also in October, the Rochester (N.Y.) YMCA *Bulletin* promised "some royal sport can be had this winter with the introduction of basketball" and by December the same paper was crowing, "It's all the go!" The Geneva (N.Y.) Branch noted that same December that two teams had been organized "and so far only one [window] pane has been broken." By February basketball had "jumped into popularity" and was attracting large crowds to the branch on Wednesday and Saturday nights. Noting the dangers to the building from basketball, the Bedford Branch of Brooklyn told its members the game would be added to the program "as soon as guards can be placed over some of the windows." By the next January, the growing popularity of basketball had spurred the Zanesville (Ohio) YMCA to build a new gym, at a cost of $1,250.

About this time, the Pine Bluff

Game and equipment as used in 1892.

Early instructions in how to pass and to defend from Naismith and Gulick's early guide on how to play the game.

(Ark.) Y declared "basketball has done more to advance the physical department . . . than anything yet tried," and modestly named its new team The Invincibles. The title proved appropriate. Organized in October, 1892, the team played "about forty games" over the next two years and lost only one. (That defeat was due to "carelessness," a team partisan related.)

The Camden (N.J.) Y was the first to sponsor basketball in the Philadelphia area, a city that quickly developed into a literal hotbed for the sport, as it is to this day. Dr. Albert Doran, the Camden coach, is credited with organizing a team in the fall of 1892. The first candidate to try out was Randolph Carmer, about five feet

eleven. "A very fast dribbler and good long distance shot, he was the kind of player that would fit in nicely with the present style of play," one old-timer recalled only a few years ago.

Basketball soon became a thriving sport in the middle Atlantic states. In January, 1894, Trenton, the New Jersey YMCA champion, challenged the Pennsylvania kingpins from Naticoke. As they arrived in Naticoke the Jerseyites were greeted with banners reading "Welcome Trentons." The game was to be played in the local opera house with the main orchestra seats removed to make room for the court and fans sitting on the stage and in the balcony. Three twenty-minute "games" were scheduled to determine the bi-state champion.

Trenton, though smaller and lighter, won the first session, but the home team took the second as three of the Jersey players were injured "falling against the steam pipes." The third game ended in a tie, so a deciding twenty-minute game was scheduled for the following night.

Tension was high as the two teams lined up the next night for the opening center jump. The Trenton center controlled the tap and batted the ball to one of his forwards, who made the basket. It was the only score of the night, and Trenton won the championship.

That March, Summit beat Morristown, 10–9, and the loser in this battle between New Jersey YMCAs complained, "One or two of their men could do as well and not endanger life and limb if they did not become so excited and lose their heads at lively points of the game." The competition,

obviously, was heating up.

The Geneva (N.Y.) Y in its bulletin printed basketball tips for its members. Soon it was charging ten cents admission for some games "to defray legitimate advertising expenses," one of the first hints of commercialism in the sport. The Geneva team must have been pretty good, because in November, 1895, it journeyed to Rochester where it defeated the Western New York champions, 4–3, even though the goal was "one or two feet" higher than the rules specified and the home team committed many fouls. The officials got grudging praise, however. "The umpire, a Rochester man, called as many as was possible with a clique hissing him every time he made a decision," the victors conceded.

Sometime later Geneva played Auburn (N.Y.) home-and-home, losing on the road, 13–7, and winning at home, 16–9. In the latter game Geneva

Sports suppliers were quick to provide equipment for the new game.

MISCELLANEOUS BALLS

BASKET BALLS

Each.

1299 Made from best English grain leather in exact accordance with official requirements. Proved perfectly round by caliper test and furnished with an extra strong pure gum bladder. Basket ball originated in Springfield and the Victor ball has always been the standard. $5 00
1300 An English grain ball with pure para bladder, official in size 4 00
1301 A regulation ball, from best American grain leather with full sized pure gum bladder 3 00
1302 A good practice ball with pure gum bladder. Made from strong olive tan dressed buck 2 50

SPRINGFIELD GOALS

1303 A strong iron frame with heavy hand woven rope basket. Per pair $4 00

BASKET BALL BLADDERS

1304 Extra heavy weight, pure gum gray, used in No. 1299 ...... $1 50
1305 Standard weight, pure gum gray, used in Nos. 1300, 1301 and 1302 ...... 1 00

led, 13–8, at the half. Auburn scored first in the second period; but when the referee announced only one minute to play, the Geneva captain, one C. Spoor, whispered to his teammates, "Now, fellows," and the home team threw in three straight baskets to demoralize Auburn and sew up the victory.

One of the first recorded leagues was set up in Hartford, Connecticut, under the sponsorship of the local Y, with five teams, divided according to the members' occupations: banking, insurance, and so on. There were ten men on each squad, seven of them starters, and they bought their own uniforms. Games were played on Saturday nights—usually an off-night at the Y—and more than 10,000 fans (an average of 550 per game) attended the competition. Admission was free, but there was a ten-cent charge for a reserved seat. The Hartford Association netted $250.

"Non Vi, Sed Saepe Cadendo, 'Not Strength but Frequent Dropping,' providing the dropping is in the basket," a correspondent wrote in the Cleveland *Young Man* of February, 1895. But, like Latin, basketball was to become a dead language to the YMCA. Success was spoiling a good thing, and the YMCA hierarchy began to campaign against the sport.

As a reason for its opposition, the directors pointed to the frequent rough play and accompanying injuries and to the bitterness the games engendered among spectators. In a New York–Brooklyn game involving YMCA teams, "small boys of the neighborhood vented their feelings by rotten egging the visiting team as they left the Association."

But there was a deeper reason. Most of the YMCA directors had been brought up under the old system of physical training, the training for which Dr. Naismith had been commissioned to find a substitute. (Remember, even Dr. Naismith insisted his sons be tumblers.) These were the real methods for staying in shape. Basketball was just a game, a diversion, and now this frivolity was beginning to take over their buildings. The tumblers couldn't even get into the gyms because of all the basketball games!

In the summer of 1894 the national YMCA's *New Era* published a two-part series, "Is Basketball a Danger?," quoting directors from all over the nation in the affirmative. "The game could never and should never be allowed to take the place of all other exercise in the gymnasium," it was written, and the directors complained that basketball players "neglected their regular body-building work and would show up just in time for games." One account stressed four areas of difficulty experienced in the Philadelphia District League's second season: Jealousies and rivalries intensified; membership lost interest in class work (traditional exercises) and desired nothing but basketball; spectators at games behaved badly; and unfair officiating caused disturbances.

At first the Philadelphia Association ruled that basketball could be played only among members of the same branch, but this didn't work as players joined several branches using assumed names to continue their rivalries. Some branches, including Cleveland, ordered that no member could play basketball unless he also regularly attended gym classes. Time for basketball was severely limited, in one case to half an hour two nights a week plus Saturday morning. And by 1898 the North Branch of the Philadelphia YMCA "refused to allow the ball on the floor at all."

By these actions the traditionalists of the YMCA made certain that their organization would never play a major role in the development of the fastest-growing sport in the world. The sport would have outgrown the YMCA in any case, but, considering basketball's impact in urban centers today, the YMCA might now have an even greater influence on contemporary city life if it had kept its gymnasiums open to the new game. But that is hindsight. The world was different then. As for basketball, tossed out of the YMCAs, it simply sought new arenas. And it found them too.

4

COLLEGE DAYS

ALMOST EVERY COLLEGE TOWN had a YMCA branch of its own during the early days of basketball, so it was natural that Naismith's disciples should early spread the new game to academia. Over the next decade and a half they gradually made the game a feature of college athletic programs, though one must bear in mind that these programs were not as structured as they are today. There was no such thing as strict eligibility rules. Teams came and went, and players went from team to team as they wished.

Amos Alonzo Stagg was one of the first of the disciples. Even though he had been away from the Springfield campus when Naismith invented basketball, he became a booster of the new sport on his return. In October of 1892 the University of Chicago began operation, and Stagg was hired to be its first athletic director and coach of

all sports. Football was his specialty, but in that first March, with the gridiron season long over and the weather still too cold for baseball, he staged a demonstration game of basketball in the school gym.

Basketball quickly gained favor as an intramural activity, for coeds as well as male students. One of the young ladies, Stella Robertson, captain of the Kelly Hall team, eventually became Mrs. Stagg. With the construction of a new gym, Stagg organized a varsity basketball team in 1894, playing mostly local teams, and in 1896 began an intercollegiate competition with a home-and-home series against Iowa. Though Stagg, who died in 1965 at the age of 102, became famous as the Grand Old Man of Football, he also coached seven Big Ten basketball champions at Chicago and boasted that his school was the first (in 1908) to rank Naismith's invention

Amos Alonzo Stagg, best known for his contributions to football, was an early advocate of basketball and added the sport to the University of Chicago athletic program. This portrait shows him as he appeared in his later years.

Charles O. Bemies, the first regular athletic director of Geneva College, believed to be the first college to introduce basketball into its program, in 1892.

Ray Kaighn, of Hamline University, is given credit for establishing the five-man game.

as a major sport. Always an advocate of good sportsmanship, he would enjoin the fans before big games: "Ladies and gentlemen! Be ladies and gentlemen."

Chicago, however, was not the first college (excepting Springfield, of course) to start a basketball program. That honor belongs to Geneva College in Beaver Falls, Pennsylvania. Charles O. Bemies of Boston, a Springfield alumnus who had seen the Flying Circus basketball team in an exhibition game, introduced the sport to Geneva's new wooden gym in February, 1892. (As Geneva's first athletic director, he had introduced football two years earlier.)

At about this same time basketball also made its appearance at the University of Iowa—again, the Springfield influence was responsible —thanks to Dr. Henry F. Kallenberg, a friend of Naismith and Stagg. Dr. Kallenberg introduced the game both at the university and at the Iowa City Y and on April 26, 1893, a combined team representing the two institutions beat the Cedar Rapids Y, 12–2. This is believed to be the first recorded game with five men on a team. The

Iowa U./Iowa Y team played its home games in a building called Close Hall. It had been opened as the YMCA headquarters in 1890 and was almost immediately closed because so many citizens showed up to witness the grand opening that the floors sagged and it was immediately condemned. However, workmen shored up the floors and the building survived for many years.

Also in 1893 Ray Kaighn, one of the members of Naismith's original group at Springfield, was serving as physical education director at Hamline University in St. Paul, Minnesota, even though still an undergraduate. He organized a team from among the eighteen male students, but it lost to the Minneapolis Y, 13–12. The first games were played in the basement of the Science Building, which had a nine-foot ceiling, and the school paper referred to it as a game supported by "cranks" (an early term for fans).

Ohio State University first saw basketball in 1894, but it did not exactly welcome the game. The organizers were almost dismissed from school for using the university's name in their first game against the Columbus

(Ohio) Y, with the players wearing baseball uniforms. The sport wasn't officially recognized by school authorities until Yale came to play the Buckeyes in 1900.

Intercollegiate competition began began during the 1894–95 season. In February of 1895 the Minnesota State School of Agriculture beat Hamline, 9–3, in the first such contest. A month later a heavily favored Temple team lost to Haverford, 6–4. Basketball had been introduced at Temple by Charles M. Williams, a student of Naismith's, and the Owls had warmed up for their big game with Haverford by playing such teams as the Purple Crescent Athletic Club, Central High School, Turngemeinde, and their own junior varsity. They played seven men on a side and compiled an 8–3 record.

Because of the friendship between Stagg and Dr. Kallenberg, Chicago and Iowa scheduled a home-and-home series in 1896, with the smaller Chicago team winning both games, 15–12 and 34–18. The first game, in Iowa City, was the first intercollegiate game played five on a side. Neither team used a substitute.

Yale, that prestigious Ivy League institution, joined the basketball parade for the 1895–96 season. The Elis, wearing football pants and socks, but new jerseys, quickly got the hang of the game. Their first season they traveled to the 13th Regiment Armory in Brooklyn and defeated The Brooklyn Central Y, three-time Metropolitan champs, 8–7. The Brooklynites played rough, but the referee refused to be intimidated by the home crowd and penalized Brooklyn Central frequently. The swift college boys used their clever "dribble game" for the one-point victory and the next year defeated Springfield, 13–12, in another rough tussle. Yale posted an 8–5 record during its first season and the next year helped form the first college conference, the Triangular League, with Trinity and Wesleyan. Wesleyan dropped out at midseason, but there is no record of whether the conference then changed its name.

Sports competition was rough and rugged on all fields in those days; Yale and Penn had broken off athletic relations after a particularly brutal football game in 1893. However, by 1897 Penn had formed a basketball team that played a sixteen-game schedule, winning six. The games against area teams were social events and newspapers relate that they often were played before a "large and fashionable audience," which included "society patronesses." The players didn't dress up for their audience, however. They wore "discarded football togs."

After the Penn team had disbanded for the season, Yale offered a challenge for a game to be played in New Haven. The Faculty Athletic Committee of Penn opposed the game and so did track coach Mike Murphy, who was waiting for the basketball players to come out for his team. But the athletes decided to go ahead on their own. The floor of their own gym was obstructed by pillars, so, for this big game, the Quakers obtained the use of a riding academy for workouts. The contest, played five on a side, has been called the first modern college game. Yale won, 32–10. The next season, although a captain was elected and a schedule drawn, Penn decided to drop basketball because of inadequate facilities. It would not be revived there until 1902. The growing sport survived Penn's defection. The Yale basketball team went on a tour of the Midwest to play the first intersectional games.

That first year of the new century, John Kirkland Clark, a graduate of Yale, where he had been captain and star of the basketball team, enrolled in the Harvard Law School and proceeded to organize an informal team. The following season the sport was officially recognized by the university and Clark became its first captain and coach. (It would be years before Harvard had a full-time basketball coach, however, although in 1902 the Crimson hired Thomas Riley of Webster, Massachusetts, to provide special instruction for two weeks before the Yale and Princeton games.)

Eligibility rules were not as stringent in those days as they are now. Graduate students and even teachers could participate on various teams no matter how much ball they had played as undergraduates elsewhere. But for one game Clark declared himself ineligible. That was the game between Harvard and his old school, Yale. Clark's brother George was captain of the Eli squad and the Harvard coach and star did not want to play against his brother or his old school. As if this situation wasn't incongruous enough, he was nonetheless allowed to serve as referee as the Crimson lost to Yale, 41–16.

Basketball was clearly booming. In 1901 the Eastern League, forerunner of today's Ivy circuit, was formed, with Yale winning the first championship over Princeton, Columbia, Cornell, and Harvard. The same year Amherst, Dartmouth, Holy Cross, Williams, and Trinity formed the New England League. The season before, Dartmouth had beaten Boston College, 44–0. (In 1905 Potsdam Normal beat Plattsburgh Normal, 123–0. And in a 1903 mismatch, John Anderson scored eighty points as Bucknell beat Philadelphia College of Pharmacy, 159–5.)

In 1902 a cadet named Joseph Stillwell, later to play a major role as a World War II general, introduced basketball at West Point. Two years later, he was referee as Army lost to Swarthmore, 27–26, in four overtimes.

In 1905 the Western Conference, forerunner of the Big Ten, was organized with Indiana, Chicago, Purdue, Wisconsin, Minnesota, and Illinois as members. Minnesota had begun its basketball program in 1895–96, joining a full-fledged league in the Twin Cities area that also included Macalester College of St. Paul, the State School of Agriculture, Company A of the Minnesota National Guard, and the Minneapolis YMCA. By 1900 Minnesota had advanced to the first rank, for on February 3 of that year it defeated Iowa, 30–4, to claim the championship of the West. A band concert, drill team exhibition, and a contest between freshman and sophomore coeds preceded the big game, which could be witnessed from a reserved seat for thirty-five cents. Then, in 1902, Minnesota went undefeated, with a 15–0 record that included one forfeit decision; the streak continued through thirty-four games into 1904. And in their first season of Western Conference competition Minnesota won the championship.

Illinois, too, had an unusual basketball history. At first the sport was played informally by coeds in the loft of the Natural History Building. Men

College girls played basketball too, as shown in this illustration of a game between students of Stanford University and the University of California in 1896.

students used to sneak up to watch the games, and soon the couples were dancing, not dribbling. When the school president discovered these carryings-on, he abolished the sport. Basketball made a comeback in 1903, however, again for girls only. Not until two years later did the male students form a team to enter the new Western Conference.

But the real power in the Conference was Chicago, which won the championship four out of five years from 1906 to 1910. In 1908 it had beaten Penn in a home-and-home game to claim the "national title."

In traditional fashion basketball was caught up in the "booster" movement. As soon as two teams began to emerge as winners, boasts about best in the nation also emerged. Very quickly various college teams tried to lay claim to the "national champion-ship," though there was not always a fully representative tournament held (as there is today) to prove which team was actually the best in the nation. In 1904 a national outdoor tournament was held in St. Louis and Hiram College won. In 1905 Columbia, which had won twenty-six games in a row over two seasons, beat both Minnesota and Wisconsin and claimed the national title.

Kentucky, which was to become one of the great college basketball powers, took up the sport in 1903 when a group of students chipped in three dollars to buy a ball. "If something [had] happened to that ball, we couldn't have played," Thomas G. Bryant, a member of that original team, once recalled. Basketball at Kentucky, and elsewhere, was often a hit-or-miss proposition then. Kentucky's 1906 schedule, for instance, shows twenty games, but the records indicate that only fourteen were played. "You made the schedule and then hoped to fulfill it," the Kentucky team manager explained.

However, behind the growth of basketball lurked trouble. Play was becoming rougher and rougher (hardly what Dr. Naismith had envisioned), and there were conflicts over administration of the sport. Dr. Gulick and YMCA officials had realized early that the sport was growing beyond them, and had gradually handed its administration over to the Amateur Athletic Union. However, as the twentieth century began, jurisdictional conflicts arose between the colleges and the AAU, which to that point was the only governing body of basketball.

When matters finally came to a head, Yale stood at the center of the dispute. The Elis had been briefly suspended by the AAU in the 1897–98 season for playing an unregistered disqualified team, and they were suspended again during the 1904–05 season for a similar infraction. Just before Penn was to play Yale that year, Ralph Morgan, the Quakers' athletic director, received a written warning from the AAU that his school also would be suspended if it played the game. Morgan not only defied the threat, he fired off letters of invitation to sports administrators of 365 col-

The early rules as set down by Naismith have provided the basis for the game since its invention, but there was considerable latitude for interpretation. Ralph Morgan, then of the University of Pennsylvania, provided the impetus for setting up a permanent rules committee.

One of the three greatest college players in 1909, according to a contemporary account, was Larry Keinath of the University of Pennsylvania, which in the early years of the game was a foremost college power.

A practice session in the Columbia University gymnasium in 1908.

leges to meet in Philadelphia in April during the Penn Relays to discuss wresting control of their own basketball affairs from the AAU.

Only fifteen of the invited showed up. From this group a committee of seven was formed to meet again that summer to formulate a set of college basketball rules. Of that seven, only four men, representing Penn, Columbia, Princeton, and Yale, appeared in New York in July. These men were tough and dedicated to the game. Meeting for fifteen straight hours they hammered out the first college basketball rules and provided some of the impetus for the formation of the Intercollegiate Athletic Association the following year. This organization, which in 1908 had only $100.42 in its treasury, eventually grew into the gigantic (and some now say arrogant) National Collegiate Athletic Association, which is still fighting the AAU.

Theodore Roosevelt was president of the United States at this time, and he was upset by the growing violence and injuries in college football. The IAA was formed in large part to combat this bloody image, for basketball was not far behind football in rough play. In 1909 Charles Eliot, president of Harvard, even though he had never seen a game, called for an end to basketball, which he said had become "even more brutal than football." And the Yale baseball captain prohibited one of his players from competing in basketball because it was "too rough."

The lights were dim in the poor gymnasiums in those days, and the single official could often barely see, much less control the game. No one school was to blame. As Ralph Morgan of Penn wrote a friend, "Strictly *entre nous*, I think Columbia is the dirtiest team playing basketball, Yale

The Carlisle Indian School was best known for Jim Thorpe and football, but it also turned quickly to basketball, as evidenced by this photograph of the 1911 team.

second, and Pennsylvania [his own school] third, and I don't think the margin separating them is very great."

Harvard, where interest in the sport had been waning, gave up basketball in the spring of 1909. Explaining the move, a member of the athletic committee declared, "The games more closely resembled free fights than friendly athletic contests between amateur teams." He added that the Yale game had been "unnecessarily rough throughout." Basketball had once been quite big at Harvard. A widespread intramural program had featured competition among student teams with such colorful names as the Loose Screws, Never Sweats, Mugwumps, Bovines, Floradoras, Rinky Dinks, and Straphangers. But even this was fading when the Athletic Council made its decision.

There was one other aspect to Harvard's decision to quit basketball. Other schools had poor facilities, sometimes minimal student interest, and found the rough play abhorrent, but they stuck it out. Harvard, though, was suffering an added indignity: the Crimsons were losing games. As the team manager put it, "We are being defeated all the time at basketball. It is a poor sport. Therefore we had better abolish it." It would be more than ten years before basketball returned to Harvard on a formal basis.

The sport, however, would survive. The Eastern League, dissolved in 1908, was revived two years later. Penn immediately led a challenge for the national championship with a twenty-two game winning streak.

In 1908 it was ruled that five personal fouls in one game would disqualify the offender; in 1910 this limit was cut to four and a second official was added to control roughness. These and other rule changes were made haphazardly around the nation. Then, in 1915, the colleges, the AAU, and the YMCA formed a joint rules committee to further stabilize the game.

College basketball had come through its first major crisis, the dispute with the AAU. There would be smooth sailing for almost the next forty years.

5

PLAYING FOR MONEY

FORCED OUT OF THE YMCAs but in no position to pursue a college education, the young men who had been so enthusiastic about playing basketball refused to give up the sport. They would find their own courts on which to play. This, of course, would involve paying rent, so they raised the rent money by charging admission. One night, after the rent was subtracted from the receipts, there was a surplus. The home team players divided it among themselves—and became professionals.

It is generally conceded that Philadelphia was the "birthplace of professional basketball," even before the turn of the century. In a 1914 report for the *American Physical Education Review,* Dr. Naismith referred to the city that way and noted that special speed-up rules were instituted to make the game more attractive "for spectators rather than players." This, of course, was anathema to the good doctor, who envisioned basketball as strictly a participant sport.

There is no clear record of when the first "professional" game was played. Ed Wachter, one of the great figures of the early pro game, says the first professional contest was played in Herkimer, New York, in 1893, when local players rented the Fox Opera House and brought in a team from Utica as their opponents. After paying all expenses, the home team had a few dollars left over, which the players split.

More substantial is the claim of Trenton, New Jersey, where players got together in 1896 to rent the local Masonic Hall for a game. The crowd was large enough that each member of the home team (even today in the NBA the visitors don't share in the gate) received fifteen dollars. There was a dollar left over, so this went to

Ed Wachter, shown here as a member of the Troy Trojans, was one of the greatest centers of early professional basketball.

the captain, Fred Cooper, later a coach at Princeton. Since at this time most teams were still playing seven men on a side, this meant the net receipts were over a hundred dollars.

This "first" pro game may have been predated by over a year, however, according to a February, 1895, account in Rochester's *Young Men,* the official publication of the Rochester (New York) YMCA. The January issue had told of a 21–3 victory over the Syracuse Y, with a return game scheduled the next month. There is no mention of that rematch in the February issue, however, except for the following item headed "An Explanation": "The Rochester basketball team is not connected in any way with the Association. A number of the team are members of the Association. They are all good fellows and have the welfare of the Association at heart. As members of the Rochester team they act in an individual capacity, not as representatives of the Association. The fact that they played with the Syracuse YMCA team in this city, caused the reporters to refer to the Rochester team as the Rochester YMCA team. A natural mistake. In view of the fact that the exhibition at which the two teams played was of a *professional* [original italics] character, it was unfortunate that the Syracuse Association officially endorsed the affair with the presence of their team. Association workers have always held aloof from professionalism in athletics. Physical Director McCormick, of Syracuse, has always vigorously protested against all connection with events of a professional character. He must have considered that he had some good reason, that we cannot understand, for coming to this city

with his team." No further documentation is provided, but it is generally accepted that during this time the line between professional and amateur was not only thin but well worn from players crossing back and forth.

The professionals played their games wherever they could find a floor and draw a crowd. Often their games were staged in dance halls as preliminaries to the night's social program. The highly waxed floors didn't make for much fancy footwork by the basketball players who then, as now, relied on fast starts and stops. And often there was a potbellied stove at one end of the floor to be avoided. If the auditorium was in a basement, a post or two might be situated in the middle of the floor, and the home team would often devise plays to take advantage of the obstructions. William J. Scheffer, a sports writer and founding president of the first professional basketball league, once wrote of "playing under the old time carbon lights that would flash brightly and then dim, with a hissing sound and sometimes dropping burnt carbon on the floor."

To keep the ball from going out-of-bounds, and to ensure continuous play, the court would be enclosed by a rope net or wire cage, hence the origin of the word "netters" or "cagers." In practice, however, the net often was used to pin the ball and opponent, as is done in ice hockey, to force a jump ball. Players also developed the technique of bouncing off the rope nets, as pro wrestlers do today. If a visiting player got too close to the net, however, fans might jab at him with hatpins or lighted cigarettes.

Rules also varied from place to place. Some areas allowed only a two-handed dribble, with both hands on

Basketball teams came to be known as "netters" or "cagers"—terms still used but puzzling to the modern fan. The Armory cage in Paterson, N.J., provides a graphic explanation. This was the site of many American Basketball League games from 1919 to 1933.

the ball; others allowed one-handed dribbling. Some rules permitted a player to dribble all he wanted; others restricted him to one dribble, bouncing the ball once off the floor before he shot, otherwise forcing him to pass off.

As could be expected, the games were rowdy and informal. The crowds, of course, contributed to the raucous scene. Usually the local dudes were already well fueled with alcohol when the basketball players came on. The backboard, in fact, had to be invented to keep fans from reaching through the net to deflect the visitors' shots. Honey Russell, one of the early pros, later the coach of Seton Hall, vividly remembers the game's rowdy infancy. "You never worried about the games, you worried about how to get out of the place alive, especially if you won," he reminisced one day. "We played with one referee, and his theory was, 'If you need any help, don't expect it from me. If you can't take care of yourself, you don't belong out there.' They believed in 'no blood, no foul.'"

Since opponents one night might be teammates the next, Russell also

John (Honey) Russell. An outstanding professional player, he later became a coach, both at Seton Hall and of the professional Boston Celtics in the NBA.

notes, "There was no real dirty play." However, he points out, "We did hit real hard, and the center tap was murderous. I've seen guys get crippled up, and I know two or three referees who ended up with broken necks. Their only object was to throw the ball up and try to get out of there in one piece."

During those early days of professional basketball the players freely jumped from team to team, performing for whichever provided the biggest immediate paycheck, small as they were. A top pro might command a dollar for a minute of playing time. But if he didn't get in the game, even because of injury in the service of his team, he didn't get paid. If the house was bad—or if the house was good and the promoter was a thief—he didn't get paid, either.

But the infant sport continued to thrive, which piqued the high-collared YMCA types who had thought of the game as their own. They had expected its rapid demise when they dispossessed it from the family home. In 1898 Dr. Gulick wrote in the Spalding *Guide,* "The game of basketball is open to numerous abuses, and unless it is held with a strong hand, it will be a detriment to all lovers of good sport. That it has not been held with sufficient firmness in the past is shown by the fact that a number of teams from Young Men's Christian Associations and from military companies have left their respective organizations and have organized independently, some of them forming professional teams. It's comparatively easy to hire a hall, get up a basketball game and then pay for the hall from gate receipts. . . . This kind of sport has ruined every branch of athletics to which it has come. When men commence to make money out of a sport, it degenerates with more tremendous speed. . . . It has inevitably resulted in men of lower character going into the game. . . ."

Early in 1898, when the AAU extended its registration requirements, the colleges weren't the only ones to object. It was reported at the time that "Philadelphia led in the protest." The correspondent was not surprised because, "This city was a hotbed of professionalism, rough play and everything opposed to clean sport . . . it felt the screws the most." Within two weeks after the AAU started to throw its weight around, an outlaw Eastern Amateur Basketball Association had been formed in Philadelphia and AAU and YMCA officials complained that "coaches and players sold their services to the highest bidders, changing their connections with teams weekly and often nightly."

In 1898 as well the first professional league was formed by William Scheffer. The players felt they needed it to give them some protection from unscrupulous promoters, but they still felt no compunction about flitting from team to team. The league was called the National Basketball League and at first it consisted of teams from the Philadelphia area: Trenton, Millville, Camden, Philadelphia, Germantown, and Hancock. The next season the circuit expanded to New York and figured it was really big time.

However, in the 1903 season the league ran into difficulty and was forced to suspend operations, being replaced by the more compact Philadelphia League, in which teams were sponsored by social clubs, including the DeNeri, Greystock, and Jasper Clubs. This league lasted through the 1906 season.

That same year the Central League was organized in western Pennsylvania, and in 1909 the Hudson River League, which lasted only three seasons, was organized. Other short-lived leagues formed about this time included the New York State, Western Pennsylvania, Pennsylvania State, In-

Philadelphia, a hotbed of early professional basketball, produced many great teams and players. Members of the original South Philadelphia Hebrew Association team (SPHAs) were (*front, sitting on floor, left to right*) Harry Passon, Lou Schneiderman; (*sitting*) Charley Newman, Mocky Bunin, Hughey Black, Chick Passon, Eddie Gottlieb; (*standing*) Bob Seitchick, the team's business manager.

ter-State, and Metropolitan.

But the greatest impact was had by the Eastern League, which was formed in 1910. The original entries were Trenton, Reading, Jasper, De-Neri, Germantown, Princeton, and, briefly, Elizabeth, which withdrew after losing its first seven games. Trenton, led by Harry Hough, who shot all his team's free throws as was then the custom, defeated Reading in a best-of-three playoff after they had tied for first place. The Eastern League, which included such soon-to-be-famous names as John Beckman of Reading and the nifty Nat Holman of Germantown, survived through the 1922 season. The final championship was won by a team called the New York Celtics.

Celtics. The most storied name in basketball!

The Celtics—today the name is associated automatically with Boston —were born in the Hudson Guild Settlement House on New York's West Side, where in 1912 Frank "Tip" Mc-

Cormack organized a team to play the city's dance hall circuit. He named his team simply the Celtics because the players were members of a social club of that name at the Guild. The original members of the team were John Whitty, Jim Calhoun, George Smith, Harry McArdle, and Jack McCormack, Frank's brother. Pete Barry joined soon after, and other early additions included Denny Morrissey, Frank Marmion, Eddie Hart, Joe Tripp, Frank Nally, and Clint Coggin. They played their home games in the Guild gym and at times competed in as many as five leagues at once.

In 1916 the name was expanded to the more formal New York Celtics —on the suggestion of John Whitty— and operations were transferred to the Amsterdam Opera House. Admission was fifteen cents for ladies, thirty-five cents for gentlemen. Top out-of-town teams were brought in and the Celtics, already building their reputation, were also in demand throughout New York, New Jersey, and Connecticut.

The Original Celtics as they appeared in 1923 (*left to right*): Johnny Beckman, Johnny Whittey, Nat Holman, Pete Barry, Chris Leonard.

Then, in 1917, the United States entered World War I. Frank McCormack joined the army. When he got back from France a couple of years later, he discovered that he had helped to win the war but had lost his team. A promoter named Jim Furey and his brother Tom had organized their own Celtics team with many of the same players, including Whitty, Barry, Tripp, Ernie Reich, Mike Smolick, Eddie White . . . and Jack McCormack.

Lawsuits followed, and Furey finally had to call his team the Original Celtics. Though McCormack won the suit, he had no team. He remained in pro basketball with another team called the MacDowell Lyceum, but his bitterness grew as he saw Furey, with the publicity help of a rising young sports writer named Ed Sullivan, turn the Original Celtics into a success. (Adding to the ill feeling was the fact that the Fureys, McCormacks, and a Whitty were related by marriage. A generation passed before the wounds were healed.)

Furey's Original Celtics first played their home games on Sunday afternoons and holidays at the Central Opera House on New York's East Side, but they were so successful they soon moved into the much larger 71st Regiment Armory at Park Avenue and 34th Street for Sunday night games. They played all comers, professional and independent, including a team called the Babe Ruth All-Stars.

At this point Furey decided to concentrate on management and he named Whitty as coach. The rest of the team consisted of Barry, Smolick, Reich, Tripp, and White. The next season Dutch Dehnert, Swede Grimstead, and Johnny Beckman, an ace foul shooter, were added. The Original Celtics were on their way to glory.

Furey was proving in his armory that money could be made in pro basketball, and that gave Tex Rickard, the boss of Madison Square Garden, an idea. He formed his own team, the Whirlwinds, with such stars as Barney Sedran, Marty Friedman, Nat Holman, and Chris Leonard. (Friedman and Sedran had played together in Philadelphia, where they were known as the Heavenly Twins.) John Murray, later a great official, was their coach.

Neither Celtics nor Whirlwinds played in an organized league at the time, and they avoided meeting until the end of the 1921 season, when public clamor forced a match at the Celtics' armory. The Whirlwinds won the opening game, 40–27, before a crowd of 11,000, but the Celtics came back to take the second, 26–24. A third game was never played. Promoters said they feared violence by the fierce partisans of the two teams. More likely they preferred to be able to carry the dispute over to another season of big gates during which each could claim to be the champion.

Anyway, the question soon became moot. Jim Furey, never one to let anything stand in his way, persuaded Nat Holman and Chris Leonard to jump the Whirlwinds and join his team. For a while the Celtics played home games at Madison Square Garden, where they had to lay out $7,500 to build a new portable combination basketball and dance floor, but by 1926 they had moved to Arcadia Hall in Brooklyn. Their greatest fame came later as a barnstorming team touring the country.

While Furey's ethics were questioned by many, there was nothing wrong with his vision. He realized that professional basketball could not possibly succeed under its current chaotic format. How could fans be expected to pay top dollar to see a game if they never had any idea who would be playing on a particular night, and for what team?

In 1922 promoters of a dozen top independent teams in New York met under the auspices of the *Evening Mail* to bring order out of the chaos. One of the objects of the meeting was to seek agreement to "confine players to individual teams in the vicinity of greater New York." The *Evening Mail* also criticized "the use of phony out-of-town names by local pickups. When you take Tom, Dick, and Harry from over the river and call them the 'Oshkosh Five' you are not fooling the public—you are just trying to bunk them and not getting away with it."

Before the next season began, Furey made certain that such charges could not be leveled against his team. With a farseeing stroke of promotional genius, he signed all of his players to exclusive contracts at guaranteed annual salaries. About this time, Horse Haggerty, a giant of his day at six feet four and 225 pounds, also joined the Celtics and assumed the role of team policeman against opposition bullies. The foundation of basketball's greatest team was completed.

This first great Original Celtic unit consisted of Ernie Reich, Horse Haggerty, Pete Barry, Johnny Beckman, Dutch Dehnert, Nat Holman, Chris Leonard, and Whitty, the coach who could fill in as a player if needed. Soon after, Davey Banks, stolen from the Philadelphia SPHAs (for South Philadelphia Hebrew Association) after they had beaten the Celtics in a best-of-three series, and Joe Lapchick were recruited, and, in a final reorganization, Nat Hickey and Carl Husta joined up. Barry, the most original Original, Dehnert, and Holman were the only players to span all three eras.

The Celtics did participate in sev-

The Original Celtics didn't win every game. This SPHA team beat them two out of three in the 1925-26 season. (*Standing, left to right*): Tom Barlow, Stretch Mechan, Charlie Schwartz, Eddie Gottlieb; (*seated*) Lou Schneiderman, Chuck Passon, Davey Banks. The Celtics later lured Banks away to play with them.

eral organized leagues at various times. Lapchick recalls that they once won 194 out of 205 games as members of the Eastern League, and they are charged with wrecking the American League with their dominance. But most of the Celtics' success and legend is built around their barnstorming years.

In 1923, their first season under exclusive contract to Furey, they won 204 games and lost only eleven. For years to follow this would be a typical record as they toured the nation taking on local opponents under the most appalling conditions. There was no coach, as such, and no trainer, and the Celtics would usually snitch towels from their hotel rooms for a postgame shower, if a shower was available. The manager was also the road secre-

tary and his job was to keep an eye on the promoter to make sure he didn't take off with the receipts. If the team happened to have an extra player along, he'd sit next to the timekeeper to keep an eye on the clock.

Fans would flip bottle caps or small bolts at the visitors and shake the baskets when they were shooting. If the Celtics were booked in a coal mining town, they could be sure the miners would wear their work hats to the game and shine the lights into their eyes. The ball was often dirty, oversized and lopsided, which made it risky to attempt a bounce pass. There was no such thing as basketball sneakers, and cheap tennis shoes would often wear out in a single game. The referees, one to a game, were often outrageously biased in favor of the

The early ball had laces.

home team, but the Celtics had their own method of handling the worst of them. On a center jump, two of the huskiest Celtics, ostensibly leaping for the tipped ball, would mash the referee like a pancake. When he came to, he usually had gotten the message.

But at least play under Furey was better than it had been in the old freelance days. The Celtics once drew 25,000 fans for a day-night doubleheader in Cleveland and their salaries often reached the neighborhood of $12,000 a year—pretty good for those days. The fact that they played hundreds of games a year together provided the Celtics with one tremendous advantage—teamwork. Their opponents were usually pickup teams.

The Celtics, of course, had no preseason training camp. As Lapchick

put it, they would show up, trim their fingernails, and be ready to start the season. They played their way into shape.

Barry was the oldest of the Celtics, smart and an aggressive rebounder. Beckman was a team leader and a great scorer from the backcourt. Once, when Dehnert's mother was ill and he couldn't leave her, Beckman came out of retirement and, at age thirty-nine, was high scorer in an important game against the Renaissance Big Five. Beckman also served as the team's volunteer trainer. His "remedies" were frightening. Celtics would keep playing despite grievous injuries rather than risk his ministrations. Leonard, the best defensive player, was called "Dog" for the way he would hound his man all over the court. Haggerty, who preceded Lapchick at center, was the muscle man whose frequent task was to protect Nat Holman after he had infuriated a larger opponent with some slick maneuver.

As they traveled the country, the Celtics had time to improve their game. They devised the give-and-go play, the switching man-to-man defense, and the pivot play, which was the personal invention of Dutch Dehnert. The older players taught the new ones and, because of their grueling schedule, they perfected the passing game in order to make the ball do most of the work. These tactics became basics of the game, a part of the fundamentals that players have to master even today. Through the teaching of the Original Celtics as players and coaches, these basic techniques

were passed on to others and developed the game.

The Celtics were not, however, invincible. One team that could challenge them was the Renaissance Big Five, a team of black players organized by Bob Douglas in 1922. However, it would be another ten years before the Rens really hit their peak, posting a record of 473 victories against only forty-nine losses in a four-year span. A barnstorming team that called New York's Harlem its home base, the Rens claimed with some justification to be the world's champions. The South Philadelphia Hebrew Association, or SPHA, also could match baskets with the Celtics, at least until the New York team stole their best player, Davey Banks. The Celtics' record also shows a number of tie

The Renaissance team was one of the greatest of all time. Robert L. Douglas, manager of the Renaissance Casino in Harlem who organized the club in 1922–23, is recognized as the winningest coach in basketball history, with 2,318 victories and only 381 losses in over twenty-two seasons. In 1933 the Rens won 88 straight games, all on the road. Members were (*left to right*) Clarence (Fat) Jenkins, Bill Yancey, John Holt, James (Pappy) Ricks, Eyre Saitch, Charles (Tarzan) Cooper, William (Wee Willie) Smith. Inset: Bob Douglas.

The original Troy Trojans as they appeared in a 1912 photograph. (*Left to right*): William Hardman, James Williamson, Ed Wachter, Chief Muller, Jack Inglis, Lew Wachter, and mascot John J. Casey, Jr.

games, but there was a reason for this. If the regulation game ended in a tie, the Celtics would not play an overtime period unless the promoter promised them extra money. Besides, Lapchick once explained, a tie meant good business for the rematch. There was also a suspicion that the Celtics would let up on an opponent so as not to win by too wide a margin if a rematch had already been booked. Some of those games got out of hand and became Celtic losses, but in the return engagement, of course, the Celtics would rout the opposition.

McCormack's Lyceum team was fairly successful during this period, but could not match the Celtics in appeal or in basketball skill. The rivals capitalized on their feud for two games in 1922, but the Celtics won both, the first, 41–15, before 9,000 fans in Madison Square Garden. One feature of the game was the duel between the two centers, massive Horse Haggerty of the Celtics and Frank (Stretch)

Meehan of the Lyceum five, who at six feet seven was billed as "the tallest man playing basketball in the East."

In 1922 McCormack's team tied the Brooklyn Dodgers for first place in the new Metropolitan League, but then misfortune struck. The players demanded more money to compete in the best-of-three playoff. McCormack had been paying them twenty-five dollars a game at home and twenty on the road and the players insisted on forty dollars for each of the playoff games. "Sooner than give up to the 'stick-up' tactics, I informed them I would default to the Dodgers," McCormack announced. And he did.

The next season the league fined each of the strikers a hundred dollars —there had been threats at the time of lifetime suspensions—and McCormack was forced to trade them. Others of his players were ruled ineligible for one reason or another and the team finished last in the league.

An earlier rival of the Celtics after World War I were the Troy (New York) Trojans, organized by Ed Wachter. He coached the team, and the star player was his brother Lew. The Trojans pioneered the fast-break offense, and Wachter insisted that all his players become adept at shooting free throws. However, established teams, including the Celtics, were able to keep the rule that one specialist, like Beckman, would shoot all the foul shots.

The Trojans won two straight championships in the Hudson River League before leaving that circuit (which collapsed) and then won three titles in four years as members of the New York State League. After that, Wachter took his team on the road; they won thirty-eight straight games before disbanding to leave the field open for the Celtics, who were just then beginning to improve under Furey. The Wachter brothers eventually became coaches in the Ivy League, Lew at Dartmouth and Ed at Harvard, where he would show up for home games wearing a tuxedo. The Trojans were originally formed to challenge the Buffalo (New York) Germans, another of basketball's most celebrated aggregations. The Germans had started as teen-agers in amateur competition around the turn of the century, and had won the Pan-American Games championship in the Buffalo Exposition of 1901. They also won a national title in 1904 and then turned professional. For two full seasons, 1909 and 1910, they were undefeated, and over four years they won 111 straight games before being defeated by one of the first barnstorming fives, Frank J. Basloe's Herkimer, New York, team. Again in 1915 the Germans were unbeaten with a 28–0

record. When they finally disbanded in 1926, they had won 792 games and lost only eighty-six.

The SPHAs, who once beat the Celtics two straight, were a club team that went into the promotion of basketball "to make a buck" for the treasury, according to Manager Eddie Gottlieb, who took this group, under changing personnel, from the dance halls to the Eastern League and eventually into the NBA. The SPHAs had been representing the South Philadelphia YMHA, but the players eventually broke away to form their own club. At first the team consisted of club members willing to put up their own money for uniforms, but later they added outsiders, paying from five dollars a night up to sixty (to Davey Banks before he jumped to the Celtics).

This was the portrait of professional basketball in the early 1920s—a smalltime operation. The Celtics, at least set in their personnel, were the closest thing to a stable force. Then, in 1926, George Preston Marshall, a Washington laundry owner, decided to organize a professional league with class. He called it the American Basketball League. The president was Joe F. Carr, who simultaneously held the presidency of the then young National Football League. (At that time Marshall was not connected with football. However, in 1932, long after the ABL folded, one of his old ABL colleagues, George Halas, owner of the Chicago Bears, introduced him into the NFL as operator, with partners, of the then inactive Boston franchise. This team, run by Marshall until his death, later became the Washington Redskins.)

At first the Celtics declined to join the new league. They were doing well

George Preston Marshall, who organized the American Basketball League in 1926.

enough as independents. But when the ABL voted to prohibit its members from playing any games against the New Yorkers, the Celtics had to give in. The new eight-team league began with the 1926–27 season. Its charter cities were Baltimore, Chicago, Cleveland, Fort Wayne, New York, Philadelphia, Rochester, and Washington.

George Halas, who for several years had operated an independent professional basketball team he called the Bruins, ran Chicago's ABL franchise. A former all-round sports star at the University of Illinois, where he at first played for and then for many years coached the football team, he

played for the Bruins when they were independents, then coached them for a while in the ABL before hiring Honey Russell as player-coach.

Max Rosenblum, owner of a department store, was behind the Cleveland team, which advertised his business. And Fort Wayne's team was run by the local chamber of commerce; over the years it liked to call itself the Green Bay of professional basketball, a boastful reference to the small Wisconsin city that for so long had operated a successful franchise in the National Football League.

The first half of the ABL's inaugural season saw Cleveland edge Washington for first place, and New York, which had joined the competition late, was a distant fourth. But the Celtics shot into high gear in the second half of the season, losing only one of twenty games, and they then swept the Rosenblums three straight in the playoff. The next season the Celtics repeated their dominance with a 40–9 record, easily the league's best.

Marshall's Washington Palace five had dropped out of the league after the first year. The laundry magnate had been taken to the cleaners after spending $65,000 in salaries trying to hire players good enough to beat the Celtics. "We'll break you yet, George," Dutch Dehnert had yelled derisively at Marshall one night as he jogged down court in still another Celtic rout.

The trouble was that the Celtics' dominance was also breaking the league. Fans stopped coming out to see their home team routed by the Celtics, who, despite the fact that they performed briefly under the sponsorship of Madison Square Garden, were never a great draw at home.

For the 1929 season, the ABL's third, the league was "reorganized," another word for breaking up the Celtics, whose players were apportioned to other teams in the league. Jim Donovan, then owner of the Celtics, was never compensated for this raid, which destroyed his franchise. Holman and Banks remained in New York as part of a new team called the Hakoahs, made up entirely of Jewish players. Barry and Dehnert went to Rochester, Beckman to Baltimore, and Lapchick to Cleveland. Later, Barry and Dehnert moved on to join Lapchick on the Rosenblums where two other one-time

Celtics, Nat Hickey and Carl Husta, were already established. Thus the old pattern was simply repeated: the Rosenblums ran away with the league. Although steps were taken during the season to "equalize" talent around the ABL, this only brought back the old days of fluid rosters.

As the league staggered into the 1931 season league owners were more determined than ever to curb the Rosenblums. They pressed legislation ordering that each team use at least two "inexperienced"—read that as "low-salaried"—players at all times, which kept Pete Barry on the bench, and they outlawed the pivot play, which was Dehnert's best weapon. The Rosies dropped out at midseason, and the rest of the league followed them into oblivion at the end of the season.

The Celtics' dominance, whether in New York or Cleveland uniforms, was one reason for the failure of the league. But the main reason was that the Great Depression of 1930 shattered the country's economy. Many enterprises a lot more solid than basketball leagues were failing. Halas, for instance, had tried to conduct a major league operation. His Bruins played in the huge Chicago Stadium, and he would spend a lot of money to buy players from the top eastern teams. In the league's next-to-last year he even obtained Nat Holman from a fading Syracuse franchise and paid him the then impressive sum of $6,000 for half a season. But times had become too hard. During their final year the Bruins were forced to abandon the high-rent Chicago Stadium for less impressive quarters, and Halas decided he couldn't go on. (The Bruins had lost $5,000 their final season, a sum as staggering then as Holman's salary. About that time the Bears won a football championship for Halas and still lost $18,000. No banks would lend him money to make up that deficit, so Halas ended up giving IOUs to some star players and his coach for part of their salaries.)

Eddie Gottlieb recalls the old ABL sadly: "We had big buildings and players on monthly salaries, and we stretched from New York to Chicago, but we were just three or four years ahead of our time."

Rising out of the ashes of the ABL, the Original Celtics regrouped with the players serving as owners and promoters. Piling into a second-hand seven-passenger Pierce-Arrow auto they had bought for $125, Hickey, Barry, Banks, Dehnert, and Lapchick resumed their gypsy life, crisscrossing the country for a guaranteed $125 a night as against 60 per cent of the gate.

Pro basketball on a league basis, however, was not destined to die. John J. O'Brien, a former player who had organized the old Metropolitan League, which had originally inspired the ABL, organized a new American League starting with the 1934 season. This compact new league took teams from the Metropolitan and Eastern circuits. (It survived into the fifties to merge into the Eastern League that exists today as a minor pro circuit.) For this action O'Brien is considered the savior of pro basketball. In 1937 Lonnie Darling, promoter of the Oshkosh All-Stars, organized a National League of midwestern teams. But despite this activity, most people figured Phog Allen of Kansas was probably right when he declared in 1937 that "professional basketball, as a money-maker, apparently has had its day."

6

INTO THE GARDEN

As THE 1912–13 SEASON BEGAN, the University of Texas basketball team embarked on an ambitious road trip from Austin to Fort Worth and Dallas to play a series of four games against different opponents. They lost three of them, blaming the defeats on "ice freezing the goals and goal posts." (Texas basketball, in those days, was an outdoor sport.) The defeats are of more than passing interest, however, because such disappointments shortly became rare for the Longhorns. Soon after they returned from the frozen north, they routed Southwestern University, 70–7, to start a winning streak of forty-four games that covered three undefeated seasons and parts of two others. They won their last three games in 1913, then added perfect records of 11–0, 14–0, and 12–0 before finally being defeated in their fifth game of the 1917 season by Rice, 24–18. No college basketball team had done anything like this before.

The Longhorns, who had introduced basketball to the Southwest in 1906, were led by Clyde Littlefield, all-America center forward, Pete Edmond, and Gus (Pig) Dittmar. Littlefield was the leading scorer and Dittmar the best defender. They manufactured their winning streak under four different coaches. The most spectacular was R. B. Henderson, the first alumnus to hold the job. He coached the Longhorns for only one season, 1916, but in their twelve victories that year they outscored the opposition 560 points to 185, opening by beating San Marcos Baptist, 102–1.

"At the outset, Coach Henderson determined an offensive system of play," a sports writer noted. "His words to each player on the eve of the battle were: 'Fellows, the score counts.' The coach stressed the idea of open play in an offensive way. It was his hobby to have Dittmar guard the opponents' basket with the re-

The unbeaten University of Texas team of 1916 ran the Texas streak to forty straight victories. The members, shown here, are (*front, left to right*); J. C. Diller, Joe Thompson, James (Pete) Edmond, Robert Blaine; (*back*) Coach Roy Henderson, Gus (Pig) Dittmar, A. B. Duncan, Clyde Littlefield, and manager Roy Wagstaff.

59

mainder of the team scoring for Texas in the offensive end of the court."

By the end of Henderson's only season the Longhorns had won forty games in a row and the athletic department thought it was time to build a new indoor gym to contain "the best floor in the Southwest." The college newspaper exulted, "Basketball can no longer be said to be one of the minor sports, both from the spectators' point of view and that of the players. Never before in the history of the institution has basketball been so popular." However, the Texas team did not live up to its new building. Too many stars had graduated and the streak came to an end.

During the seasons around World War I several powerful college teams emerged. In 1914 Wisconsin enjoyed its second undefeated season in three years, and in 1916 Utah became the first college team to win the National AAU title. In 1915 Illinois and Virginia both posted undefeated records, and starting in 1918 Oregon State, Navy, and Texas A&M were unbeaten in successive seasons. In 1923 Army, tired of taking regular beatings in its new series with Navy, hired Harry Fisher away from Columbia and the former Yale All-America coached the Cadets to a thirty-one-game winning streak that included a perfect 17–0 record his first season. In 1924 North Carolina and Texas both posted 23–0 records, the Longhorns' season beginning with an abbreviated 3–2 victory over Southwestern in which "the lights went out after eight minutes and didn't come back on."

Led by Cat Thompson and Frank Ward, Montana State parlayed a great passing game into some outstanding records. The Bobcats posted a 19–1

record in 1917 and were 13–0 three years later. In 1923 Ott Romney took over as coach and his six-year record was 144–31. His last team in 1928 was 36–2, a record exactly duplicated the following season by his successor, Schubert Dyche.

As great teams and players began to attract a following, it became necessary to find places for the games to be played that would accommodate the growing numbers of fans. A warning of what kind of crowds basketball could attract was posted in March, 1920, in New York City, where City College and New York University had developed a fierce basketball rivalry. Going into their annual game NYU had an 11–1 record with a nine-game winning streak; City was 13–2 with five straight victories. The game was booked into the 168th Regiment Armory (NYU did not have a gym and even played some of its games on a huge barge on the Hudson River). Some 10,000 New Yorkers jammed their way in to see NYU win, 39–21. It was an amazing crowd for those days—and not so bad for today, either. The Violets, incidentally, went on from that victory to beat Rutgers for the National AAU title in Atlanta, Georgia, at which time a local paper called Howard Cann, the star NYU player who later became a highly successful coach at his alma mater, "the greatest basketball player in the world."

Two years later Stanford built a 5,000-seat gym, and before the twenties had come to an end there were spacious new basketball pavilions at Minnesota, Iowa, Washington, Oregon, Penn, Butler, Indiana, Xavier, West Virginia, and Drake. They ranged in size from Drake's 6,500 capacity to more than 16,000 at Iowa. With these new gyms came the realization that basketball could be a money-making sport; in fact, it almost had to be to pay for those ambitious arenas. Dr. Naismith's vision of his game as a simple exercise for physical fitness was finished forever.

One school that didn't join the rush to build a new gym was St. John's of Brooklyn, which played its home games in a dance hall. However, this didn't prevent the Redmen—their mascot was a gaily painted cigar store Indian—from achieving big-time success. For three seasons, from 1929 through 1931, they earned the appellation of the Wonder Five with records of 23–2, 24–1, and 21–1. "They're the smartest college club in the country," marveled Nat Holman, coach at CCNY, which was quite a tribute to the Wonder Five's own tutor, James (Buck) Freeman.

The Wonder Five used the famous passing offense of the Original Celtics and a switching defense. The center jump was still in effect then, and after every basket Matty Begovich, considered huge those days at six feet two, would control the tap and the Wonder Five would slowly work the ball down court to set up a shot. If the sure shot did not materialize they would simply toss the ball back out and start over. Max Posnack, team captain for two years, was the supreme ball handler; Mac Kinsbrunner an outstanding dribbler. The other starters were Rip Gerson and Allie Schuckman. Gerson would refuse to change his socks during a winning streak—only once did he have to use more than two pairs a season.

St. John's had used the Celtics' pivot play in 1929 with Jim Collins at center. After he graduated, Begovich replaced him the following season as a freshman, and he and Posnack, who was five feet eleven, would often set up a double pivot offense and wheel the ball back and forth to their cutting teammates like the Harlem Globetrotters.

In 1930 the only game St. John's lost was at Providence, 31–21. It may not be right to blame the officials, but the record shows that the home team was given the opportunity to shoot twenty-four free throws, the visitors only six. The Redmen's only loss the next year was to NYU, 23–20, as the Violets copied their deliberate style of play. After this season the Wonder Five was declared ineligible for further college competition for having played outside games against professionals. So they just moved en masse into pro ball as the Brooklyn Jewels and were able to be immediately competitive.

The Redmen had, however, left their mark on college basketball, not only with their tremendous records but with the rule changes they forced and with at least one crowd they had helped draw. It all came to a head on January 21, 1931. The Great Depression had brought the economy crashing down on unsuspecting Americans and millions were out of work. James J. Walker, bon vivant mayor of New York, had already sponsored a football game for unemployment relief and now called for a basketball tripleheader in Madison Square Garden with the teams playing fifteen-minute halves, five minutes shorter than usual. Some 16,000 fans showed up to net about $20,000 for the needy.

After Columbia beat Fordham, 21–18, in the opener, Manhattan

Edward S. (Ned) Irish changed the focus of college basketball from small, obscure gymnasiums to large arenas by introducing doubleheaders into Madison Square Garden.

edged NYU, 16–14. Then, in the feature, St. John's routed CCNY, 17–9. In addition to their other skills the Redmen excelled on defense (in one game they had held Manhattan without a field goal). In the Garden, they allowed CCNY to score the first basket of the game and then did not permit another score from the floor until the final minute of play. But the crowd, the largest ever to see St. John's, was not impressed. They objected to the slowdown style of play and booed the victors throughout the contest. Even Nat Holman, the losing coach, criticized the Redmen because "they hold the ball back and waste too much time."

The reaction of the crowd made it clear that if basketball was to become a gate attraction it would have to give the fans a better show. Because there was no center line the Redmen had been able to control the ball almost indefinitely, using the entire court. Thus the ten-second rule was instituted the following year, setting up the midcourt line and giving a team ten seconds to bring the ball up into its offensive zone. For the time being

the double pivot offense was not tampered with, nor were offensive players, with or without the ball, prevented from camping near the basket to set up plays and block out the defense. This was changed in 1935 when offensive players were barred from more than three consecutive seconds in the free-throw lane while their team had possession of the ball.

The Garden bill produced still another result. In charge of promoting that tripleheader for Mayor Walker was veteran New York sports writer Dan Daniel of the *World-Telegram*. Assisting him was a younger colleague from the same paper, a University of Pennsylvania graduate named Ned Irish. Irish, from Brooklyn, was a go-getter. While in college he had served as school correspondent for a long string of New York papers and actually earned more at this than he did for his first few years as a big city newspaperman. He graduated from Penn in 1928 and soon was covering college sports for the *World-Telegram* while doubling as publicist for the New York football Giants. As one of the few writers to regularly cover college basketball, the sharp-eyed newsman discovered the popularity of the game in small, out-of-the-way gymnasiums. One night he received a graphic lesson when he tore his pants climbing through a window to get into the packed Manhattan gym, capacity 500 with 1,000 spectators already on the premises.

This accident, plus the success of the Garden tripleheader he helped promote, started Irish thinking. In 1934 NYU and CCNY came into their last game with undefeated records and Irish tried to book them into the Garden. The schools were willing and so was the Garden, which had a fight card arranged for that night; but one of the fighters declined to accept a change in date and the project fell through. NYU went ahead and beat City, 24–18, before 5,000 fans in an armory, and tickets were at such a premium that one NYU star had to be bailed out of jail to play the game —he had been arrested for scalping.

Irish then went to work on plans for the following season. Again he approached the Garden and this time he asked them to set aside six dates for college basketball doubleheaders. Irish actually wanted the Garden to hire him to promote the games, but the arena management wanted no part of such a risky venture. They said he could have the dates if he personally guaranteed the $2,000 rental, and he would also have to lay out the $2,500 to build a portable floor.

This, a few hundred dollars for printing the tickets, and minimal guarantees to the teams, marked the last financial risk Irish had to take. As soon as the tickets were printed he knew he had a hit on his hands. As December 29, 1934, the date of the first doubleheader, approached, Irish became busier and busier. His phone at the *World-Telegram* was ringing constantly, and not about newspaper business. "You'd better decide whether you want to be a promoter or a sports writer," sports editor Joe Williams warned him. Irish made perhaps his first and last instantaneous decision—he was making less than fifty dollars a week as a sports writer, so he chose the potential riches of promoting.

For that first doubleheader Irish booked St. John's against Westminster, a colorful Pennsylvania power

Klein of New York University blocks a shot by Ford of Notre Dame in the featured game of the first college doubleheader at Madison Square Garden. NYU won, 25-18.

with a star center named Wes Bennett, and, for the feature, NYU against Notre Dame. Coming into the doubleheader NYU had a two-year winning streak of nineteen straight. Notre Dame, led by two future big-time coaches, Johnny Jordan and George Ireland, was billed as champion of the Midwest. Westminster, champion of its conference, was unbeaten and St. John's had won nine in a row. It was perfect matchmaking. Frank Lane, a Big Ten official later to win fame as a baseball executive, was imported to assure Notre Dame a fair break at the foul line.

As the big night approached Irish was hoping for a crowd of 10,000. Everett Morris wrote in the New York *Herald-Tribune:* "Metropolitan college basketball will step out of its cramped gymnasiums and gloomy armories tonight into the bright lights and spaciousness of Madison Square Garden for the first of a series of six doubleheaders arranged in the hope of proving this winter that the sport deserves and will thrive in a major league setting."

Competitively, the doubleheader was a success. In the first game Wes Bennett scored twenty-one points to lead Westminster to a 37–33 victory over St. John's. In the feature, although many in the crowd of so-called subway alumni were rooting for Notre Dame, NYU came from behind for a 25–18 victory. But these were not the important numbers. The important numbers were 16,138, the paid attendance; and $20,000, the gate. Irish had succeeded beyond his greatest anticipation. As Charles Hoerter wrote in the *Daily News* the next morning: "College basketball made its big-time debut in Madison Square Garden last night and scored a smashing success."

A week later Irish put on his second program. CCNY beat St. John's, 32–22, in a rough game that saw Redman coach Buck Freeman bench one of his players, Frank McGuire, for "growing overly pugnacious." In the second game NYU defeated Kentucky, 23–22, when, with thirty seconds to go, Kentucky star Leroy Edwards was called for fouling NYU's Sid Gross, who made the winning free throw. The foul, called blocking, resulted in a week-long controversy, and Kentucky coach Adolph Rupp used a biblical quotation to explain what had happened to Edwards: "He was a stranger and they took him in."

Despite his complaints, however, Rupp would bring his team back to the Garden. Schools loved the money they got from the huge New York crowds and they liked the exposure, which helped their stars make All-America and aided them in recruiting new players. And the officiating, as a rule, was a lot fairer than they were used to receiving on the road. Even Huey Long, governor of Louisiana, tried vainly to get his Louisiana State University team into the Garden "if a suitable opponent could be found." Before long Irish was also promoting doubleheaders in Philadelphia and Buffalo, and he could bring teams east from great distances by promising them games in all three cities.

That first year Irish drew 99,995 fans to a total of eight Garden programs. This represented more than 50 per cent of all the people who saw college basketball in all of New York that season. He had reason to be proud

Adolph F. Rupp, of the University of Kentucky, was one of the most successful coaches in the college game.

of the success of his doubleheaders, so scheduled because one game just didn't provide a long enough evening to command the top dollar, but he typically sought to underplay his role. "Why shouldn't basketball be a good drawing card?" he asked an interviewer soon afterward. "It's a fast game with lots of action and scoring. It's easy to understand. I wasn't surprised by the big crowds. For years I've seen hundreds of thousands turned away from games in college gymnasiums. Those who were lucky enough to get in often had to endure the most uncomfortable conditions. In the Garden they get a comfortable seat and they don't have to travel to an out-of-the-way spot at the risk of not being able to get in."

However, as the first year of the

Long Island University didn't have a gymnasium in which to play its games, but Clair Bee produced outstanding teams nonetheless.

Garden doubleheaders bounced to a successful conclusion, Irving T. Marsh pointed out in the *Herald-Tribune* that when Irish scheduled his doubleheaders "he inadvertently also filled in open dates in the business schedule of the betting gentry. . . ." There was talk of betting coups. It was said that $50,000 was bet on an NYU-Temple game in which Temple suddenly switched from a 13–5 favorite to a 9–5 underdog. (Only later was it learned by the public that one of Temple's star players was ill.) But this was just a small cloud on a distant horizon. There was a new sporting wheel in town, and the world of college basketball was only worried about getting on for the ride and maybe some day soon building their own arenas to attract some of that money.

There was some talk about betting coups in the following years, too, when NYU went into a slump after its winning streak was halted at twenty-six straight by Yale—and Howard Cann, the coach, was forced to deny the rumors publicly. But all this was soon forgotten. Irish and Madison Square Garden scheduled ten doubleheaders, which drew near-capacity crowds for the season, and while NYU slumped, another local team, Long Island University, began to engage the interest of New York fans.

LIU had been an outsider in New York City basketball for many years, not rating with such powers as CCNY, NYU, or St. John's. The little school in downtown Brooklyn didn't even have a proper nickname. For a while they were the Blue Devils, then the Red Devils, and finally they became the Blackbirds.

More important than a new nickname, in 1932 the school hired lean and ambitious Clair Bee as its coach. Bee had suffered from tuberculosis as a child but went on to become an outstanding athlete in his native West Virginia. Burning with a fierce desire to excel, he became one of basketball's greatest coaches, an innovator and an author of texts on his sport, as well as a writer of fiction about athletic heroes for young readers.

Although Bee coached his boys to a 26–1 record in 1934, they still didn't earn general recognition until they left their tiny "home" gym at the Brooklyn College of Pharmacy—where at one point they won 139 straight games—and moved into the Garden the first year of the doubleheaders.

Led by their nearsighted center, Arthur Kameros, the Blackbirds won their last seven games in 1935 and then proceeded to conquer all opposition the following season. Julie Bender, LIU's first All-America, was one of the guards, a six-footer, fast, and a great dribbler, alongside Leo Merson, deadly with a two-hand set shot from way out. Merson was the defender who stayed back as Bender drove for the basket. Marius Russo, later to be a fine big league pitcher with the Yankees, and Ben Kramer were the forwards. Art Hillhouse, at six feet six the biggest man Bee had ever coached, replaced the graduating Kameros at center. Bee recalls that Hillhouse, who lived in New Jersey, was the only player whose house he ever visited to sell him on coming to LIU. "And even then I didn't go inside, we talked at the front gate," Bee points out, proud that most prospects came to him to see about joining the Blackbirds.

LIU won all twenty-six games in 1936, including a victory over its

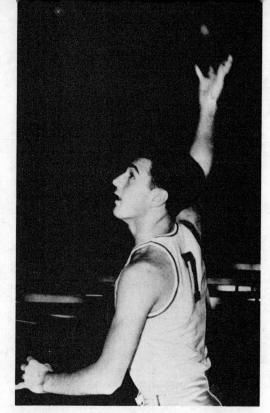

Hank Luisetti, the rangy star of Stanford's quintet, about to let go one of his famous looping one-hand basket shots.

alumni, and, as the next season began, the Blackbirds won their first ten games for a three-year winning streak of forty-three. But, on December 30, 1936, they were scheduled to play in the Garden against Stanford and its highly publicized star, Hank Luisetti.

On the Ned Irish–sponsored Eastern swing, Stanford played Temple in Philadelphia before coming to New York. Although Stanford would go on to post a 25–2 record that season, Bee thought so little of them that he didn't bother to scout the Californians personally. Instead, he sent two players, Russo and Bill Schwartz, a substitute, to do the job for him. They came back reporting that Stanford had used a zone defense in routing the well-regarded Owls, 45–38.

Bee was impressed by Stanford's easy victory over such a strong team. The Indians had a well-balanced squad and played a fast-moving game in contrast to the deliberate New York style. Luisetti was their leader. A great ball handler, he may have been the first to popularize the behind-the-back dribble. However, he is known for making famous an even more startling innovation, the one-handed shot. Until Luisetti showed the way most players shot one-handed only on lay-ups. All other field goals were made on two-handed sets. Most coaches would jerk a player from the lineup if he tried to shoot with one hand from farther than a few feet from the basket. But John Bunn, the Stanford coach, was wiser than most. Luisetti had learned to shoot one-handed in high school in his native San Francisco. When he enrolled at nearby Stanford he asked Bunn if he could continue the unusual style, and then he demonstrated that he could shoot as accurately his way and also get the shot off more quickly.

"Stay with it, boy," Bunn told him and the boyish-looking, dark-haired Californian became the most publicized star on the West Coast as he led Stanford to one championship after another. Luisetti usually shot one-handed with both feet planted on the floor, but occasionally he'd take what is known today as a running jump shot. In those days fifteen to eighteen feet was considered long shooting because most players had learned to play in basement gymnasiums with low ceilings that prohibited putting any arc on a shot.

From the opening tip-off against LIU, Luisetti was the dominant figure on both ends of the court. Bee, in fact, recalls him more for his defensive skill than for his offense. LIU players, and Garden fans, marveled at Luisetti's dexterity and at his one-handed shot, which they literally could not believe.

Bee, however, was stunned for still another reason. He quickly saw what his player-scouts had missed. The Stanford "zone" was really a disguised man-for-man, which had to be attacked quite differently from a zone. Before he could make the necessary adjustments at half time, Stanford had taken command of the game. The Indians scored an easy 45–31 victory, breaking LIU's winning streak at forty-three, and Clair Bee vowed never again to leave his scouting to others.

Taken from the game with thirty seconds to go, Luisetti received an ovation from the crowd of almost 18,000. The six-foot-two-and-a-half forward had scored fifteen points, high for the game, and had set up his teammates for countless baskets. (A year later he showed what he could do when going all out. As his teammates insisted on setting him up, he scored fifty points in one game against Duquesne.)

The one-handed shot had, to be sure, been used previously by Luisetti and by other players around the nation. But playing in the Garden had given the handsome, always smiling star and his unique shot unprecedented exposure. Newspapers grabbed Luisetti for feature stories, and magazines wrote about his life. He became a national sports hero. This was what playing in Madison Square Garden meant then, and continues to mean to this day. As for LIU, by the following season more than one Blackbird player was practicing the one-handed shot.

From Curt Gowdy, the noted sports announcer, comes first-hand evidence that Luisetti was not the sole inventor of the one-hander. Gowdy, later a star at Wyoming, says he set a state high school scoring record shooting a one-hander in the early thirties and that Les Witte, a star at Wyoming between 1931 and 1934, scored over a thousand points during his college career shooting a one-hander. (Coached by his brother, Willard [Dutch] Witte, Les, a left-hander, became known as One Grand Witte after making his thousandth point.) In 1934 Wyoming put together a 26–3 record, losing in the finals of the National AAU tournament, and Witte, Ed McGinty, Art Haman, John Kimball, and Haskell Leuty, the starters, all made the AAU All-America. Most of them shot one-handers, as did many Rocky Mountain area players. Henry Iba has called this Wyoming team one of the greatest passing aggregations he ever saw. "They passed the ball like a bubble," he said.

Luisetti's performance against LIU was only the start of a basketball revolution. For years there had been discussion of ways to speed up the game, and for the 1937–38 season the rule makers adopted one suggestion that had been bruited about for some time—they eliminated the center jump following every basket. From now on the team that had been scored against would immediately put the ball into play under its defensive basket.

Many coaches feared the boys would burn themselves out playing a full forty minutes without the respites provided by the center jump after each score, but their worries, of course, were groundless. Few remember this, but the clock was kept running during the center jump, which cut from nine to twelve minutes of playing time from every game. Elimination of the center jump put most of those minutes back in the game, and scoring increased proportionately at once.

With the offense now becoming a more important part of the game, scoring increased even more; and the full-court "pressing" defense, which the elimination of the center jump made possible, added to the excitement. In the first Garden doubleheader of the new season, for instance, Illinois and St. John's set arena scoring records as the Illini won, 60–45, aided by nine points from Lou Boudreau, a dark-haired youngster who one day would become a baseball immortal.

From the very beginning Ned Irish had dreamed of a tournament—to be held in Madison Square Garden, of course—that would decide a national college champion. In the winter of 1938 the plans were formalized. The Metropolitan Basketball Writers Association would act as sponsoring agent for what they labeled the "Rose Bowl" of basketball, and the first National Invitation Tournament was born.

The field was set up on a modified East-West basis. NYU, LIU, Temple, and Bradley were invited to play in the first round with Oklahoma A&M and Colorado drawing byes into the semifinals. LIU and NYU had never met before; they were paired in the first round. The Violets were official city champions, but many called the Blackbirds more deserving. NYU, however, dispelled all doubts about its claim with a 39–37 victory while, in the other game, Temple defeated Bradley, 53–40. The Bradley Braves with their left-handed hook shooting star, Dar Hutchins, had been favored. But they appeared nervous in their first big city appearance—"Garden-itis" would freeze many a mighty invader over the years—and the Temple zone limited Hutchins to only three points. In the semifinals Colorado, led by its football All-America, Whizzer

The first National Invitation Tournament in 1938 came to an end with Temple beating Colorado, 60–36. Don Henderson (3) of Temple and Jack Harvey (22) of Colorado battle for a rebound. At left, watching the action, is Byron (Whizzer) White, an All-American as a football player and later an associate justice of the U.S. Supreme Court.

White, later to become a Supreme Court justice, nipped NYU, 48–47, and Temple clubbed Oklahoma A&M, 56–44. Temple than prevailed in the finals, 60–36.

The NIT was a complete success, and the Garden, Ned Irish, and the New York writers made plans to stage another tournament the following season. But they would have company. The National Collegiate Athletic Association, which has never hesitated to get in on a good thing, decided to stage its own national tournament in Evanston, Illinois, on the campus of Northwestern University.

In the first National Collegiate Athletic Association tournament, in 1939, long-armed John Schick (11), the Ohio State center, tips in two points. Oregon won, 46–33.

After two "off" years in which they lost seven games against fifty victories, Long Island University had another powerhouse for the 1939 season. All-America Irv Torgoff was the leading player, but Clair Bee was two deep in stars at every position. He had wise veterans to start and eager sophomores for speed and dash. He would shuffle his lineup each game to get the best matchups. Danny Kaplowitz, Dolly King, George Newman, six-foot-four Mike Sewitch, and Torgoff were the senior starters. The great sophomores included Ossie Shechtman, Solly Schwartz, and Cy Lobello.

The Blackbirds cruised easily through their regular schedule, winning the first twenty-one games before going into the season windup against LaSalle in Philadelphia's jammed Convention Hall. The Explorers, who had lost five games already, felt they might upset LIU by holding the ball,

and the strategy seemed to be working. LIU went along with the stall and La-Salle led by a slim margin most of the way. However, the Blackbirds hung close and the crowd grew hostile as late in the game Johnny Bromberg of LIU prepared to take a foul shot that would put the Blackbirds in front. He never got the shot off. A frustrated La-Salle player stepped up, punched Bromberg in the nose, and a full-scale riot began. With the game almost over, local police had already left the arena to direct the homeward traffic, and fans poured out of the stands to attack the LIU team. Bromberg's nose was broken from the initial blow, Torgoff suffered a gash in his head, and Sewitch's arm was broken.

The Blackbirds managed to fight their way to their dressing room and lock themselves in until order was restored and the game could be resumed. Bromberg, of course, was in no condition to shoot his free throw and the opposing coach had the right to pick his substitute. Leonard Tanseer, the LaSalle coach, tabbed Arthur Gurfein, a big LIU sub, to take the shot. Gurfein was definitely no shooter, but he airily told Bee, "Don't worry about a thing, coach," as he strolled to the line and converted not only on the personal foul but also on the technical to put LIU on top for good in what ended as a 28–21 victory. The Blackbirds' second undefeated season in four years was assured (over nine years their record would be 216–19) and now they went into the second NIT against a field that included Bradley, New Mexico A&M, Roanoke, St. John's, and undefeated Loyola of Chicago.

From the start Bee knew Loyola was the team to beat, and he flew out to scout them twice in late-season games. He was right, for both undefeated teams easily made the finals. The Loyola star was six-foot-eight Mike Novak, who played under the basket in the Ramblers' 2-2-1 zone and, as was legal then, specialized in blocking shots as they approached the hoop. However, on his scouting trips Bee had noted that Novak was slightly handicapped in blocking shots from his right. In the days before the NIT final, Bee painted a star high on the backboard and had Torgoff and Kaplowitz practice banking shots off the star so they would rocket into the basket out of Novak's reach.

On offense, Novak, a consistent scorer, liked to get his points from in close. Bee wondered whether Sewitch, with his recently broken arm, could handle him. He had nothing to worry about. Sewitch, his arm held against his chest in a cast like a rock, could not be budged. Eventually Novak had to move outside, scoring only one point as LIU capped its perfect season with a 44–32 victory. Bee still calls this his greatest victory and the 1939 five his greatest team. LIU's winning streak ran to thirty-four in a row before Southern Cal's great ball handlers stopped them, 57–49, with a five-minute freeze at the end of the game the day before Christmas of 1939.

Dr. Naismith had died a month earlier and one can only wonder what his reaction would have been late that season when the game he had invented to promote physical fitness extended its frontiers to turn still more thousands—eventually millions—into armchair spectators. The occasion was little noted at the time, but on February 28, 1940, a doubleheader from the Garden (Pitt-Fordham, NYU-Georgetown) was televised by W2XBS. The experimental program was hardly a success—the picture was even lost for parts of both games—but it was the first of many.

This was not the only sign that the game was still growing. The New York basketball writers realized that the NIT was getting too big for them, so they turned the tournament over to an organization of coaches formed to work with the Garden in picking teams and promoting the annual event.

John (Honey) Russell, coach at Seton Hall.

Indiana, which had finished second in the Big Ten, but gained the tournament position because it had beaten conference champion Purdue twice, won the 1940 NCAA title and Colorado triumphed in the NIT; but for some reason the hottest team in the country did not appear in any tournaments. This team was the Pirates of Seton Hall, with a perfect 19–0 record. The Pirates had actually jelled the year before, when their star player, six-foot-seven Ed Sadowski, broke his leg. With his big man out for the season, coach Honey Russell decided to go the rest of the way with sophomores and promoted five of them to the starting lineup. The best of these was a blond, baby-faced guard who looked like a choirboy, but would match an opponent elbow for elbow if necessary. His name was Bob Davies and you'll find him in the Hall of Fame. In high school Davies read magazine articles about Hank Luisetti and copied the Stanford star's behind-the-back dribble, even adding a few extra tricks of his own. He was the complete ballplayer, a great feeder as well as shooter. Bob Holm, John Ruthenberg, Ken Pine, and Bob Fisher were the other sophomores who became starters with Davies and they won their last four games in 1939. A great defensive team, with the free-lancing Davies intercepting passes all over the court, the Pirates won all nineteen games on their schedule during the 1941 season, and this time they did get a bid to the NIT where they were paired against Rhode Island State in the first round.

Frank Keaney was the Rhodies' coach, one of the first to popularize a wide-open, race-horse style of play. (He also had his players work out while smudge pots burned in his gym to get them ready for the cigar smoke in Madison Square Garden.) Keaney's center was his son, Warner (Flip) Keaney, a hulking six-foot-four 250-pounder, and his dad joked, "He's the only subsidized player I have. I give him room and board and even slip him a few bucks now and then." The Rhodies played a strange one-man defense. Young Keaney would hang under the basket to block shots and rebound; his teammates would stay up court waiting for his long passes to start their fast break offense.

During Seton Hall's pretournament practice, Russell had a lanky freshman named Chuck Connors imitate young Keaney for the varsity. (The old coach says this was probably the future TV Rifleman's first job of acting.) The strategy was simple: the Pirates' defense would ignore Keaney, who seldom crossed the center line on offense; and they would use the extra man to block off his outlet passes. Keaney thus had nobody open to pass to and Seton Hall won easily, 70–54.

Seton Hall was matched in the semifinals against the LIU Blackbirds, who were enjoying another of their great seasons. Solly Schwartz held Davies scoreless in the first half and the Seton Hall star fouled out in the second half with almost seven minutes to go after scoring only one basket and four points. The 49–26 defeat ended the Pirates' winning streak at forty-three games. LIU then became the first team to win two NIT championships by routing Ohio University, 56–

Seton Hall's Bob Davies.

In the NIT finals Ohio was routed by LIU, 56–42, but Frankie Baumholtz, shown battling Richard Holub for a rebound, was named outstanding player of the tournament.

The semifinals matched LIU against Seton Hall. Hank Beenders of LIU gets the rebound from Rothenberg (13) of Seton Hall. Bob Davies (11), watching at right, had a disappointing game, with only four points. LIU won, 49–26.

42, in the finals. Frankie Baumholtz, later a major league baseball outfielder, starred for Ohio U.

The NCAA Tournament had a story of its own. Wisconsin had finished ninth in the Big Ten the previous year, but this season the Badgers won their last dozen games to sweep the conference title and tournament berth. They moved into the NCAA final by defeating Dartmouth and then Pitt, and in the finals at Kansas City downed Washington State, 39–34.

With these tournament victories by LIU and Wisconsin, basketball completed its first half-century. In the years before his death Dr. Naismith had come out against roughness and the zone defense, but the game was strong and thriving. Ned Irish even felt secure enough to surrender his second job as publicity man for the football Giants. Basketball clearly could make it on its own.

7

THE GIANTS ARRIVE

THE START OF BASKETBALL'S second fifty years coincided with America's entry into World War II, but at the outset, at least, the war had little effect upon the sport.

At Rhode Island State, Stanley Modzelewski—later, as a professional, known as Stan Stutz—concluded his four-year varsity career with a record 1,730 points, and at West Texas State Price Brookfield set a single-season high with 520. The West Texas Miners averaged six feet six and a half in height and billed themselves as the world's tallest basketball team. But when the Miners came east they lost to Long Island University by two points in overtime. Stanford won the 1942 NCAA championship even though its star player, Jim Pollard, missed the 53–38 finals victory over Dartmouth because of the flu. West Virginia edged Kentucky, 47–45, for the NIT title.

But the most captivating basket-ball gang was performing at the University of Illinois, where coach Doug Mills had put together a starting line-up of five sophomores. "Gee, those kids really whiz down the floor," a Midwest radio announcer exclaimed one night, and thus were born the Whiz Kids.

There were four players generally accepted as Whiz Kids—Andy Phillip, six-foot-two-and-a-half center, un-emotional, a great ball handler and shooter who had once scored 101 points in a recreation league game, and the star of the team; Gene Vance, a handsome, hard-driving guard; Jack Smiley, a tenacious defender as the other guard; and Ken Menke, a speedy forward, whose bad feet, which occasionally kept him on the bench, disqualified him for the Marines but were deemed perfectly fine for the infantry.

In the Whiz Kids' first season Art Mathisen and Vic Wirkowits alternat-

Illinois' Andy Phillip was the star of the Whiz Kids.

ed as the fifth man. The next year Mathisen held the job alone. After their third season, the Whiz Kids went to war, and when they returned in 1946 Fred Green became the fifth man. Phillip, a high school baseball star who had been steered to Illinois by Lou Boudreau, continued to play both sports in college, but he earned All-America honors his first year in basketball as he led Illinois to an 18–5 record and the Big Ten title.

The Whiz Kids lost to Kentucky by two points in the first round of the NCAA Tournament that year, but came back even stronger in the 1943 season with a 17–1 record; but the school declined tournament bids. (So did 15–0 Army.) Phillip again made All-America, not bad for a kid who used to be chased off the court by the big boys when he started playing basketball as an eleven-year-old in Granite City, Illinois. He then joined the Marines and served in the Pacific as a first lieutenant. Although he returned at age twenty-four to play one more year of college ball with his old teammates, and then enjoyed a ten-year pro career, Phillip's glory days remained those when he and his young fellow Illini had "really whizzed down the floor."

Even without Illinois and Army the tournaments went on in 1943. In the NCAA Tournament the hot team was Wyoming, led by a quick-starting forward named Kenny Sailors, one of the first of the one-handed jump shooters. (A couple of years earlier Johnny Adams of Arkansas had made All-America with a two-handed jumper.) The Cowboys spent long hours of practice adapting their play to tighter eastern rule interpretations, and beat Georgetown easily in the NCAA fi-

Kenny Sailors of Wyoming outmaneuvers Hy Gotkin of Long Island University in the 1943 Red Cross benefit game. Wyoming, earlier winner of the NCAA tournament, took the "national championship" by beating LIU, 52–47.

nals with Sailors being named tournament MVP. St. John's, coached by former Celtic Joe Lapchick, won the NIT by routing Toledo in the finals, 48–27. Fuzzy Levane had been the big gun in leading the Redmen to a 21–3 record, but the tournament star was really mustachioed Harry Boykoff, a hulking six-foot-nine sophomore.

Following the tournaments Wyoming and St. John's played for the national championship in a Red Cross benefit game in Madison Square Garden. The hometown Redmen were heavily favored, but the Cowboys' big man, six-foot-seven Milo Komenich, the only non-Wyoming resident on the squad, scored twenty points and Wyoming won the undisputed national title, 52–47, in overtime.

At the same time as Boykoff was starting to gain notice at St. John's, in

DePaul's George Mikan.

Chicago's DePaul University, an awkward, nearsighted freshman named George Mikan was breaking in as a part-time starter. He stood six feet ten. And at Oklahoma A&M still another giant freshman was learning to keep his feet from tangling as he ran up and down the court. He was Bob Kurland; they called him "Foothills" and he stood an even seven feet tall.

Mikan and Kurland were men who would change the game of basketball. Despite their awkward beginnings they would become polished players before they finished college. Thanks to personal determination they would learn to dribble and shoot as well as smaller men, but their big advantage remained in rebounding and on defense where it was still legal to bat the ball away from the basket to prevent the opposition from scoring. By 1945 the rules were changed to

limit goal tending, but by then the big man had learned to play the game. Despite still-continuing attempts to legislate against him, he is here to stay. (Phog Allen, at the time the outspoken coach at Kansas, thought the best way to curb the big man was to raise the baskets to twelve feet. He tried it once in an experimental game and seven-foot-one Elmore Merganthaler of New Mexico State scored forty-one points. The big man was still closer to the basket than anyone else.)

As coaches saw that big men could be taught the game and could develop the necessary coordination, they began to start working with these gawky youngsters at an earlier age. The ordeal that Mikan and Kurland went through as college freshmen is no longer necessary. Today a kid who shows signs of growing tall starts to get coaching in junior high.

Although Mikan made All-America in 1945, he wasn't the whole story of that season. By then the war had stripped many colleges of their eligible young men. More than a few schools dropped sports altogether. Others continued on a makeshift basis with personnel changing from day to day as students were drafted or as athletes, enrolled in a campus armed forces training program, were transferred.

Vadal Peterson, coach at Utah, had plenty of problems. The army had taken over the school gym, and every other team in the Big Seven had dropped basketball. However, Peterson found a church auditorium that would be suitable for practice, collected six freshmen and sophomores to make up his team, and pieced together a schedule of college, service, and industrial teams.

The Utes did well, and with an

Arnie Ferrin (22) struggles to retain possession in the 1944 NCAA finals. Utah won the title with this victory over Dartmouth.

18–3 record they had their choice of two tournaments. Since the NIT offer was financially more attractive that's where Utah elected to compete. (Today, the situation is reversed; an NCAA bid is worth far more than one to the NIT.) The trip to New York was long and tedious. The Utes lost their basketball shoes en route and had to play in plain sneakers. As the last-invited and bottom-seeded team they were matched against powerful Kentucky in the opening round. The Utes made a game of it, but they lost to the Wildcats, 46–38, and Peterson told reporters, "The kids were a little tight playing here for the first time; a little gawky-eyed at all the people. But they're a young bunch. They only average eighteen. I wish we could play here again."

That night, as the Utah party was packing for the trip home, the phone rang in Peterson's room. It was the NCAA calling from Kansas City. Members of the University of Arkansas team had just been involved in an automobile accident. Could Utah replace them in the tournament? After

getting agreement on a better financial deal than had first been offered, Peterson called his young squad together and told them of the new bid. "It's up to you. We can play, or go home," he told them. They quickly accepted the second chance. "We'll be back here in a week to play the Eastern champ [for the title]," Arnie Ferrin, a young Utah star, vowed as the team headed for Kansas City and the NCAA Western Regional playoffs.

Because of wartime travel difficulties, it took Utah two and a half days by train to get to Kansas City where they defeated Missouri and then Iowa State for the Western crown. Then it was back on the train for New York to play Dartmouth, the Eastern winner, for the national championship in Madison Square Garden.

Dartmouth was an imposing rival. The Indians were led by their All-America captain, Aud Brindley, and their team had recently been augmented by two navy transfers, Dick McGuire of St. John's and Bob Gale of Cornell. Fred Sheffield, Utah's six-foot-one center and leading scorer, had a bad ankle and Dartmouth was an eight-point favorite. The morning of the game a gambler approached Peterson in his hotel room, to see if Utah would be willing to lose by twelve points or more, but the coach belted him and threw him out. The only gambling Peterson had planned was a risky "pickup" defense that involved double-teaming the ball whenever it went to one of the Dartmouth stars.

The defense seemed to work until the final minute when Gale and McGuire scored for Dartmouth to send the game into overtime. The game was still tied going into the last seconds of the extra period when Utah called time-out to plan its final shot. Dartmouth was certain the Utes would set up Arnie Ferrin, the slender freshman who had already scored twenty-two points, but Utah gambled that another player, Herb Wilkinson, might be left unguarded and would be better able to get off a good shot. They were right. Wilkinson, left free, took a one-hander from behind the free-throw circle that hit the back rim, hung for an instant, and fell in for a 42–40 victory. The baby-faced Utes —they were called the Blitz Kids— had redeemed themselves after their NIT loss by winning the NCAA championship.

Utah still had one game remaining, though—the annual Red Cross benefit against the NIT winner. This game had been arranged some time before the NCAA final, and the sponsors expected Dartmouth to be that tournament's winner. However, at the last minute, the Navy Department ruled that leave could not be extended for its trainees at Dartmouth, win or lose, so the Red Cross knew it was stuck with Utah, no matter what happened in the final. The charity game's sponsors had to be just as happy as Utah fans when Wilkinson's final shot dropped in.

The NIT champion for an unprecedented second straight year was St. John's. The Redmen, playing without Boykoff, were underdogs in every game they played. (Boykoff had entered the service, even though he towered over the armed forces six-foot-five height limit. When the time had come for his measurements during his physical exam, he had simply stepped off the scale, straddling it, and had come in under the limit.) But even without him the Redmen beat Bowling Green and then Kentucky before entering the finals against DePaul. The Blue Demons were led by Mikan, but the powerful giant fouled out with fourteen minutes to go after scoring thirteen points (high for the game) and the Redmen rallied to win, 47–39. (During the St. John's comeback, Lapchick, the Redmen's intense coach, passed out on the bench. St. John's trailed when he fainted and was in front when he came to only minutes later. "Well, I guess I just dealt strategy a helluva blow," he joked afterward.)

Joe Lapchick, a member of the Original Celtics and a distinguished coach at St. John's University for twenty years.

Giants met for the first time in the NIT semi-finals of 1944: Bob Kurland (*under the basket*) vs. George Mikan (99). Kurland won the battle for individual honors, but DePaul won the game, defeating Oklahoma A&M, 41–38.

Even against St. John's, a local team, the young Blitz Kids got a big hand from Garden fans as they took the floor before a packed house that raised $35,000 for the Red Cross. St. John's led early, but Utah, paced by the dazzling Ferrin, fought back to tie at half time, 19–all. With eleven minutes to go, Utah led, 35–26. The Redmen rallied to pull within two, but then Ferrin took over again.

Born to wealthy parents, the slightly built six-foot-four 170-pounder had the competitive fire of his pioneer ancestors. He stole the ball to set up one Utah basket and then scored two more field goals and a free throw himself to assure the 43–36 victory. The Blitz Kids, who had left New York as losers only days before, now owned the city and the basketball world.

Henry P. (Hank) Iba, coach of Oklahoma A&M.

For a preview of the future, however, fans would better have noted the semifinals of that 1944 NIT. Here, before more than 18,000 awed spectators, one of the first battles of the giants was waged. Oklahoma A&M with seven foot Bob Kurland against DePaul and six-foot-ten George Mikan.

Kurland, from St. Louis, was six feet seven when he started high school. His high school coach, who had played for Henry Iba at Oklahoma A&M (now Oklahoma State), recognized potential in the awkward redhead. He started working with the boy and tipped off Iba about him. By the time Kurland was a six-foot-ten high school senior, dozens of colleges were interested in him, but Iba had the inside track—he had been working with Kurland for two years at a summer

The Aggies' Bob Kurland.

camp. His enrollment was assured, Kurland recalled later, one night when Iba "fed me the biggest steak I'd ever seen."

It took some doing to make Kurland a college star, but the big fellow was willing to work. One weapon Iba thought he needed was a left-handed hook. The coach recalls his first experiments: "The first day he tried 600 left-handed hook shots. The first 100 didn't hit either the backboard or the rim. The next 100 didn't go in. After that he started to connect." As a freshman eligible for the varsity during wartime, Kurland was a part-time player, but he came into his own as a sophomore and made All-America three straight years. His assets were height, perseverance, and quickness, if not speed. After one game, Dolph Schayes, then a six-foot-five-and-a-half NYU freshman, complained, "Kurland was always a step ahead of me going for the ball."

Kurland had intelligence too. Iba thought this was important. "The main reason he came along is that he's brilliant mentally," Iba related one day late in Kurland's college career. "He's been able to take shortcuts by correcting his own mistakes. He's an A student and brings that same brain onto the court with him. Whenever I see a giant who doesn't make progress, I know that he is either lazy or dumb. Bob is neither."

If Kurland's beginnings were inauspicious, Mikan's were even less promising. He not only was oversized and awkward as a youth, he was also nearsighted and brittle. His playmates teased him cruelly, and in his loneliness he often thought about becoming a priest. The highlight of his childhood was winning a marbles championship at age ten and being taken from his home town of Joliet, Illinois, to Chicago to see the Cubs play the Boston Braves and have his picture taken with Babe Ruth. Few reckoned he would one day become the Babe Ruth of his own sport.

Mikan started playing basketball in a Catholic Youth Organization league in Joliet before he began high school, but he did not go out for his high school team until his junior year, at which point he broke his leg. It was a terrible injury—for a year and a half he couldn't walk. Doctors warned he would never play games like basketball again. But by the time the injury healed, George had grown from five feet eleven to six feet seven, and he once again returned to the high school basketball coach who earlier had cut him from the team because he didn't think kids who wore glasses could ever compete in the sport.

Eventually George was sent to a prep school where he was able to play some basketball. By the time he graduated, he stood six feet eight and a half and had hopes of attending Notre Dame. However, a tryout found the Fighting Irish coach, George Keogan, no more sympathetic than Mikan's first high school mentor. "You'll never be a basketball player, you're too clumsy," Keogan told the disappointed youngster, taking note also of the quarter-inch-thick eyeglasses Mikan needed to keep from tripping over the foul lines.

Keogan's graduate assistant, Ray Meyer, was also at the workout, and as Mikan left the floor he offered the lad some encouragement. "Don't let it get you down," he said, "Stick with it and someday you'll be a fine player."

Then came one of life's coinci-

dences. Mikan, still determined to get his education through basketball, enrolled at DePaul. Three weeks later Meyer quit at Notre Dame to become head coach at DePaul and he found Mikan already enrolled there and waiting for him.

Injuries continued to harass Mikan. He even dislocated a kneecap on the bus ride from Joliet to the DePaul campus, but this never checked his drive to become a basketball player, the only way he could turn his height to an asset in this little man's world.

Meyer had Mikan out for four weeks of drills before the rest of the basketball squad showed up, and he used him as a forward through his freshman season. Whenever Mikan got into a game, his orders were to pass off immediately if the ball came his way. But, daily in practice, for an hour after the regular squad left, Meyer had his awkward freshman put in the extra work that eventually turned Mikan into a star and a two-time All-America.

As a freshman George averaged eleven points a game and DePaul made it to the NCAA Tournament, only to lose in the second round. That same season, Kurland, also a freshman, averaged only 2.5 points a game, but by the time they were sophomores both had matured to be stars of their teams and dominant forces in the game.

DePaul didn't even think it would field a team in 1944, but somehow the Demons managed, and that March the two sophomore giants met in the semifinals of the NIT. DePaul won the game, 41–38, but Kurland outscored Mikan, who fouled out early in the second half, 14–9. This confrontation with Oklahoma A&M may have marked DePaul's emotional peak for the tournament. In the finals Mikan was clearly not himself as the Demons lost to St. John's. Later Meyer found out why. The morning of the game George had taken a walking tour around Manhattan. When they retraced his giant strides, they found he had covered ten miles! No wonder he was weary.

The next year, even with goal tending outlawed, DePaul and Oklahoma A&M both posted tournament-worthy records, but went different ways, the Aggies to the NCAA, the Demons to the NIT. Oklahoma A&M had an easy time of it, routing two opening foes and then stopping NYU's crack team, 49–45, for the NCAA championship as Kurland scored a record sixty-five points in the three games.

Meanwhile, DePaul started off by blasting West Virginia, 76–52, in the first round of the NIT as Mikan scored thirty-three points. The DePaul team, which practiced in a ratty little campus gym, was not very imposing, except for Mikan's height. One starter was sixteen years old. Four of the regulars, including Mikan, wore glasses. Gene Stump, a forward, was nearly blind in his left eye. Stump usually assumed the task of needling Mikan before a game so he'd be psychologically primed to attack the enemy after the tip-off. However, Stump didn't have to say a word before DePaul met Rhode Island State in the semifinals. That afternoon Meyer had overheard Rhode Island State coach Frank Keaney telling a friend: "We're going to drive Mikan nuts with our fast break. We'll have him stumbling over his own feet. He'll be ready to go back to Chicago with his tongue hanging

Don Otten of Bowling Green scores against Mikan in the finals of the 1945 NIT. DePaul won, 71–54, as Mikan continued his outstanding play, with 34 points in the game. His 120 points in the tournament broke the existing scoring record.

out before we're through with him." Meyer's pep talk merely consisted of repeating Keaney's words. The Blue Demons won the game, 97–53, and Mikan scored a record fifty-three points—as many as the entire Rhode Island team!

In the finals DePaul trailed, 11–0, after almost five minutes against Bowling Green and its six-foot-eleven-and-a-half center, Don Otten, but rallied to win going away, 71–54. Mikan scored thirty-four points.

The tournament victories set up still another meeting of the giants in the annual Red Cross game. The Garden was packed with more than 18,000 fans who had contributed more than $50,000 to the Red Cross. But the individual battle was disappointing. Mikan fouled out after only fourteen minutes of play with nine points. Kurland went all the way but his fourteen points weren't even high for his team in a 52–44 victory.

But the two big men had proved something that season. The goal-tending rule hadn't bothered them a bit. They still had a role to play in basketball. They were big players, not limited freaks, and they were here to stay.

One test still remained, however. Thus far Mikan and Kurland had been achieving their record feats against limited wartime competition. But now peace had come and the veterans were returning to school and sport, physically mature and mentally tough. Still the two big men showed that their skills were their own and not relative to weak competition. Although DePaul did not defend its NIT championship, the Demons still posted a fine 19–5 record and Mikan led the nation for the second straight year by scoring more than twenty-three points a game. Kurland and the Aggies were even stronger. Bob's 643 points were the most ever scored by a college player in one season, and for Kurland's last regular-season home game Coach Iba instructed his players to help the giant have a big-scoring game. Fed by his teammates Kurland responded with fifty-eight points against St. Louis. The Aggies then went on to defend their NCAA championship with a defensive display to warm the ball-control heart of their fundamentalist coach. They shut off Baylor, 44–29, in the first round; muzzled California, 52–35, for the Western title, and, in the finals in Madison Square Garden, trumped North Carolina, 43–40.

Mikan and Kurland, who played such a major role in transforming college basketball, went separate ways after graduation. Mikan, turning down bonus offers to become a baseball pitcher, became a basketball professional and had a profound influence in the acceptance of the National Bas-

In 1946 Oklahoma A&M won its second consecutive NCAA title with a victory over North Carolina, 43–40. Here J. L. Parks passes to teammate Blake Williams (77).

Ernie Calverly of Rhode Island lofts a one-hander against Bowling Green in the 1946 NIT. Later his fifty-five footer at the buzzer tied the game. Rhode Island won in overtime, 82–79, but Kentucky won the tournament.

ketball Association. (And later, on its emergence, as the first commissioner of the American Basketball Association.) Kurland went to work for Phillips Petroleum, played many years for its famed 66ers basketball team and in Olympic competition, and now holds a major executive position with the firm.

As a footnote to the giant achievements of Mikan and Kurland, one moment stands out in their senior season of 1946. In the first round of the NIT, Rhode Island State, humiliated the year before by DePaul, was playing against Bowling Green which had six-foot-eleven-and-a-half Don Otten playing center. Ernie Calverley, a foot shorter, led the running Rhodies, who were heavy underdogs. They didn't play like underdogs, though. In a blistering match the score was tied twenty times and the lead changed hands on twelve occasions before Otten, high scorer with thirty-one points, fouled

out with 3:20 to go and his team on top, 68–66.

With a minute to go the Falcons led, 72–70, but Calverley tied on a long one-hander. Bowling Green went back in front, 74–72, on Vern Dunham's layup with ten seconds left, and only two seconds showed when Rhode Island State was able to call time out to stop the clock, then put the ball in play at midcourt. There was no time for strategy. Center Bob Shea took the ball out-of-bounds, Calverley broke into the backcourt, took the pass-in and, as he vividly recalls today, "I immediately let fly with a two-handed set shot that had very little trajectory. The ball never touched a part of the rim or the backboard."

What Keaney, his coach, called "a hoper" and what Calverley calls "this lucky shot," tied the game as time ran out and the crowd sat in stunned silence. Later it was estimated that Calverley's shot had traveled fifty-five feet. Others say fifty-eight feet or fifty-one feet, but none argue with the claim that it was the longest shot ever made in the Garden, and one of the most important, too, since it saved Rhode Island from defeat. The Rhodies went on to win in overtime, 82–79.

Rhode Island then defeated Muhlenberg in the semifinals, but in the title game ran into Kentucky and its freshman star, Ralph Beard, who scored thirteen points and held Calverley to eight as the Wildcats won a 46–45 thriller. But Ernie Calverley did not have to feel too badly about the defeat. The years would establish Beard as one of the great college players and the memory of Calverley's shot would long outlast the defeat. (To this day Calverley will run into one of the hundreds of thousands of fans who claim to have been in Madison Square Garden that night, and who will even vehemently dispute his own version of "the shot.")

DePaul had managed to scale the basketball heights out of a grubby little gym. But Holy Cross had no gym and played no games at home. Alvin (Doggie) Julian, the Crusaders' coach, still built fine teams with intensive recruiting, mostly in the New York City area, but unlike most coaches, who like to show off their gymnasiums to young prospects, Julian's task was to hide his. After the kids had enrolled, it was presumably too late for them to change their minds. Among those who stuck it out were George Kaftan and several of his pals from New York, and it was a good thing they did. By 1947 the Crusaders were so loaded with talent that Julian had two full units he could throw at the opposition. One of the guards on the second group

was a shy freshman with a slight speech impediment named Bob Cousy; the veterans were led by Kaftan, who was anything but shy. The handsome six-foot-three 200-pounder had a smile and a wisecrack for everyone. When he came on the floor, he would announce, "You can relax now, Kaftan's in the game."

Kaftan had gone out for basketball in high school because a friend with whom he walked to and from school had decided to try out for the team. Before long he was impressing college scouts with his cool, effortless style of play. By 1947 college ball was becoming more and more wide open, but Julian still stuck to the conservative game. Kaftan was his clutch star.

The Crusaders were no better than 4–3 early in the season, but they won their last twenty games to clinch an invitation to the NCAA Tournament. After watching Kaftan lead Holy Cross to an opening victory over Navy, Nat Holman, coach of CCNY, the Crusaders' next opponent, vowed, "We'll take care of Kaftan, we'll wall him in." But after the Holy Cross star had scored thirty points in a 60–45 rout, Holman could only lament, "What we should have done was walled him out . . . out on the street."

In the finals the Crusaders drew Oklahoma, which was led by Gerry Tucker, a twenty-six-year-old returning serviceman. "So you're the nineteen-year-old hotshot who scored thirty points the other night?" Tucker said in greeting—to which Kaftan breezily replied, "Yes, it's a young man's game, you know." And he proceeded to lead Holy Cross to the NCAA championship with eighteen points in a 58–47 victory.

"Nineteen-year-old hotshot" George Kaftan defends against Gerald Tucker in the 1947 NCAA title game. Holy Cross won, 58–47.

Kentucky's Adolph Rupp thought his 1947 NIT team was even stronger than the unit with which he had won the same championship the previous year but in the finals the Wildcats ran into that gang of upsetters, the Utah Blitz Kids. Arnie Ferrin was back from the service by now and was joined by Vern Gardner, who had been in the service himself when the Utes had won a national title in 1944. Gardner's father had died when he was eleven, and he had been brought up along with twelve brothers and sisters by their mother on a small Wyoming farm. His background was quite a contrast to Ferrin's comfortable childhood, but they meshed to form an outstanding team. Unseeded in the NIT, the Utes beat Duquesne and West Virginia before facing Kentucky in the finals as eleven-point underdogs. However, with little Wat Misaka holding Ralph Beard to a single free throw and Gardner and Ferrin scoring fifteen points apiece, the Utes slowed Kentucky's fast pace for a 49–45 upset victory.

It would be a long time before anybody else stopped the Wildcats. Adolph Rupp would see to that. The thought of failure was anathema to the autocratic Baron of the Blue Grass and he saw his teams and players as instruments for building an unmatched coaching record for himself. Rupp's success was based on discipline, fundamental concepts of the game, and a keen tactical sense. His game plans were masterful. His players, through countless hours of drills, responded to his pattern play perfectly. "At Kentucky, we open with the 'Star Spangled Banner' and then No. 6," he'd say, referring to a basic guard-around play that disclosed whether the opposition was using a zone or a man-to-man defense.

Discipline was absolute. No visitors were allowed at practice because "teachers don't have people walking in and out of their classrooms and I'm a teacher." Players were ruled with an iron hand and Rupp demanded perfection. He'd tell players, "You're only at Kentucky to do two things, get an education and play basketball. And if you flunk either one, you have to go home." Once Kentucky was leading Arkansas at the half, 38–4. "Who's guarding No. 12?" Rupp demanded in the dressing room, referring to the man who had scored Arkansas' only field goal. Jack Parkinson glumly acknowledged his responsibility. "Well, get *on* him," the Baron exhorted. "He's running wild." When one of his teams lost to Georgia Tech in a major upset, Rupp told his players, "In my time there have been two national disasters. One was Pearl Harbor. This is the other."

In 1948 Rupp had the perfect team, a well-matched blend of skills and experience. Alex Groza, six feet seven, was the center; Wah Wah Jones, later to be a sheriff of Lexington's Fayette County, and Cliff Barker played the forwards; Ralph Beard and Ken Rollins were the guards. Rollins was the only senior, the others were juniors, and together they played fast-break basketball to such perfection they became justly known as the Fabulous Five.

In Beard and Jones's freshman year, 1946, the Wildcats were 28–2

Colgate's Ernie Vanderweghe and NYU's Dolph Schayes fight for a loose ball in 1948 season action.

Kentucky's Ralph Beard puts the ball in the air in action against Georgia Tech as teammates Alex Groza (15) and Wallace (Wah Wah) Jones (27) watch.

and won the NIT. The next year, joined by Groza, they were 34–3. In 1948 they swept to a 36–3 record and only two of the losses were to college teams. The third was to the powerful Phillips Oilers in the finals of the U.S. Olympic Trials, after which the two teams were combined to form the American Gold Medal team. Included in this magnificent campaign, almost as an afterthought, was an NCAA championship.

The Wildcats started their 1949 campaign just three and a half months after returning home from the Olympics in London. The graduating Rollins was replaced by Dale Barnstable with no loss in efficiency, and Ken-

The 1948 NCAA title went to Kentucky as it beat out Holy Cross 60–52 in the title game. Here Ken Rollins (26) loses the ball to Bob Cousy. At left is Ralph Beard (12), at right, Cliff Barker (23).

tucky won its first eight games before bowing to St. Louis, the defending NIT champion led by smooth-as-silk Ed Macauley, 42–40, in the finals of the Sugar Bowl Tournament. The Wildcats then reeled off twenty-one straight victories and Rupp stunned the basketball world by announcing that Kentucky would compete in both the NCAA and the NIT. Critics accused the Baron of seeking to collect championships the way he gathered purebred Herefords for his several farms, and of asking too much from his boys. No team had ever intentionally tried for such a grand slam, and the only school ever to play in both tournaments had been Utah in the unusual year of the Blitz Kids.

The critics were satisfied, however, when Loyola of Chicago, one of the last teams invited to the NIT, summarily ousted the proud Wildcats in the first round, 67–56. "We were flat and dead," Rupp lamented (all too soon he would learn why), and for the next week, while he waited for the NCAA Eastern Regionals to begin at Madison Square Garden, he got his team ready to play.

Villanova and Illinois both fell to the Wildcats by one-sided scores. Rupp told New York sports writers, with whom he often feuded, "I guess we vindicated ourselves," as Kentucky left for Seattle to whip Oklahoma A&M in the national finals, 46–36. Groza scored twenty-five points in that final game and for the second straight year was named tournament MVP. The wire service All-America teams reflected Kentucky's dominance, listing Jones, Beard, and Groza, along with Macauley of St. Louis and Tony Lavelli, Yale's colorful, accordion-playing hook-shot virtuoso.

St. Louis University's Ed Macauley.

For 1950 Barnstable was the only returning regular, but a new potential superstar had just joined the Wildcats. He was seven-foot Bill Spivey, a sophomore who had come to Kentucky with little natural ability, but who had successfully put in long hours under Rupp's grinding tutelage to become an accomplished basketball player. With Spivey scoring almost twenty points a game, the Wildcats posted a 25–4 record and prepared to enter the NIT.

Meanwhile, in New York City another basketball powerhouse was emerging. Adolph Rupp, raised on a farm, had his "country boys from down the road." But at the City College of New York (CCNY), Nat Holman, a slender and dapper New Yorker from his neatly combed hair to his freshly shined shoes, had built no less of a reputation as a coach with players from the city's asphalt playgrounds. City College was a free institution with high academic standards. There were no scholarships. Big name players went elsewhere. Holman and his assistant, Bobby Sand, combed the five boroughs of New York for the leftovers, and it is a tribute both to the depth of talent in New York high schools and their own coaching skills that these little-known players became stars on winning teams.

Rupp had learned his basketball from Naismith and Phog Allen. The five-foot-eleven Holman had been schooled on New York's Lower East Side and later with the Original Celtics. Turning down a baseball offer from the Cincinnati Reds, he became one of the biggest names in pro basketball, the game's first big scorer, and a slick ball handler.

In 1919, while still playing pro ball, Holman was named coach at City College, and it is a measure of his skill that he was successful at both tasks. For years he scorned the Western-style wide-open game. "I'll quit before I teach one-handed shooting to my boys," he once said, but in the early forties he realized that perhaps he was being too rigid in sticking with the old Celtic short-passing game. Just as critics were whispering "basketball has passed him by," Holman switched.

And, in the years after World War II, CCNY began winning again. As the 1950 season approached, Holman thought he had put together a squad that could make "my greatest team." The only seniors were Irwin Dambrot, a six-foot-four forward who would prove the "perfect" captain, star defender, ball handler, and rebounder, and Norm Mager, a sixth man who could pick up any team with his outside shooting. Opening with Dambrot were four sophomores. The other forward was Ed Warner, six feet two and a half, a great leaper and driver, and possibly the most natively talented of them all. The center was six-foot-six Ed Roman, the tallest man Holman had ever coached. Al Roth and Floyd Layne, both six feet three, were the guards.

CCNY broke from the gate by winning thirteen of its first fifteen

Nat Holman conducts a "skull session" with the 1950 CCNY team that achieved an unprecedented "double," championships of both the NCAA and NIT. Kneeling are (*left to right*) Nat Holman, Norm Mager, Joe Galiber, Irwin Dambrot, Mike Wittlin, Ed Roman. In back are Ed Warner, Al Roth, Seymour Levy, Herb Cohen. Floyd Layne is not shown.

games and even Ned Irish, the cool and aloof Garden impresario, predicted, "Potentially they are one of the great college teams of all time." But then the Beavers surprisingly ran into trouble. They lost to Canisius and Niagara, beat St. Joseph's and Fordham, but then fell again to Syracuse. Holman was perplexed, mystified. "You need a psychiatrist, not a coach," he told his boys.

But in the Syracuse game, even though they lost, City's season turned around. Roman, who had been one of the worst offenders in the slump, fouled out. Holman replaced him with Warner, the smallest man on the team but a great jumper with pivot experience in high school. The team began to jell again. Even though the Beavers barely beat a so-so Manhattan team by two points in their next game, they closed their season with a 64–61 victory over arch-rival NYU for a 17–5 record.

Holman feared that the late slump had cost his team any chance for a tournament invitation, but the NIT had trouble completing its twelve-team field. The spot remaining open was handed to CCNY. Four teams were seeded in the NIT—Bradley, Kentucky, Duquesne, and St. John's. CCNY had to be considered the last of the least. Odds were 7-to-1 against City winning the tournament.

As his unheralded Beavers prepared to go out to meet defending champion San Francisco in the first round, Holman told them simply, "You've grown up. I know you can do it." San Francisco employed a deliberate offense, so Holman tried an unusual strategic ploy. He abandoned City's fast break and beat the Dons at

their own game. With Warner scoring twenty-six points, CCNY won easily, 65–46. But City fans had only a temporary reason to celebrate because mighty Kentucky was next in line.

To start the game, Holman used his third-string center, six-foot-eight Leroy Watkins, to oppose the seven-foot Spivey for the opening tap, but then he quickly moved Roman into the lineup and the Beavers began to roll. Going back to their fast-break offense, they blew the Wildcats off the floor. Warner, shooting from inside and then from far out when the Kentucky defense began to sag on him, scored twenty-six points for the second straight game. Dambrot added twenty and Roman seventeen in the 89–50 victory, the most one-sided loss in Kentucky history. This crushing victory made fans begin to take CCNY seriously and basket fever mounted in New York as the Beavers then gained the finals by upsetting Duquesne, 62–52.

Meanwhile, Bradley had been moving along in the opposite bracket, enjoying its bye and then knocking off Syracuse and St. John's by comfortable margins. The championship confrontation was a classic with the Braves sparked by two All-Americas, Paul Unruh and little Gene (Squeaky) Melchiorre. But it looked as if Holman would have to miss the biggest game in his coaching career: he was running a high fever and doctors warned that he'd probably have to remain at home. A television set was placed by his bed so he could watch the action, and a direct phone line was installed from his bedside to the bench so he could relay instructions to his assistant, Sand. However, at the last

Al Roth (7) of CCNY grabs a rebound from Elmer Behnke of Bradley in the
second meeting of the teams, the finals of the NCAA tournament.

minute, Holman's fever abated and he joined his players in the locker room just before the tip-off.

At first it looked as if he might as well have remained in bed. The Beavers, missing their foul shots, fell behind by eleven points, 29–18, but then they abandoned their fast break for ball control and slowly worked their way back. Going into the last two minutes City led by 64–61, but that year a rule was in effect stating that in the final minutes there would be a jump ball after every foul shot, made or missed. Bradley started fouling, knowing the Beavers were missing their free throws and also confident that six-foot-seven Elmer Behnke would control the tap against six-foot-three Ed Warner. Seven times they jumped for possession and seven times Warner controlled the tap as City held on to win, 69–61, for its first national championship. Dambrot was high scorer in this game with twenty-three points, but Warner, who had scored eighty-seven points in four games, was named tournament MVP.

The season wasn't over for the Beavers, however. The NCAA invited them to their own tournament and City elected to go for the sweep. Ohio State was City's first NCAA opponent and Norm Mager had to come off the bench to help Floyd Layne break the Buckeyes' zone with long shots for a one-point 56–55 decision. North Carolina State, which had recently become a national power under coach Everett Case (and would drag the rest of the mid-South along with it in a couple of years), was City's next foe in the Eastern Regional finals. Holman had seen how the Wolfpack, led by Dick Dickey, had outrun the Holy Cross press in the first round. So this time the Beavers played a set, conservative defense to win, 78–73.

By a twist of fate and scheduling Bradley had also gone from the NIT to the NCAA's Western Regional, and with close victories over Brigham Young and Baylor had qualified for another match with CCNY for a national title. This game also was scheduled in Madison Square Garden where CCNY would be playing its seventh tournament game in eighteen days.

The tension was unbearable and the pace swift as the climactic game got under way. Bradley opened with a zone defense, but after nine early lead changes City had taken a 39–32 halftime lead. Forrest Anderson, Bradley's young coach, knew he had to make an adjustment. The change was a return to the Braves' standard man-to-man defense, but the Beavers, rebounding inches taller than their height, retained command. With less than two minutes remaining, City led by 69–61 and Anderson made another tactical switch. Speedy Joe Stowell and Gus Chianakas were inserted into the lineup, and with the five-foot-eight Melchiorre leading the way, Bradley went into a full-court press. The crowd was stunned as their hometown team, already national champions from one tournament, seemed to lose its poise. Again and again Melchiorre stole the ball from the flustered Beavers. In one minute Bradley had scored seven straight points and Melchiorre had five of them as the Braves closed to within a point at 69–68.

Suddenly Melchiorre had the ball again, and again he dribbled swiftly toward the basket. But this time, as he left his feet for the layup, the ball flew from his grasp. Had he been fouled? There was no whistle. The ball was in play, Dambrot grabbed it and flipped it up court to Mager, who was unguarded and who put in the clinching basket in a 71–68 City victory. The Beavers had completed their grand slam.

As the whole city of New York exulted, for truly this was a victory for all the millions in its teeming boroughs, Holman reflected on the unprecedented achievement. It was something he still couldn't believe as he harked back to that unexplainable slump in late season that had almost destroyed City's chances to win anything. After the grand slam was completed, the eloquent coach told his players, "It took us an hour to play each game, it will take a lifetime to forget them." Later he wrote, "Now that it is over, I am grateful. But going through two tournaments was a horrible strain—on the boys and on myself. Maybe it was too much to ask of a team." Less than a year later those words would be given a prophetic ring.

8

SCANDAL

AT FIRST ONLY A FEW RIPPLES disturbed the smooth surface of the prospering sport of college basketball. In the spring of 1944 a gambler had suggested that Utah coach Vadal Peterson throw an NCAA championship game to Dartmouth and had been punched for his troubles. An important lesson was learned—stay away from coaches.

Then, a year later, shocking news broke that five Brooklyn College basketball players had taken $1,000 to deliberately lose an upcoming game with Akron in Madison Square Garden. They were promised an additional $2,000 after the game, but one regular, Bill Rosenblatt, refused to go along. The fix was aborted, the game canceled. The two fixers were sentenced to a year in jail, and the five players were expelled from school. For one player, expulsion was a gesture: he was not even a bona fide student.

New York laws were strengthened to provide more severe penalties against players who took bribes, but, generally, the public glossed over the few kids who went wrong and lauded Honest Bill Rosenblatt, who had nixed the fix.

Out in Kansas Phog Allen warned of additional skulduggery at the Garden, and he even sent Ned Irish the name of a player he felt was doing business with gamblers. Allen blamed college presidents and faculties for wrongdoing in basketball. "They have been afraid to face facts," he charged, but he was ignored. Phog Allen had an opinion on everything; but basketball administrators, and the press, ignored the bellows of the western windbag.

The following year, another ripple appeared on the surface, but this one, too, was quickly forgotten. Four gamblers approached Dave Shapiro, a

Max Kase, sports editor of the New York *Journal-American*, broke the scandalous story.

97

There was a hint of things to come when Dave Shapiro, co-captain of the George Washington basketball team, reported to DA Frank Hogan a $1000 offer to throw a game. The fixers were caught, and Shapiro was congratulated by Hogan.

twenty-five-year-old law student from Brooklyn who was the co-captain at George Washington University. They offered him $1,000 to throw a game with Manhattan in the Garden and up to $10,000 if he would manipulate scores to their order in the Colonials' final sixteen games. The pretty young sister-in-law of one of the gamblers was enlisted as a "feminine decoy" to keep Shapiro's attention.

Shapiro, however, reported the bribe attempt involving the Manhattan game to New York district attorney Frank Hogan. He was told to pretend to go along with the fix, which he did, and he set up the arrest of all four men before the game. One of them, William Rivlin, was said to be an admitted bookmaker. GW, supposed to lose by eighteen or nineteen points, according to the fixers, actually beat Manhattan, 71–63. It was estimated that the gamblers, who thought the fix was in, lost $5 million. The fixers all pleaded guilty and received sentences ranging up to two and a half years.

And again basketball went its merry way, although betting was wide open in arenas like Madison Square Garden, newspapers printed all the point spreads, coaches discussed them with their players, and crowds often cheered not the winning basket but the basket that put their team over the spread. Some college players from poor families were seen driving fancy cars, and after one game in a New York armory, one of the stars was publicly bawled out by a former player for letting his team go over the point spread.

Betting on basketball is different from most sports although today football has adopted the same principles. Instead of betting on a team to win or lose and giving or taking odds (i.e., 3-to-1, risking one dollar to win three) as in racing, prize fighting, and presidential elections, the bookmaker handicaps the game with a point spread. Usually this opening line comes from a mysterious central source in the Midwest. In the supposedly fixed George Washington–Manhattan game, George Washington opened as a seven-and-a-half-point underdog. To win a bet on Manhattan, the Jaspers would have had to win by eight points or more. If they won by seven or less, it was the same as a loss to their supporters and the GW bettors won.

The bookmaker normally is not a gambler himself. If you lose a ten-dollar bet to a bookmaker, you pay him eleven dollars. If you win, he pays you ten dollars. The dollar difference —the "vigorish"—is the bookmaker's profit. He sets up his line, not so much to predict the outcome, but to handicap the event in such a way that an equal amount of money will be bet on both teams. If too much comes in for one team, he may try to "lay it off," that is, send the money to another bookmaker who is overloaded the other way, or he will adjust the spread to attract more money from the other side.

As money poured in from gamblers on "sure-thing" Manhattan, the bookmakers raised the Jaspers from seven-and-a-half-point to nine-and-a-half and finally to twelve-point favorites, hoping to make a bet on George Washington more attractive and thus lure more money to counterbalance the Manhattan flood. Eventually they just "took the game off the boards," meaning they would accept no more bets. When the fix failed, the sure-thing guys were out the $5 million. But it was a close call for the bookies, who, although they operate illegally on the fringe of the underworld, depend more than anyone on honest games to survive.

The use of point spreads was what gave the gamblers their in with the ballplayers. "We're not paying you to

Junius Kellogg, star of the Manhattan team, was another player to report an attempted bribe. His schoolmates gave him a hero's welcome to campus as a result. At his left is Manhattan coach Ken Norton.

lose, just hold down the score," they would croon seductively. The stars on a bad team would be told that their school was going to lose anyway, so why not make the score a little more one-sided? Nobody would be hurt and the players could share in some of the wealth they saw going to their coaches, colleges, and the big-time arenas. Once a player was snared, however, he would also lose on order.

By January of 1951 Junius Kellogg had established himself as the best player on the Manhattan varsity even though he was only a sophomore. The first black athlete ever to perform for the Jaspers, he was a six-foot-eight 205-pound center and the team's leading scorer. One of eleven children, the Portsmouth, Virginia, native was twenty-three years old and attending the college as a service veteran under the G.I. Bill of Rights.

One day Henry Poppe, a former Manhattan star who had been co-captain the year before, dropped by Kellogg's dormitory room. This wasn't

Picked up and accused in the effort to bribe Kellogg were former players Henry Poppe (*left*) and John Byrnes (*third from left*). Charged with paying bribes were Cornelius Kelleher (*between the players*) and Irving Schwartzberg (*dark suit, hand to face*) and his brother Benjamin (*right, hand to face*). Seated are Bronx district attorney George DeLuca (*right*) and assistant DA Edward Breslin. Glaring at his former players is Coach Norton.

unusual, but what Poppe had to say shocked Kellogg to his toes. Manhattan would be the underdog in its next game against DePaul in the Garden, and Poppe offered Kellogg $1,000 to make sure the Jaspers lost by at least ten points. Stunned, Kellogg turned down the proposition, but Poppe would not accept his refusal. "I'll see you tomorrow," he said.

The next day Poppe told Kellogg how he and another former Manhattan player, John Byrnes, who was in with him on this particular fix attempt, had thrown three particular games "among others" the year before and had earned $5,000 each without a hint of exposure. When Byrnes broke his leg and could not finish the season, he still got paid off by the fix-ers, Poppe said. Poppe also told Kellogg how to go about the business of dumping. Miss a shot here and there "but don't be so bad you stink out the joint," Poppe warned. He had forgotten to tell Kellogg not to go to his coach, however. After the very first approach, Kellogg had alerted Manhattan coach Ken Norton, and the district attorney's office was kept apprised of all developments.

DePaul opened as a four-and-a-half-point favorite, but the spread soared all the way to ten and a half before frightened bookies "took it off." Although Kellogg, obviously upset by his ordeal, played poorly, Manhattan won the game, 62–59. The fixers lost their bets, and their liberty, too. All of them, including Poppe and Byrnes, were arrested.

Questioned by police, Poppe implicated other players. He even told of one game where he learned that another syndicate had bribed Manhattan's opponents to dump, too. Poppe was able to call off Manhattan's dive, but later there was supposed to have been an actual game in which both teams were trying to lose. The news was stunning. "I'm shocked and surprised," Norton said. "I had no idea last year that some of my boys were throwing games, although I knew the kids weren't doing so well." Even non-involved Manhattan players were surprised. "When we lost those games, I just thought we were having one of our bad nights," one reflected.

Again college authorities reacted with the decisiveness of an ostrich. Kellogg was hailed, and rightly, as a hero. The two dumpers were excoriated as bad apples. Dr. Tristan Walker Metcalfe, president of Long Island University, called a meeting of eight of his colleagues from the New York area to discuss what could be done to head off future basketball scandals. The only man who showed up was the president of recently tarred Manhattan.

As universities and arena managers continued their complacent way, bookmakers became strange allies with the law. The bookies were tired of taking regular financial beatings on fixed games. One day in early January a bookmaker entered the rundown Lower East Side offices of the New York *Journal-American* and sought out the paper's astute sports editor, Max Kase. Kase, short and round faced, had been in the newspaper business for a lot of years. He, and many sports writers on the basketball beat, had heard all the rumors about fixed games. They had covered a lot of "upsets" that defied explanation, but the laws of libel prevented them from printing the rumors and voicing their own suspicions. Besides, if coaches like Norton could be fooled by their own players, how could outsiders tell when a game was being fixed? Kase, and the others, were looking for something solid, and the veteran sports editor sensed he had succeeded when his bookmaker friend sat down at his desk. "Watch _____," the bookmaker said, naming a former local college star. "He's the go-between."

Kase could have had himself a pretty good scoop, even without naming names. Instead, he went to district attorney Frank Hogan with the tip and promised not to write a word until the prosecutor had built his case. Hogan, in turn, agreed to let the *Journal-American* break the story. (Kase later received a Pulitzer citation for his role.) Exactly a month after Kellogg's disclosures the *Journal-American* broke its story. A new major basketball scandal was about to be revealed, the paper headlined. Among the people pulled in for questioning was Eddie Gard, a former Long Island University star. Gard was the go-between whose name had been whispered to Kase. Harvey (Connie) Schaff, a New York University player, was also called in and later sentenced to six months in jail for dumping games and trying unsuccessfully to involve a teammate in the fix. Within hours the world of college basketball began to crumble.

The CCNY team that had scored that unbelievable grand slam the year before was on its way back from Phil-

Former LIU star, Eddie Gard (*left*) leaves court with a detective.

CCNY players Ed Warner, Al Roth, Connie Schaff (*at left*), Ed Roman (*second from right*), and Eddie Gard (*hidden behind Roman*) are booked after being picked up. Booked at the same time (*with hats over faces*) were Sollazzo and Sabbatini.

adelphia after a victory over Temple. As their train rolled through New Jersey, a representative of the district attorney's office called coach Nat Holman aside. He said he had orders to pick up three of his players when they arrived in New York and he felt they'd all like the matter to be handled discreetly. "Just tell them the truth," Holman told the three players. The truth would break his heart.

The three players arrested that night in Penn Station were Ed Roman, Al Roth, and Ed Warner. After twenty-one hours of questioning, they confessed. They had accepted bribes ranging from $500 to $1,500 a game for throwing three games the previous year. Holman finally learned the rea-

son for his great team's mysterious slump. Eddie Gard had been the go-between. The money had been put up by Salvatore (Tarto) Sollazzo, a forty-five-year-old jewelry manufacturer and former convict. Sollazzo had met Gard at a Catskill Mountain resort a year earlier while Gard was playing in the high-pressure hotel summer basketball leagues that attracted hundreds of top college players and thousands of dollars in wagers. Sollazzo entertained Gard lavishly and enrolled him in the plot. Later, with his pretty young wife, a former model, acting as hostess, and attractive dates available for the players, Sollazzo continued to entertain and entrap top college stars. He would take them to his

Salvatore Sollazzo.

plush apartment overlooking Central Park or to New York's top night spots.

"You have corrupted these young men and it is a disgrace," Chief Magistrate John Murtaugh said when he refused bail at Sollazzo's hearing. The justice also pointedly noted that he was an alumnus of City College. Other unsavory characters were involved with Sollazzo, it was later determined, along with still another former LIU player, Jackie Goldsmith, a great set shooter who had starred despite his five-foot-eight height. Gard, who turned informer once his role in the conspiracy was uncovered, was held under protective custody.

When he had first met Sollazzo, Gard was still playing at LIU and he involved teammate Adolph Bigos, a guard. Bigos came from a well-to-do family, but he agreed to go along. He and Gard each got $1,000 for losing a 1950 game to North Carolina State.

Soon after, Sherman White, a six-foot-seven forward who was conceded to be an outstanding professional prospect, approached the two conspirators. "You guys laid down in that game. You didn't feed me the ball," he charged. At first Gard denied everything, but then he decided White should be included in the ring. When Gard's eligibility expired, even though he was still enrolled in school, he realized the fixers would need another ball handler to control the game, so he signed up his replacement, Leroy Smith.

Soon the fixers were able to control their games as if they had been choreographed like ballet or professional wrestling. They would win, just barely, right under the spread. "Real marksmen," Hogan called them. But they had to lose one of the games in the NIT. That one hurt. Clair Bee, LIU's coach, suspected nothing. The 1950–51 Blackbird team opened with sixteen straight victories, some of them surprisingly close. And yet they won by 84–52 over Duquesne! This game was supposed to be shaved, but this time rumors of fixes and investigations were widespread and the players told Sollazzo they wanted out. (He reputedly lost between $50,000 and $65,000 because he had already placed his bets.) "This team could have been a great one," Bee said sadly years later, ranking the playing potential of the fixers as the equal of his earlier undefeated fives. Instead, they shattered him emotionally—friends feared he might not live through the shock—and for seven years destroyed basketball at LIU.

The three LIU players—Smith, Bigos, and White—were arrested one afternoon as they left their classes. Only that morning, questioned by Bee, they had denied everything. Under police interrogation, Bigos cracked first, then White and Smith. A couple of days earlier, after the arrest and confessions of Warner, Roman, and Roth, there had been a mass rally at CCNY. Students vowed to support the remaining members of the team. Few of them were cheered louder than Floyd Layne, another of the veterans of the grand slam, when he made an inspirational speech. A week later Layne was also arrested and he admitted taking $3,000 to shave points in two Garden games.

In the next month three more City players, Irwin Dambrot, Norm Mager, and Herb Cohen, were arrested and confessed. Also three former LIU players, Nathan Miller, Louis Lipmann, and Dick Feurtado, for fixes dating back to 1948, as well as Goldsmith. William Rivlin, the bookmaker who had been convicted of trying to bribe Dave Shapiro some years earlier, and a shadowy figure named Eli Klukofsky (alias Eli Kaye), were tabbed as the men behind these particular fixes.

The players never even got to enjoy the money. Warner, an orphan who lived with his aunt, had taken $3,050 for shaving points. The money—twenty-eight hundred-dollar bills and five fifties—was found tightly folded in an envelope stuffed in a shoe box. Roth had taken $5,060 and it was in an envelope in his mother's safety deposit box. She didn't know it was there. White had $5,500 in a drawer in the room he occupied in a Brooklyn YMCA. Bigos had $5,000 in the pocket of a topcoat in his closet.

Smith had stashed $1,930 in a safety deposit box and in his room at the Y. Layne, who said Warner had recruited him into the ring, had hidden $2,890 in a flowerpot. He had wrapped the bills in a handkerchief before refilling the pot with dirt. Only Roman's money had apparently been spent. "I knew something like this was going to happen," the remorseful Leroy Smith said. "I got about $2,000 and I spent about twenty-two dollars of it immediately on ties and shirts and things like that. When the cops asked me for the money, I threw it over to them."

The players not only failed to enjoy the money, they were often shortchanged by the fixers. Many times a player would shave points in the final game of his college career and then not be given all that was coming to him. The fixer didn't need him any more. To whom could he complain? There was also the element of physical danger. "One more basket and you would have gotten us killed," players in one ring told an uninvolved teammate after he got hot in a particular game. From then on he was a member of the gang.

The district attorney's disclosures brought down a torrent of abuse on New York basketball and particularly on Madison Square Garden and Ned Irish. The big city was full of sin and corruption. Bradley's basketball team voted unanimously to never play in the Garden again. Adolph Rupp, coach at Kentucky, blamed big-city newspapers that printed the point spreads, boasted that "gamblers couldn't touch my boys with a ten-foot pole," and urged leniency for players who only shaved points but didn't throw games.

The Bradley vote and Rupp's complacent pronouncement would come back to haunt them. Before the summer was over, four of the five starters from Bradley who had taken that pious vote to avoid the contagion of Madison Square Garden, including All-America Gene Melchiorre, were arrested and found guilty of taking bribes to fix several games. Only two of the fixes had come off, both of them involving games played in Bradley's new and supposedly incorruptible field house. Four players at Toledo were also involved.

That fall came the biggest blockbuster of them all—some gambler had apparently found an eleven-foot pole. Dale Barnstable, Ralph Beard, and Alex Groza, stars of the Fabulous Five, Kentucky's NCAA champions, admitted sharing $2,000 in bribes to shave points in the 1949 NIT game against Loyola. The Wildcats had been favored by ten points, but in trying to hold down the score had lost control of the contest and were defeated in a stunning upset. An assistant district attorney said "practically every game" Kentucky played that season was involved in gambling. The players admitted only one fix, however.

By this time Beard and Groza were stars and co-owners of the professional Indianapolis Olympians. Both were suspended immediately by Maurice Podoloff, commissioner of the National Basketball Association, and their lucrative careers ended.

Later, three more Kentucky players were named in the spreading scandal. Jim Line, a former Kentucky star serving as an assistant at his alma mater, was accused of being an intermediary in offering bribes to Walter

Hirsch and seven-foot Bill Spivey. Hirsch was nailed on the fix charge and Spivey was indicted for perjury, his dreams of a rich pro career ruined. Now that the scandal had "hit in the family," Rupp no longer urged leniency for players who "only" shaved points.

The fixers involved in the Kentucky-Toledo-Bradley scandals were a mixed bag. Nick Englisis, briefly a Kentucky football player, and his brother Tony were the contact men hooked up with one Jack (Zip) West, identified by police as a former associate of New York hoodlums. Joseph Benintende, identified as a Kansas City gunman, was later fingered as the real kingpin of the operation. The ubiquitous Eli Kaye got wind of the ring late and tried to get involved, so the brothers Englisis tipped him off on a couple of fixed games.

The fixers were rough customers. Once West kidnapped Tony Englisis and ordered Nick to change a fix. Instead of going over the spread, West wanted an under. Nick, frantically signaling his stooge players from the sidelines just before the opening tap, managed to make the change, which saved his brother from a beating and provided West with a big payoff. The hapless Kaye took a financial thumping. Nobody bothered to tell him about the change. Another time, the brothers and West deliberately doublecrossed Kaye by giving him the wrong side in a fixed game.

College basketball staggered under the continuing disclosures of corruption by highly admired players. The grand jury that had been called into session in February of 1951 to investigate the scandals wasn't dissolved until April 30, 1953. All told, thirty-two players from seven colleges were involved. Between 1947 and 1950 eighty-six games had been shown to have been fixed.

Among the fixers, major sentences went to Sollazzo, eight to sixteen years; Benintende, four to seven; Goldsmith, two and a half to five; and Gard, a maximum of three years. Among the players, Sherman White was sentenced to a year, Schaff, Warner, and Roth to six months each. Sentence was suspended for the others, but for all of them the punishment only began in court. In terms of ruined lives, wasted careers, and heartbreak, their punishment was indeed cruel.

When it came time for their sentencing, the blame was spread beyond the greedy players and unscrupulous gamblers. In some of the most scathing language ever directed from the bench, general sessions judge Saul S. Streit excoriated the universities and their coaches for permitting big-time sport to run unfettered through the halls of ivy. Phog Allen had called the turn; Judge Streit documented those charges as he passed sentence on the various fixers. "The responsibility for the sports scandal must be shared not only by the crooked fixers and corrupt players, but also by the college administrations, coaches and alumni groups who participated in this evil system of commercialism and overemphasis," Judge Streit declared.

He said he had closely studied the backgrounds of all the players involved and the athletic programs of their schools. "The conditions revealed were, to say the least, most shocking," Judge Streit pointed out. "I found, among other vices, that the sport was commercialized and professionalized; devices, frauds and probable fraud were employed to matriculate unqualified students to college; flagrant violations of amateur rules by colleges, coaches and players; and illegal scouting, recruiting and subsidization of players."

The stern jurist then detailed how some of the players had been enticed to their respective colleges. Leroy Smith, he said, was given a full scholarship at LIU, plus a job, but was told "it was not necessary to put in time at the job, and if he had given a good athletic performance during that week his pay slip would be marked extra hours." He recounted that White had an IQ of eighty-two when he finished high school, had failed admittance at Duquesne, and flunked out of Villanova before enrolling at LIU. "In some miraculous manner, despite the demands made by a severe basketball playing schedule, daily practice and his illicit summer activities [the resort league], White showed 'remarkable scholastic improvement' at LIU," the judge said sarcastically. "Among the courses he pursued his senior year at LIU were music seminar, oil painting, rhythm and dance, public speaking and physical education."

Layne and Warner, both with poor high school records, also showed "miraculous improvement" once they enrolled at CCNY after qualifying with special evening courses. Roth, the judge revealed, graduated from high school with an average of 70.43, but his high school transcript as recorded at CCNY showed 75.5. "This discrepancy has never been explained," the judge declared. There were also changes in Cohen's record from the time it left his high school until it was recorded at CCNY. "I suggest that in the cases of Roth and Cohen there was deliberate fraud and probable forgery," the judge charged.

"In brief, all of the players entrusted to the care of LIU were only exploited in behalf of Mr. Bee and the university," he concluded. "The naivete, the equivocation and the denials of the coaches and their assistants concerning their knowledge of gambling, recruiting and subsidizing would be comical were they not so despicable."

Judge Streit also noted that players earned up to $2,000 playing basketball in the Catskill resorts while ostensibly working as bus boys, waiters, and life guards. He also said "gambling was rampant" at the Garden. He quoted figures to show the financial importance of basketball to the various schools.

He added that corruption of basketball players was "not local by any means." And, in passing sentence, the judge pointed out that the players, all of whom were twenty-two years of age or older, were not merely innocent victims. "Here is no isolated mistake in a moment of temptation, no fall from grace because of undisciplined passion. Here is callous, careful, schemed cheating time and time again."

Later, when handing down suspended sentences against the University of Kentucky stars (the type of sentence appeared to depend on whether a player had enmeshed any of his teammates in the fixes), Judge Streit unleashed a blast at that school and its coach, Adolph Rupp. The judge called the university "the acme of commercialization and overemphasis." And he especially scored Rupp for his association with Ed Curd, acknowledged as the biggest bookmaker in Lexington, Kentucky. He quoted

Rupp as admitting that Curd's illegal activities were "general knowledge." He charged that Rupp had called Curd several times for information on point spreads of Kentucky games and said that Curd had been a dinner companion of the Kentucky traveling party, which included players, on at least two occasions at New York's Copacabana night club. (Kentucky insists Curd did not pick up the check.)

Judge Streit said in his investigation of the athletic program at Kentucky, "I found covert subsidization of players, ruthless exploitation of athletes, cribbing at examinations, 'illegal' recruiting, a reckless disregard of their physical welfare, matriculation of unqualified students, demoralization of the athletes by the coach, alumni, and townspeople and the most flagrant abuse of the athletic scholarship." (Some of these violations later caused Kentucky's basketball program to be suspended for a year.) Not in the history of sport had there been such wholesale revelations of corruption.

It was a terrible ordeal, but the college basketball family thought it would prove worthwhile if the lessons it had taught would be remembered. That was the cruelest joke of all. A mere ten years later still another scandal swept through the sport. This time New York City and "venal" Madison Square Garden could not be blamed.

The front men in what proved to be a huge ring were Aaron Wagman, who already had been convicted of trying to bribe a University of Florida football player, and Joseph Hacken, who had once been implicated in trying to fix a prizefight. They toured the country, mostly in the South, to recruit fixers. The ring's mastermind was Jack Molinas, a former Columbia star who had been thrown out of the National Basketball Association as a rookie in 1954 for betting on games played by his Fort Wayne team. One Philip LaCort bankrolled the operation. Eventually all received jail terms, the most severe being a ten-to-fifteen-year sentence for Molinas.

Seton Hall was the first school implicated in the new scandal but then the net spread north and south and on into the Midwest. Before it was over, forty-nine players in twenty-seven schools had been implicated, some of them, to be sure, merely for not reporting bribe attempts. A total of twenty players had been paid $44,500 to fix forty-four games over a five-year period. Six other players, including some getting ready to enroll as college freshmen, got $800 in softening-up money. The twenty-six players represented fifteen schools. There were reports that the ring even tried to fix a high school game in New York.

Some of the players, all of whom were granted immunity to testify against the fixers, seemed to treat the affair as a lark. Jerry Graves, the Mississippi State captain, took $4,750, but insisted he had never shaved a point and had used the money for a good time. "I gave Wagman nothing but my opinion. I took the crooks in, you might say," he gloated.

A sadder and more typical case was that of Ray Paprocky of NYU, a married army veteran who said he got involved because "I was in debt and my wife was expecting a baby." Hacken learned of Paprocky's financial straits and moved right in. "I am aware that what I did was wrong and I don't expect anyone to condone it," Paprocky said later. "But if I were in the same circumstances, I'd do it again, not because I'd want to, but because I'd be forced to. It was better than robbing a grocery store. Others wanted the money for cars or girls, I wanted it for my family."

From March, 1961, through May, 1962, the revelations of this latest scandal flowed from the various district attorney's offices throughout the nation. Again, everyone vowed that lessons had been learned, abuses would be corrected. Never, never again.

Then, in April of 1965, players at Seattle University were expelled for involvement in bribes. Chicago syndicate money was supposed to be involved, but the scandal was a small one. Only a single school, only three wrecked lives.

It would never happen again . . . until the next time.

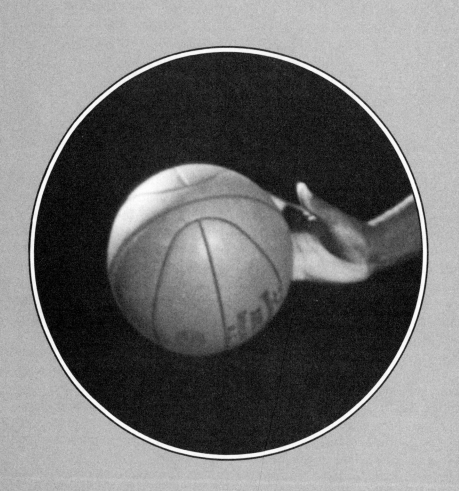

9

THE COMEBACK

SOME FOUR DECADES BEFORE the basketball scandals, baseball had been staggered by the infamous "Black Sox" incident. Public confidence in the sport had been shattered when it was revealed that the Chicago White Sox had thrown the 1919 World Series to the Cincinnati Reds. To regain that confidence the club owners hired Judge Kenesaw Mountain Landis to be their first all-powerful commissioner. Landis fulfilled that role, but of considerably more importance was the emergence of a bandy-legged home run hitter named Babe Ruth, whose gargantuan feats captured the public's imagination and made them forget all about the scandals.

College basketball hired no czars. The only apparent change was the strengthening of the NCAA Tournament vis-à-vis the NIT and the avoidance by some schools of the big-city arenas. As in baseball, it was not the administrators who saved the game, but the players. In the postscandal decade of the fifties, dozens of glamorous new stars burst upon the college scene, literally leaping to new heights and shooting with an accuracy that would have put even the fabled Hank Luisetti on the bench.

Bill Russell, Wilt Chamberlain, Dick Groat, Bill Mlkvy, Tom Gola, Bob Pettit, Frank Selvy, Hot Rod Hundley, Jerry West, Elgin Baylor, Oscar Robertson, Jerry Lucas, the O'Brien twins—these were some of the stars of this era, probably the most exciting in the history of college basketball. In 1970 *Sport Magazine* polled one hundred college coaches to name an all-time All-America team. Four of the starting five played in this decade: West, Baylor, Russell, and Robertson. These were the players who wiped away the original taint of scandal and who kept fans from

brooding when it recurred ten years later.

At one end of the player spectrum were the dominating giants, Bill Russell and Wilt Chamberlain, who forced rule changes, just as Bob Kurland and George Mikan had done before them. At the other end were the exploits and antics of the bantam-sized twin brothers from the University of Seattle, Johnny and Eddie O'Brien.

The O'Briens hailed from South Amboy, New Jersey. Johnny, the shooter, stood five feet nine; Eddie, the feeder, was half an inch shorter and four hours younger. No eastern schools offered them scholarships when they finished high school, but they were approached by Seattle coach Al Brightman while competing in a national baseball tournament in Wichita, Kansas. Brightman wanted to turn Seattle into a national basketball power. He signed the O'Briens to combination baseball-basketball scholarships and the boys went on to play major league baseball for the Pittsburgh Pirates.

The lads were an immediate hit at Seattle, which made the most of them: one home game was advertised as "O'Briens vs. College of Puget Sound tonight." In his junior year, 1952, Johnny O'Brien became the first college player to score more than a thousand points, topping that figure by fifty-one with the aid of a record 361 free throws. He also led the nation in scoring and made All-America as a senior. One of Johnny O's biggest games was an Olympic benefit contest when he scored forty-three points as Seattle upset the then mighty Harlem Globetrotters. Despite his lack of size Johnny played center in this game, and after the defeat Goose Tatum, the

Globies' legendary star, could only mutter in disbelief, "That Johnny O, he's not a little man, he's a big man."

Meanwhile, across the nation, another small-of-stature sharpshooter, Dick Groat, was breaking records at Duke. Groat, a six-footer, had been turned on to basketball at the age of six by his older brothers, who had been all-around athletes at Pitt. Although he grew up in the Pittsburgh suburb of Swissvale, Pennsylvania, he went to Duke instead of Pitt because of its fine baseball program. In 1951 Groat led the nation in scoring and he completed his basketball career by setting a national three-year scoring record. He credited some of his success to little tricks taught him by Red Auerbach, an assistant coach at Duke. Groat was also able to star in baseball for the Blue Devils and signed with the Pirates on graduation. After a service hitch, he joined them in Pittsburgh and became the regular shortstop. The man whose job he took was Eddie O'Brien.

Duke's Dick Groat.

"That Johnny O, he's not a little man, he's a big man," said the Globetrotter's Goose Tatum, and the five-foot-nine-inch Johnny O'Brien proved it by becoming the first collegian to score a thousand points in a season.

Bill Mlkvy of Temple.

One of Groat's rivals for scoring honors was Bill Mlkvy, a slender six-foot-four dental student at Temple, who was known as the Owl without a Vowel. Mlkvy, whose older sister taught him the set shot, scored a record seventy-three points against Wilkes College in the final game of his junior year, which helped him set another national record of 29.2 points for a season's scoring average. That same year Groat set a record with 831 total points. When they met head-to-head the following season, Duke won easily, 85–48, with Groat outscoring his rival, 33–17.

Kentucky, led by Bill Spivey, Cliff Hagan, and Frank Ramsey, won a record third NCAA championship in 1951, after getting a pass into the field. In past years the winner of the Southeastern Conference postseason tournament automatically received the NCAA bid, and in 1951 the Wildcats were upset by Vanderbilt in the finals. But, for some reason, it had been voted that this year the regular-season champion would go, and that was Kentucky.

The Wildcats' toughest game in the NCAA was in the Eastern Regional finals when they edged Illinois, 76–74. In the tournament's first round the Illini had eliminated Columbia, which had gone undefeated through twenty-two regular-season games under Lou Rossini, a last-minute choice as coach.

Kentucky, playing without the indicted Spivey, fell to St. John's in the Eastern Regional finals of the 1952 NCAA Tournament, but Adolph Rupp could find some sentimental satisfaction in the eventual result as his alma mater, Kansas, and old coach, Phog Allen, beat the Redmen in the finals, 80–63.

Allen had grown up in Independence, Missouri, on the same block as Harry S. Truman. He had learned his basketball directly from Dr. Naismith at Kansas, where at one time he coached three different colleges simultaneously to winning records. (They were the U. of Kansas; Haskell Indian School, also in Lawrence, which won the National Aboriginal Championship; and Baker University, in Baldwin, Kansas, fifteen miles away.) He later received a degree from the Kansas City School of Osteopathy, for he felt this knowledge of the human body would help his coaching career. After he returned to Kansas as full-time coach in 1919, he became famous for his winning records, his outspoken comments on all subjects, and his sometimes-bizarre training rules. The latter included an afternoon pregame nap for all the players, and himself, and an unending war against cold feet. "I never saw a man with cold feet who wasn't nervous and jumpy," Allen proclaimed, and he would often group his players around an open fireplace, their feet facing the flames.

Allen's proper name was Dr. Forrest C. Allen. He received the nickname of Foghorn in his youth when he worked as a baseball umpire, but the name eventually was shortened to Phog. Allen warned others early about the basketball scandals, and despite his dictum that "a good big man is always better than a good little man," he tried to minimize the effect of the big man on basketball. Yet when he won his first national title, his star was a hulking six-foot-nine center named Clyde Lovellette, known variously as "Man Mountain" or the "Big White Whale."

Lovellette was not overly graceful when he enrolled at Kansas, but Allen was determined to make the big guy into a scorer and built his offense around him. "He's closer to the basket than anyone else on the floor, so I'd rather see him go for it than anyone else," Allen explained logically. Lovellette responded with a record 141 points in four NCAA games, including forty-four in the regional finals. He also broke Groat's career scoring record by two points only two days after the Duke star had established it.

There are some who maintain that the best college basketball played in the 1953 season took place in the in-

Forrest C. (Phog) Allen, outspoken coach of the University of Kansas.

Clyde Lovellette.

Bob Pettit (50) pulls down a rebound for Louisiana State in the 1954 Southeastern Conference title game against Kentucky. Kentucky won, 44–43.

trasquad games at the University of Kentucky gymnasium. The abrasive Adolph Rupp had never made any friends in his conference, and when they got the chance Southeastern Conference officials went after him. With information revealed in the scandal testimony, the SEC, backed by the NCAA, barred Kentucky from basketball for an entire year because of recruiting violations. These included a rather standard practice of giving players some spending money for participating in holiday tournaments. "I won't quit until the fellow who told me I couldn't have a team this year hands me the NCAA championship trophy," Rupp vowed as he pondered the powerhouse he had assembled with Cliff Hagan and Frank Ramsey as the key performers.

The next year the Wildcats burst from their cage with a vengeance, sweeping undefeated through their twenty-five-game schedule and beating LSU in a playoff for the SEC title. But the NCAA had one card still to play against Kentucky. The Wildcats' best players had remained in school and earned their degrees during the season of suspension. Although they could play out their final year of eligibility in regular games, as graduate students they were barred from NCAA tournament competition. Kentucky stayed home; LSU went instead and was eliminated in its first game.

During Kentucky's eclipse, one of the nation's greatest players, Bob Pettit, came out of the Wildcats' own conference. During his career at Louisiana State he averaged more than twenty-seven points a game. As a senior he averaged 31.4, which would have been a record if Frank Selvy up at Furman hadn't been scoring ten points higher that same season.

An only child, Pettit actually failed to make the junior varsity of his high school team the first time he tried, but he refused to accept the rejection. He improvised a basket in his back yard and practiced for hours. Eventually, his father, who had played at Westminster himself, put up a real basket for his son. When it grew dark, Bob would put two lamps in the window so some light would fall on his little court. By the time he was a high school senior, Pettit had grown to six feet four and spent the summer before his final season at a basketball camp run by Ray Meyer of DePaul. There, for hours, he studied old movies of George Mikan in action. More than a dozen colleges sought Pettit's services when he graduated at his full growth of six feet nine, but the easygoing yet dedicated athlete chose to stay in Baton Rouge to attend LSU. There were no regrets on either side, except that LSU's strongest team was in Pettit's junior year when Kentucky was barred from competition, and Bob wished he could have tested himself against the Wildcats under the best conditions.

Pettit's major rival for college headlines was Frank Selvy, handsome son of a Kentucky coal miner, who was born as the third of seven children the night of Franklin D. Roosevelt's election to his first term as president. Selvy was only five feet four as a high school freshman and couldn't make the team until his junior year. He was an even six feet as a senior

Frank Selvy of Furman University.

and too small for Adolph Rupp. By the time Rupp had a chance to see Selvy shine against the state's best (and bigger) players in an All-Star game, Selvy had already committed himself to Furman.

As a six-foot-three junior at Furman, Selvy averaged almost thirty points a game and scored a high of sixty-three against Mercer. As a senior he surpassed even these figures and included in his record 41.7 average the greatest game any major college player had ever put together. The occasion was a contest with state-rival Newberry, played in the second-floor arena of the Greenville, South Carolina, Textile Hall. Included in the four thousand fans were several hundred of Selvy's neighbors who had driven down from Corbin, Kentucky, to see him play. This would be the first and only time his parents would see him play in college or as a pro. (This was also the first college game to be televised in South Carolina.) Frank, who had scored twenty-five points against Newberry in a previous meeting that year, was just anxious to have a good game so as not to disappoint his parents and neighbors. From the beginning it was obviously Selvy's night. He scored twenty-four points in the first quarter and thirteen more in the second for an NCAA record half-time total of thirty-seven. During the intermission the Furman players decided to see just how many points their star could score, so they set him up for twenty-five more points and a total of sixty-two in the third quarter.

Now the Furman players, the crowd, and Selvy were caught up in the excitement. When Newberry came down court with the ball, they were allowed to shoot at will so Furman could quickly regain possession and set up Selvy for another shot. (The Newberry players made no effort to stall, either, for which Selvy was grateful.) Firing from all over the court, Selvy was making the scoreboard blink like a Las Vegas pinball machine as the public address announcer kept track of his increasing personal total after he reached eighty. Mlkvy's college record of seventy-three points was far behind, and with thirty-five seconds to play, Selvy had scored ninety points. With five seconds remaining he had ninety-eight, took the inbounds pass, dribbled to midcourt under double coverage, then pivoted to his right and heaved the ball toward the basket with two seconds showing. "There was no way I could really make that shot. I just threw the ball,"

Selvy related years later—but the ball went in and Franklin Delano Selvy had scored a hundred points in a single game.

Meanwhile, in the small-college ranks, another scoring star flashed briefly across the scene to eclipse even Selvy's totals against much weaker opposition. His name was Clarence (Bevo) Francis. He grew up on a farm in Ohio and he and his friends would spend their winter weekends engaging in nonstop basketball games in his barn. Bevo came to the attention of Newt Oliver, the peppery little coach at Rio Grande College in Ohio, who persuaded him to enroll at that tiny institution. Rio Grande had only ninety-four students and thirteen teachers, but Oliver seized on Bevo Francis as the means to make the school, and perhaps himself, famous.

Bevo, six feet nine, did just that. Playing against business colleges, seminaries, junior colleges, and some four-year schools, Francis averaged 50.1 points a game as Rio Grande won thirty-nine in a row in 1953. His high was seventy-two points against California State. Bevo's totals broke all the records, but the shocked NCAA refused to accept them and threw out all his achievements against non-four-year schools. That left him with a 48.3 average in twelve games. Francis and Oliver were crushed, but only temporarily. Oliver determined to make up a better schedule for 1954 and Francis spent the summer in his back yard practicing his shots. The results were even more spectacular. In a 134–91 victory over Hillsdale, Bevo scored 113 points, a small-college record, and he scored fifty or more points on no less than eight occasions. His season average was 46.5. However,

Bevo Francis, of tiny Rio Grande College in Ohio, set all sorts of scoring records in 1953. When the NCAA refused to accept them, coach Newt Oliver (*above right*) sought tougher competition, and Francis's 1954 records stood.

after this season of vindication, Bevo and Oliver disappeared from the college scene.

There were some other great moments during these years as scoring totals soared. One reason was the introduction of the new bonus free throw rules, allowing an extra penalty shot when the offending team had fouled excessively. ("Only alcoholics want two shots for one," growled dissenting Phog Allen.) The new rules, however, didn't help Siena and Niagara come to a decision one February night in 1953. Niagara, well regarded in the East, had just been eliminated from a possible NIT bid with a loss to St. John's in Madison Square Garden. En route home to their campus near Buffalo, the Eagles stopped off to play Siena in Albany. Niagara had a couple of future pro stars in Ed Fleming and Larry Costello, but the Eagles were cold and uninspired, and the score remained tied at 54–all after the regulation forty minutes (a basket at the buzzer, which would have won for Niagara, was disallowed).

After one overtime period the score was tied at 61–all and the opposing coaches, Taps Gallagher of Niagara and Dan Cunha of Siena, instructed their players to perform cautiously. Each team scored one basket and the second overtime ended at 63–all. Play opened up in the third overtime, which ended 70–70. The fourth overtime again saw only one basket giving each team seventy-two points. The game turned into a grinding endurance contest. There were no real rest stops and when one player had to relieve himself, his teammates bunched around him and he used a paper cup. The fifth overtime ended at 76–all, but in the sixth five-minute extra session of what turned out to be the longest college game in history, Niagara finally prevailed, 88–81. The usual seventy minutes of basketball required three hours and two minutes to complete. It was past midnight when the last spectators could finally head home.

The next year Kentucky's streak of 129 straight home-court victories, dating back to 1943, was broken, 59–58, by a Georgia Tech team with a losing record; and George Linn, a pretty fair college player at Alabama, set a distance record against North Carolina with a shot that traveled eighty-four feet eleven inches.

Over at Furman, Frank Selvy had graduated, but his replacement was right on hand. Furman won no championships, but the sharp-shooting Darrell Floyd led the nation in scoring for two straight years, 1955 and 1956. At St. Francis of Loretto, a little school in Pennsylvania, six-foot-seven Maurice Stokes, son of a Pittsburgh steel worker, developed into an outstanding all-round performer who sparkled in the spotlight of the NIT against overwhelming competition. He actually frightened teams off the St. Francis schedule until he graduated.

On the national scene, Indiana, led by Bob Leonard and big Don Schlundt, won the 1953 NCAA title, while the following year national honors went to LaSalle of Philadelphia and its great star, Tom Gola, who beat Bradley, 92–76, in the first NCAA title game ever televised.

Gola, six feet six, was an instant success in college basketball. One of seven children born to a Philadelphia policeman, he scored 2,222 points for LaSalle High and then spurned dozens of offers from out-of-town schools to attend LaSalle at home. A well-coordinated youngster who excelled in all phases of the game, he moved right into the Explorers' starting lineup as an eighteen-year-old freshman and for a while caused some resentment among his older teammates. But Gola had learned to play in the tough playground leagues and could handle it. He proved his value his first season by

leading LaSalle to a 25–7 record and an upset victory in the finals of the 1952 NIT. Gola, who was named co-winner of the tournament's MVP award with teammate Norm Grekin, diplomatically credited his fellow players for the victory. "We did it as a team, not as individuals," he said. "If they had asked Tom Gola to go out on the court as an eighteen-year-old by himself and play against a twenty-one-year-old, it would have been a little difficult."

Adding the 1954 NCAA title to LaSalle's NIT crown, Gola made All-America three straight years. He also led the nation in rebounding for two straight years—his career total of 2,-201 rebounds still stands as an NCAA record despite the assaults of bigger stars later on. "I've never seen any one player control a game by himself the way Gola does," said his college coach, Ken Leoffler.

The Explorers had a shot at two NCAA championships in a row when they battled into the finals in Gola's senior season of 1955, but their way was blocked by the University of San Francisco. The Dons, only 14–7 the year before, had won their first two games of the season, lost to UCLA, and then swept into the NCAA field with twenty-one straight victories. West Texas and Utah fell easily to the Dons in the opening rounds and an impressed Jack Gardner called them "the greatest college team ever assembled." After edging Oregon State, 57–56, USF made the national finals by routing Colorado, 62–50.

San Francisco was led by an oddly matched pair. The center was six-foot-nine Bill Russell, a gaunt defensive wizard who would have a tremendous impact on the game, both on a college and professional level. The other USF star was K. C. Jones, a six-foot-one guard. As a young child Russell had moved with his family from Monroe, Louisiana, to Oakland, California, and his memories of those early days were etched with bitterness. His basketball beginnings were inauspicious. He was a junior before he even made the McClymonds High junior varsity and he went to nearby USF "because it was the only school that offered me a scholarship." Hard to believe today, but self-doubt shackled his development in those early days.

K. C. Jones had been an outstanding high school football star in San Francisco and, as with Russell, went to USF because that was the only school interested in him. In fact, he'd almost given up on the idea of going to college and had applied for a post-office job when the Dons' offer came through a year before Russell was enrolled.

At one point in high school Jones had been a shooter. But one day his coach chewed him out for letting his man score a lot of points and from that day he dedicated himself to defense. Jones and Russell made a perfect match. "Go after that ball," Phil Woolpert, the intense Frisco coach, would tell K.C. "Make some blind stabs. If you miss, remember, you have the big guy parked under the basket as a second line of defense." And so, as the Dons prepared to challenge defending champion LaSalle for the NCAA championship in Kansas City, they boasted the best defensive record in the nation. Russell, called by Henry Iba "the best defensive player ever," was the headliner, dominating the backboards and blocking shots, but he credited his smaller teammate,

Bill Russell battles for a rebound with Tom Gola as San Francisco and LaSalle compete for the 1955 NCAA title. San Francisco won, 77–63.

the playmaker in USF's deliberate offense, with making the team go. "The team was like a slingshot," Russell said. "I was the fork, K.C. was the rubber band."

Most experts predicted that Russell would guard LaSalle center Gola in the 1955 NCAA finals, but Woolpert pulled a switch. He assigned Jones to shadow Gola, reasoning that his smaller man could leap high enough and had the extra quickness to do the job. Russell would then be free to roam and protect the basket. The strategy worked perfectly. Jones held Gola scoreless for the first twenty-one minutes until the issue was decided and the Dons swept to a 77–63 victory. Uncharacteristically Jones ended up the game's high scorer with twenty-four points while Russell scored twenty-three. (Some observers, however, felt that Russell should have been credited with half a dozen additional baskets on which he had tipped in teammates' shots.)

Russell's overwhelming display knocked the rule makers into a state of shock and they moved to legislate against his dominance. The free-throw lane was doubled in width from six to twelve feet to keep the likes of Russell away from the offensive basket. As Doggie Julian of Dartmouth confessed, "We weren't planning to make any changes in the foul lane, but after some of the coaches saw Russell's performance they got scared and pushed through the twelve-foot lane." The change hardly bothered Russell. The Dons, who had won their last twenty-six games the previous year, swept through the regular schedule undefeated with twenty-five more victories, and for the second straight year led the nation in defense. If anything, Woolpert felt the wider foul lane may have helped Russell, opening things up so he could better use his great speed.

Some of the nation's top independent teams elected to go to the NIT that year rather than challenge San Francisco in the NCAA. Despite the absence of K. C. Jones, who was ruled ineligible for the tournament, the Dons rolled into the finals where they easily defeated Iowa for the championship. No other undefeated team had ever won an NCAA title as San Francisco stretched its two-year winning streak to fifty-five games. "Let's face it, he's the best ever," George Mikan said of Russell, and Joe Lapchick called USF's two-time champions "the best college teams I have ever seen."

Their college careers finished, Jones and Russell both played for the 1956 U.S. Olympic team and remained together as pros with the Boston Celtics. The Dons won their next five games the following season, but

then were humiliated by Illinois, 62–33. Still, their winning streak of sixty stood as the longest in college history until 1973. Amazingly, only one of their games was in doubt going into the final minute, the one-point victory over Oregon State in the 1955 NCAA semifinals.

In addition to marking San Francisco's second straight championship, the season of 1956 represented another milestone in the history of basketball. Phog Allen, at the age of seventy, reluctantly retired as Kansas coach. Five years old when basketball was born in Springfield, Massachusetts, Dr. Allen had a forty-six-year coaching record of 771 victories and only 233 losses. No other coach had won so many games. (Rupp, his pupil, subsequently passed him.)

In addition to his impact on the game, Allen left a legacy at Kansas, a well-coordinated, powerful seven-foot legacy named Wilt Chamberlain. Allen had fought hard to recruit Chamberlain out of Philadelphia's Overbrook High. Hundreds of colleges had wanted to sign him, including some in the South that were willing to break the color line for Wilt. Even the pros were interested, with the Philadelphia Warriors of the NBA actually exercising their territorial draft rights (since abolished) to him as a high school senior. They knew he could be worth waiting for.

Although Allen had landed Chamberlain in this bitter battle, he had still been forced to retire after Wilt's freshman year. Dick Harp, the old master's successor, would coach Chamberlain with the varsity. His biggest burden was the prediction that Wilt's presence would make any college team unbeatable. The experts weren't far

The University of Kansas's Wilt Chamberlain shows his stuff. A decade later, however, the "dunk shot" was outlawed in college play.

wrong. As a sophomore Chamberlain averaged almost thirty points a game, and Kansas lost only twice—to teams that used a stall against them. As Big Seven champions, the Jayhawks qualified for the NCAA Tournament and they moved into the finals with one-sided victories over Southern Methodist, Oklahoma City, and San Francisco.

Meanwhile, North Carolina, undefeated through the regular season, was having its problems. Frank McGuire, who had been hired away from St. John's after his Redmen had lost to Kansas in the 1952 NCAA finals, had recruited a fascinating array of basketball talent for his new school. McGuire still retained his New York accent and his New York roots, and it was New York his players came from. Len Rosenbluth, a six-foot-six jump shooter with a soft scoring touch, was the Tar Heels' outstanding player. Although North Carolina presented a well-balanced starting five, its bench was suspect and many observers felt the Tar Heels were finished when they had to go three overtimes to beat Michigan State, 74–70, in the semifinals.

On the basis of their undefeated record, the Tar Heels were top ranked in the national wire-service polls. But, on the basis of Wilt Chamberlain, the second-ranked Jayhawks were slight betting favorites as the two teams met in the national finals. The dapper and personable McGuire knew his main problem was how to nullify the seven-foot Chamberlain when his own tallest man, Joe Quigg, was only six feet nine. So he started the championship game by trying to unbalance the Kansas giant. Instead of letting Quigg jump center, McGuire sent five-foot-eleven Tommy Kearns to the center circle. The crowd roared with laughter, and although Chamberlain controlled the tap the Tar Heels ended up with the ball.

Kansas opened up with a four-man-and-chaser zone defense. Chamberlain stayed back under the basket while the fifth Jayhawk guarded Rosenbluth man-to-man. Fortunately for the Tar Heels, their own big men, Quigg and six-foot-six Pete Brennan, could score from outside and they popped for a 19–7 lead before Harp abandoned his zone. But when Chamberlain came out to guard Quigg, Rosenbluth moved into the pivot and scored fourteen quick points. At half time North Carolina held a 29–22 lead.

The Jayhawks refused to panic, however, and as the second half began they moved in front by five points. McGuire ordered his players to slow the action and steadily they cut the Kansas margin. Even though Rosenbluth fouled out with 1:45 to go after scoring twenty points, the Tar Heels managed to tie at 46–46 and sent the game into overtime. This was the first NCAA title game ever to require extra time. North Carolina scored first in overtime, but Kansas tied on a Chamberlain jumper, and when the Jayhawks missed a chance to win on a last-second shot, the score was still tied at 48–48. The second extra session was fraught with tension, but scoreless. Both teams played for the unmissable shot and neither one got it.

North Carolina broke in front by four points as the third overtime began, but led by Chamberlain the Jayhawks rallied to tie at fifty-two, then went in front by 53–52 with thirty-one seconds to play. However, with six seconds left, Quigg was fouled trying to follow a rebound. Two shots. He made the first, bounced the ball, took aim for his two-handed shot, and made the second. North Carolina had won, 54–53, its thirty-two victories marking the most ever achieved by a championship team.

The following season Kansas dropped to an 18–5 record and failed even to win its conference championship. Chamberlain scored slightly over thirty points a game, but was unhappy. Feeling that slowdown defenses were ruining his game, he dropped out of school and toured with the Harlem Globetrotters for a year until he became eligible to join the NBA, where for one of his pro seasons in Philadelphia he was coached by Frank McGuire.

There was nothing classic about Kentucky's victory in the 1958 NCAA Tournament with coach Adolph Rupp using what he called his Fiddling Five, comparing them unfavorably with violinists. True, their 23–6 record was the worst ever posted by an NCAA champion, but it marked the first time any school had ever won four titles, and the Wildcats did it by defeating such teams as Miami of Ohio with Wayne Embry, Notre Dame with Tom Hawkins, Temple, which had won twenty-five straight, with Guy Rodgers, and in thé finals, Seattle with Elgin Baylor.

The 1958 season, however, was most noted for the debut of two outstanding sophomores, Jerry West and Oscar Robertson. Robertson, born on a farm in Tennessee, was raised in the basketball-happy city of Indianapolis. West actually lived in a tiny dot on the map called Cheylan, West Virginia, but the nearest post office was in Cabin Creek and that's generally accepted

Elgin Baylor prepares to move off a pick in a 1956 NCAA regional game against the University of San Francisco.

Jerry West of West Virginia.

Oscar Robertson of the University of Cincinnati.

as his home town. Born six months apart in 1938, both represented the complete ballplayer. Robertson played at six feet five, West at six feet three. To those familiar with just their great professional accomplishments, it need only be said that these men were even more dominant in college.

Robertson, great-grandson of a slave who lived to be 116 years old, grew up in a grimy Indianapolis ghetto and learned his basketball at the local YMCA. He had two older brothers who also played ball, and Oscar's motivation was to some day be good enough so they'd have to let him play with them. Only five feet eight when he entered Crispus Attucks High, Robertson reached his full height by his junior year and led the school to two straight state championships—quite an achievement in Indiana where every crossroad has a crack high school team and every home a back-yard basket. Deluged with college offers, the quiet, introspective Robertson chose Cincinnati, less than a hundred miles from his home. His

decision was booed by Indiana boosters who felt he should have remained at home, but cheered by Cincinnati fans who rightly predicted a new era in basketball with Robertson as their first black athlete. (It also has been speculated, not unreasonably, that the NBA Royals moved from Rochester to Cincinnati soon afterward to lock up Robertson as a territorial pick.)

Robertson did nothing to disappoint Bearcat fans. In 1958 he became the first sophomore ever to lead the nation in scoring with a 35.1 average. As a junior and senior he also led the nation by scoring more than thirty points a game and he made All-America three straight years. In the Big O's three varsity seasons, Cincinnati posted a combined 79–9 record and Phog Allen called Robertson "the greatest player of all time for a fellow his size." Despite his scoring records, John Wooden of UCLA said the real measure of Robertson's greatness was that he always "first looked for the pass."

West's basketball career started

just as early as Robertson's, but instead of playing at the YMCA, his first basket was perched on a neighbor's garage. Hour after hour, sometimes through pouring rain and despite a parental spanking or two, West devoted himself to mastering the jump shot that would be his signature. Jerry, like Robertson, also led his high school, East Bank, to a state championship, and he was also deluged with dozens of college offers. But West knew from the beginning that he would remain at home and attend his state university where Hot Rod Hundley, a dazzling star with a vast array of shots and tricks, was already gathering headlines. The year Hundley graduated, West became eligible for the varsity, and while he didn't turn the school's already fine program around, as Robertson had, he raised it to an even higher plane of success.

Robertson's first big public splash came during his sophomore year when he scored an arena record, fifty-six points, to lead Cincinnati past Seton Hall, 118–54, in Madison Square Garden. West also established himself early in his varsity career in the University of Kentucky Invitational Tournament where he led the Mountaineers first to a 77–70 victory over the host team, causing Rupp to say, "I've seen a million basketball players in my time, but this boy is one of the best." Then, in the UKIT final, West Virginia ended national champion North Carolina's winning streak at thirty-seven straight, leading Frank McGuire to call West "the greatest pure shooter in basketball." West's scoring average steadily increased during his college career from 17.8 as a sophomore to 29.3 as a senior, and he made All-America his last two seasons. West

Hot Rod Hundley of West Virginia.

Virginia posted a total 81–12 record while West was on the team.

Ironically West and Robertson never played against each other in college, but they were teammates on this country's gold-medal Olympic team in 1960, and they became adversaries later on as professionals. In

Ohio State's Jerry Lucas (11) manages to block Paul Hogue's shot in the NCAA finals in 1961.

another irony, neither star, like Chamberlain, was able to bring his school a national championship. West came closer than Robertson. In Jerry's sophomore year the Mountaineers were rated the top team in the nation by both wire-service polls, but they were upset in the first round of the 1958 NCAA Tournament by Manhattan. The next season, West & Co. came within a point of going all the way, losing 71–70 in the finals to California, the national defense leader, despite West's twenty-eight points. Jerry scored 160 points in his five tournament games and was named MVP. West's senior year the Mountaineers lost in the NCAA's second round.

Cincinnati, with Robertson, also fell short. They lost their first game in the regional semifinals Oscar's sophomore season, then lost two straight years to California in the national semifinals. Cincinnati's frustration

was doubled because national honors in 1960 went to another school from just up the road, Ohio State.

As the sixties began, the Buckeyes had put together one of the great college teams of all time sparked by one of the great stars, Jerry Lucas. Lucas was literally a phenomenon from the beginning. At birth in Middletown, Ohio, he stretched twenty-one inches and weighed ten pounds. By the time he attained his full growth, he was six feet eight. In one of the most spectacular high school careers ever recorded, Lucas broke Wilt Chamberlain's career record as he led Middletown to two straight state titles and, at one point, seventy-six straight victories. Naturally he was also a straight-A student and it was no wonder that 150 colleges sought his services. Still, he turned down all kinds of under-the-table offers, including jobs for his father, to accept an academic scholarship at Ohio State.

Darrell Imhoff hooks over Bob Smith and Bob Clousson in the 1959 NCAA championship game. California won, 71–70.

John Havlicek shows perfect form in a jump shot against Georgia Tech.

If Lucas had a fault as a player, it was his reluctance to shoot. He averaged just fifteen shots a game, but as Frank McGuire once pointed out, "whenever Ohio State needed points, he got them." His favorite shot was a soft hook with either hand. In addition he was tough under the boards, using his height and his 230 pounds to get the rebound or to tip in shots missed by his teammates. And what teammates he had as the Buckeyes swept to a 78–6 record over three glorious years. John Havlicek, Larry Siegfried, and Mel Nowell, all of whom went on to professional careers, shared the court with Lucas, but he was the bellwether and became the first college player ever to win five NCAA statistical titles in his career—field-goal percentage three times and rebounding twice.

The 1960 NCAA finals provided a rare matchup. California, coached by Pete Newell, led the nation in defense. Ohio State, coached by young Fred Taylor, was tops in offense. But this was one case where a good, and balanced, offense beat a good defense. All five Buckeye starters scored in double figures and Ohio State hit fifteen of its first sixteen shots for a 75–55 victory. Later that year Newell would tutor the U.S. Olympic team that included Lucas, Robertson, and West, and he rated the deadpan OSU star "the best player I ever coached."

Ohio State had won its last five games en route to the NCAA championship, and the Buckeyes picked right up the following year with Lucas, Nowell, Siegfried, and Havlicek all returning as tough as ever. Overpowering all opposition, the Buckeyes easily held top position in both wire-service polls as they took a thirty-two-game winning streak into the NCAA finals against Cincinnati. These two schools did not play each other in regular season, and this marked the first time two teams from the same state had ever met for the national championship. The Bearcats were no pushovers. They ranked second in the polls, sported a twenty-one-game winning streak and a 26–3 record.

The game went into overtime, but this time Ohio State failed to show the balanced scoring that had won for them the year before. Lucas scored twenty-seven points and was named the tournament MVP, but next high for OSU was Siegfried with fourteen. Havlicek scored only four. With Bob Wiesenhahn, Tom Thacker, and Paul Hogue leading the way under new coach Ed Jucker, Cincinnati accomplished what it had never been able to achieve with Robertson, beating Ohio State, 70–65, for a national championship. "We don't have All-America players but we have an All-America team," Jucker said happily.

The next year marked a replay and the first time two teams had ever met two years in a row in the finals. Ohio State, with Lucas, Nowell, and Havlicek still around, posted another giddy 26–1 record and was top-ranked going into the finals. The Bearcats were rated second with a 28–2 record, but had been forced to survive a playoff with Bradley to make it to the NCAA since both of its losses were to rivals in the Missouri Valley Conference.

In the national semifinals at Louisville, Ohio State routed Wake Forest, 84–68, while the Bearcats had to struggle past UCLA, 72–70. Lucas

suffered a heel injury in that game and in the finals he scored only eleven points while burly Paul Hogue doubled that total for Cincinnati's 71–59 victory and a second straight championship.

The 1962 season marked quite a year for Ohio basketball. Cincinnati won the NCAA title, Ohio State was runner-up, and Dayton, after finishing second five times, finally won the NIT.

The next year the Bearcats lost Hogue to graduation, but returned Ron Bonham and Tom Thacker and showed no signs of relaxing their hold on the national title. Once again Cincinnati powered into the NCAA Tournament with a 23–1 record and led the nation in both polls and defense. Loyola of Chicago, tops in offense with an amazing 92.9 points a game, earned an at-large berth in the NCAA with a 24–2 mark and showed its credentials by beating Tennessee Tech in the first round, 111–42.

Neither team had difficulty making the finals, and at first it appeared as if tournament-wise Cincinnati would run Loyola off the floor. But midway through the second half the Ramblers began to pull their game together and they closed in despite Cincinnati's deliberate style of attack and tight defense. Using only five players the whole time, Loyola caught Cincinnati at the buzzer on a shot by Jerry Harkness to send the game into overtime. The Ramblers then won it, 60–58, with three seconds left in the extra session when Vic Rouse put in the rebound off a Harkness shot.

The Cincinnati dynasty had ended. But there would be others to come.

⑩
BIGGER THAN EVER

THERE WAS LITTLE TO INDICATE the formation of any dynasties during the 1964 season. Howard Komives of Bowling Green, only six feet one, led the nation in scoring with a 36.7 average, but six other players—the most ever—also averaged thirty points or better. Fans couldn't be blamed for wondering what had happened to defense in Dr. Naismith's Grand Old Game. The emphasis seemed to be on individual brilliance rather than team excellence in college basketball.

Out in the West, though, one school seemed to be bucking the trend. The University of California at Los Angeles (UCLA), coached by scholarly John Wooden, was showing that defense remained an important part of the game and that a fast-moving, well-drilled team could win without a big man. The Bruins had no starter taller than six feet five. They had no standout scorers. What the Bruins did have was a disconcerting zone press with which they were able to win . . . and win . . . and win.

Starting with a 113–71 victory over Brigham Young University, UCLA swept past its first eighteen opponents with startling ease before being forced to work to beat California by two points, 58–56. However, in the rematch, the Bruins won by thirty points and closed their season with a perfect 26–0 record. The same five men started every game: Keith Erickson, Gail Goodrich, Jack Hirsch, Walt Slaughter, and All-America Walt Hazzard. Key men coming off the bench were Doug McIntosh and Kenny Washington. Goodrich, Hazzard, and Erickson all went on to successful pro careers.

Although the polls rated UCLA as number one, the Bruins were not that highly regarded as they entered NCAA competition, and they strug-

John Wooden as a player at Purdue University. Outstanding in high school and college as a player, Wooden became the nation's foremost college coach in the 1960s and 1970s and was uniquely honored by being elected to Basketball's Hall of Fame for his contributions in both capacities.

gled into the finals by winning three games by a total of fifteen points. Meanwhile, heavily favored Duke, led by Jeff Mullins and with two six-foot-ten players in the frontcourt, was walloping its tournament opposition. The huge Blue Devils were in for a shock, however. The speedy Bruins literally ran them off the court, and, with sixteen straight points late in the first half, UCLA sewed up a 98–83 victory. Goodrich led both teams in scoring with twenty-seven points with Washington scoring twenty-six. But Hazzard was the true architect of the victory and he was named the tournament's outstanding player. Speaking later about this, his first championship team, Wooden would say, "It exemplified unselfish team play to a remarkable degree and it came closer to realizing its full potential than any team I have ever seen."

Goodrich and Erickson were the only starters returning for the 1965 season. McIntosh moved up to a starting berth where he was joined by Fred Goss and Edgar Lacey, the latter a sophomore of vast potential. Washington was again the sixth man. Few expected the Bruins to be able to match the previous season's mini-miracle, especially after a 110–83 opening loss to Illinois, but they reckoned without the genius of Wooden and his demoralizing zone press. After that opening defeat the Bruins won twenty-four of their next twenty-five games, losing only when Erickson was injured and could not play.

This time in the NCAA Tournament they didn't let anyone come close. They scored a hundred or more points in each of their first three victories and in the finals routed a good

Michigan team led by All-America Cazzie Russell, 91–80. Russell led his team with twenty-eight points in the final, but Goodrich scored forty-two; Wooden thought Goodrich should have been named the tournament's outstanding player instead of that young man from Princeton, Bill Bradley. Bradley had scored a tournament record fifty-eight points in the third-place game against Wichita State. Bradley and Russell, later teammates and competitors for the same forward position with the professional New York Knicks, were easily the dominant figures of the tournament as the individual excellence of Goodrich and Erickson were submerged in UCLA's concept of team performance.

Russell and Bradley were much alike and yet very different. Both were six feet five, both played forward, and both could shoot the bottom out of any peach basket. Russell, from Chicago's South Side ghetto, followed the playground route to basketball stardom. In warm weather he would play for long hours on the outdoor courts, and later, when he entered high school, would plead with the janitors to leave the lights on in the gym and let him into the locked building so he could practice on his own, perfecting his line-drive jump shot. (When the college offers starting pouring in, Russell would credit his high school coach, Larry Hawkins, and the "friendly janitors" for his success.) After turning down a pitch by Oscar Robertson to enroll at the Big O's alma mater, Cincinnati, Russell chose Michigan, where he was credited with reviving the Wolverines' basketball program. The crowds Cazzie drew inspired Michigan to build a new gym,

Gail Goodrich of UCLA driving against Southern California.

which Russell never got to play in as a collegian—it was completed after he graduated.

Bradley's background was different from Russell's, but the dedication he brought to basketball was the same. Russell said that basketball had saved him from "driving a cab, working in the steel mills, or pushing rocks on a construction gang." No such alternatives awaited Bradley. His father was a bank president in Crystal City, Missouri. A comfortable future was assured even if he never shot a basket. But Bradley's inner fires burned as fiercely as if he needed basketball for survival, and in a way perhaps he did. While his classmates were playing football, he practiced shooting for two hours a day. During the basketball season he stayed late for extra work. In summers he virtually wore out his back-yard basket as he practiced until perspiration made him slip out of his sneakers. He set up an obstacle course of chairs on the court, then donned special eyeglass frames fitted with cardboard so he could practice dribbling without looking at the ball or the floor. Scholarship offers flooded the Bradley home, too, but Bill elected to accept an academic scholarship at Princeton (over Duke) because of the Ivy League institution's school of foreign affairs.

Bradley and Russell met twice in the 1965 season. Their first confrontation, in the Holiday Festival Tournament in Madison Square Garden at midseason, resulted in one of the all-time classic games. Princeton wasn't expected to excel in big-time athletics, but Bradley had made the Tigers an exciting and competitive team. He captivated the near-sellout crowd by

leading Princeton to a 79–69 victory over Syracuse in the first round. Meanwhile, Michigan, the nation's top-ranked team, had advanced by beating Manhattan, 90–77, and there was a full house of more than 18,000 when these two great All-Americas met in the featured semifinal two nights later. The throng was rewarded with one of the greatest individual efforts in basketball history. Michigan was a powerful team, with six-foot-seven Bill Buntin to complement Russell. Princeton played well, too, but only because of Bradley's skill and his uncanny knack of bringing out the best in his teammates. This would prove the key to the game.

Bradley and the Tigers started strongly. The Princeton star scored his team's first twelve points and had twenty-three at the half. The man he was guarding had scored only one and Cazzie had but eight as the Ivy Leaguers took a commanding lead. With five minutes left in the game, Princeton was on top, 75–63, and an incredible upset seemed assured. At this point disaster struck Princeton. Bradley, who had scored forty-one points, fouled out. The crowd gave him a sixty-second ovation, but the cheers failed to inspire his teammates. The Tigers collapsed before Michigan's pressing defense as they missed Bradley's ball handling even more than his shooting. The Wolverines went on a 16–1 closing tear, and Russell, who ended up with twenty-seven points, scored the clinching basket in an 80–78 victory with three seconds to go.

The victory may have taken too much out of Michigan, however, for in the finals they collapsed in the second

Cazzie Russell of Michigan and Bill Bradley of Princeton twice engaged in head-to-head confrontations as college players. Here Russell scores in the meeting at the Holiday Festival Tournament in Madison Square Garden. Bradley is at far right. Though Michigan won the game 80–78, Bradley was Most Valuable Player of the tournament.

half against St. John's, just as the Tigers had done against them. Underdogs by as many as ten points and trailing by sixteen with less than nine minutes to go, St. John's rallied for a 75–74 victory. Russell, who scored twenty-four points, had been in foul trouble (just like Bradley), and when he had to sit out three minutes in the second half the momentum had passed from Michigan. Bradley, who had scored 110 points in three games, even though his team had won only one of them, was named the tournament's MVP. Joe Lapchick, coach at St. John's, called Bill's performance against Michigan "the greatest one-man job I've ever seen."

Both Michigan and Princeton went on from the Holiday Festival to outstanding seasons. Princeton, 23–6, moved into the NCAA Tournament as Ivy League champions. Michigan, 24–4, qualified from the Big Ten. At Portland, Oregon, they met again in the national semifinals and this time the issue wasn't even close. Michigan won, 93–76. But again the victory turned sour for the Wolverines and Russell. As had happened in the Festival, Michigan was beaten in the finals (by UCLA) and Bill Bradley earned all the individual honors.

When Bradley's college career ended after the 1965 season, he accepted a Rhodes Scholarship to study in England before turning professional. Cazzie, with one more year of eligibility, made All-America the following season and scored more than thirty points a game as he led Michigan to another Big Ten championship. But this time the Wolverines didn't even make it out of their region in the NCAA Tournament.

Michigan's defeat in the finals of the Holiday Festival had also been part of another sports story. Before the 1965 season began, it was announced that this would be the last campaign for St. John's coach Joe Lapchick who had turned sixty-five, the school's mandatory retirement age. Lapchick, who had come out of Yonkers, New York, as a six-foot-five "giant" with the Original Celtics, later became a giant in the coaching profession for two terms at St. John's, divided by a successful run with the professional Knickerbockers. But now university authorities ordained that he must step down. Everyone close to Lapchick, especially his players, wanted to see the not-so-old man retire a winner.

Lapchick's last St. John's team was inexperienced and erratic. Its best player was a sophomore, six-foot-seven Sonny Dove. The Redmen were not expected to do great things, but emotion means a lot in college sports, and emotion—and defense—helped St. John's overcome Michigan in the Festival finals. This victory was nice, but the best retirement present for Lapchick would be an NIT championship. The Redmen almost didn't make it at all, losing three of their last five games, but, finally, they did get the invitation. Their chances of winning were rated as slim.

They opened the tournament by routing Boston College, 114–92, and then concentrated on tight defense to defeat second-seeded New Mexico, 61–54. Excitement began to mount on the St. John's campus. Perhaps the Redmen *could* win it for Lapchick. Army's rugged team was next in line and again St. John's played it close for a 67–60 victory to gain the finals against top-seeded Villanova, which had gained the final round by routing NYU, 91–69. Now the Wildcats were up against another New York team playing at home. But the Redmen had more going for them than the hometown crowd. This was Joe Lapchick's last game, capping half a century of basketball. The years had not been easy for him—the pressures of a basketball season were physical torture and his body had paid the price. The second round of scandals had touched St. John's while he was there, and each defeat had stung like salt on an open wound. But there had been championships and hundreds of victories, too, and good boys turned into good men as they passed through his hands. Hundreds of boys, thousands of games, and this was the one that could wipe the tears from his farewell.

From the opening jump the Redmen were on top as they raced to a fourteen-point lead. But Villanova and its astute coach, Jack Kraft, refused to submit passively. The Wildcats fought back, whittled at St. John's margin, and moved to within a single point. Would the young Redmen crack? Lapchick prepared himself for the worst so the disappointment would not destroy him. He continued his ritual trips to the water cooler. As the minutes ticked away, St. John's held on, refusing to surrender the lead.

With three seconds left the Redmen still led, 53–51. Jerry Houston, one of the co-captains, had scored only three points all game and was now at the foul line with a foul shot in a bonus situation—if he made the first, he would get a chance at a second. But if he missed that first shot, Villanova might get the rebound and have one last shot at a tie. The Garden, a bedlam moments before, grew still. Houston went to the line, put up his first shot and made it—then he made the second. The final buzzer signaled not only a 55–51 victory and a record fourth NIT championship for Lapchick, but a massive outpouring of affection for the tall, lean coach. St. John's students rushed the floor, cheerleaders wept as they embraced the coach, and his players lifted Joe Lapchick to their shoulders to receive his championship watch. Many minutes later Lapchick was finally able to compose himself to meet the press. His voice hoarse with emotion, he could only whisper, "What a way to go!"

There were those who felt that Adolph Rupp, approaching sixty-five, might emulate Lapchick and leave in a blaze of glory the next year. Rupp's Wildcats had struggled through a 15–10 season in 1965, but in 1966 they were loaded with talent. Led by Louie Dampier and Pat Riley, they won their first twenty-three games and entered the NCAA Tournament with a 24–1 record. Dayton, Michigan, and Duke all fell before the Wildcats, and then came the finals in College Park, Maryland, with tradition-laden Kentucky facing the unlikeliest of opponents, the upstart Miners of Texas Western. The Miners, who had also lost only one game all year, were led by a gang of players nobody had ever heard of, culled from here and there around the nation. The aptly named Willie Cager was one of them, and five-foot-seven Willie Worsley, too small to be a ball boy for Rupp, was another. And yet these Willie-come-latelies were able to humble the mighty Wildcats, 72–65, for the NCAA title.

Rupp had already won four NCAA championships, more than any other coach. His ambition was to be the first to win a fifth. But even as the Baron was making his bid against Texas Western, events had taken place that would foil this particular dream. Away from center court, UCLA's John Wooden, as self-effacing as Rupp was flamboyant, had beaten Kentucky and hundreds of other schools to the most sought-after high school prospect in the nation, an introspective seven-foot New Yorker named Lew Alcindor. Not since Wilt Chamberlain had there been such competition for a high school prospect. Chamberlain had promised great things for Kansas, but never really delivered. Lew Alcindor promised even more, and for three years he would doom the rest of the college world to the role of also-ran.

Alcindor, from Manhattan, stood six feet four when he was eleven years old, and had already drawn notice for his height and skill in a CYO All-Star game. Two years later he stood six feet six as he entered Power Memorial High School, which he led to an overall 95–6 record with five of the losses coming his freshman year. At one point Power won seventy-one straight games. Already a seven-footer while still in high school, Alcindor was the target of hundreds of college recruiters. For not only was he big, he was also well-coordinated—an athlete in the truest sense. His high school coach, Jack Donohue, had insulated him completely from both press and college recruiters; he also instilled in the young giant a complete sense of team basketball. The other little tricks of the game Alcindor learned on the pub-

Lucius Allen was another player during the UCLA reign who went on to an outstanding career in the professional arenas.

lic playgrounds of New York, where at age fifteen he was already competing with older and tougher opponents.

UCLA's coach Wooden realized it would take more than superplayer Lew Alcindor to turn his team into a sure champion. Wilt Chamberlain had proved that. So, recruiting carefully, Wooden assembled a perfect supporting cast to surround his star. He already had one backcourt player, Mike Warren, who would be the ball handler. Lucius Allen was recruited to be the shooting guard who would insure that defenses could not sag back on Alcindor. Lynn Shackleford, deadly

Lew Alcindor, later known in the professional ranks as Kareem Abdul-Jabbar, shows the shot that made UCLA virtually unbeatable during his college career.

from the corner, was enrolled to be the shooting forward so Alcindor could not be double-teamed up front. The fifth starter was an unselfish defender, Ken Heitz. As Alcindor was unveiled in varsity competition and immediately acclaimed as an instant All-America, he was surrounded by three other sophomores and one junior, Warren.

Opposition coaches correctly resigned themselves to three years of UCLA dominance. Wooden installed a low post offense to take advantage of Alcindor's height and skills, and the Bruins easily became the most dominant college team in history. Their regular-season record was 30–0, and they brushed through the NCAA championship field as if playing their jayvees. No opponent that year could come closer than five points, and Wooden became the first coach to win two NCAA titles with undefeated teams. With three victories in four years, he matched Kentucky's showing in 1948, 1949, and 1951.

The next year, coaches paid Alcindor the ultimate honor. Just as they had done with Russell and Chamberlain, they legislated against him and outlawed the dunk shot. It really hurt. UCLA lost all of one game all season and swept to still another NCAA title. And the next year they won another, suffering only one loss during the regular season.

In Alcindor's three years the Bruins had won an unprecedented three straight NCAA championships (and enabled Wooden to beat Rupp to that personal fifth title) with a combined record of eighty-eight victories against two losses. They had winning streaks of forty-seven and forty-one straight.

Through it all Alcindor was the era's premier player, bested individually only once, but never in a game that counted, and drawing huge crowds at home and on the road as the greatest attraction in college ball. Thousands of fans trudged through snow-choked streets after a massive Chicago blizzard just to see him play. And, his junior year, he would perform before the biggest crowd ever to see a college basketball game.

The place was the Houston Astrodome, "the eighth wonder of the world" as modest Texans call it. The occasion was a basketball game between UCLA and the University of Houston, which had a major star of its own in Elvin (Big E) Hayes. Hayes was from the small town of Rayville, Louisiana, and the youngest of six children. Shy and awkward, the closest he came to athletics during his first two years in high school was as drum major for the band. But by his junior year he was ready to play, and as a senior he attracted dozens of scholarship offers from major schools throughout the country. The University of Houston, just desegregating its athletic program, recruited him, and soon the school's five-thousand-seat gym was too small to hold the crowds he was attracting as a full-blown six-foot-nine 235-pound All-America.

Hayes led the Cougars into the NCAA Tournament his first two varsity campaigns; in his junior year Houston fell to UCLA, 73–58, in the national semifinals. A rematch was booked for the Astrodome the following season. The Bruins came in with a forty-seven-game winning streak. They had not been beaten since Alcindor had joined the varsity. The

Houston's Elvin Hayes, along with Alcindor a giant of the college game, helped end the UCLA winning streak, 71–69, as he scored thirty-nine points.

Cougars had won seventeen in a row and had not been beaten since the previous season's tournament loss to UCLA. Both teams returned virtually the same personnel for the rematch.

Some 55,000 fans converged on the Astrodome for this game—52,693 of them paid, for the biggest gate in basketball history—and a nationwide television audience was looking in. The floor, shipped in from the Los Angeles Sports Arena at a cost of $10,000, was set in the middle of the vast playing field. The players worried that they might exhaust themselves traveling to and from the distant dressing rooms; Wooden worried about the unusual shooting background.

There was a major element of mystery as the big game approached. Eight days earlier, in a game at the University of California, an opponent had accidentally poked Alcindor in the left eye, scratching the eyeball. The injury was serious enough to put Alcindor in the infirmary for almost a week. Two days before the game he was released and permitted to practice briefly with the eye bandaged. But only the day before the game, as the Bruins were preparing to leave for Houston, did doctors give Alcindor permission to play. There was no telling how effective he would be.

The Cougars came out with a 1-3-1 zone designed to negate Alcindor as much as possible while the Bruins stayed in their usual man-to-man with Alcindor parked under the basket where Hayes usually operated. However, Houston coach Guy Lewis made his strategic move early and pulled Hayes outside, around the foul circle. If Alcindor came out to guard the Big E, the middle would be opened up,

and Houston had six-foot-nine Ken Spain, bigger than any other Bruin, to rebound. If Alcindor stayed in, Hayes would shoot from outside, which he did, again and again.

Enjoying the greatest half of his life, Hayes looped in one one-hander after another for twenty-nine points in the first twenty minutes. At the half Houston held a 46–43 lead, though it had been on top by a greater margin most of the time. Alcindor, on the other hand, appeared unsure on defense. He wasn't banging under the boards as he usually did, and his shooting was off target. The eye injury and the recent hospitalization were obviously affecting him. But still the Bruins made a game of it.

Hayes cooled off in the second half—who could continue such shooting?—and, with ten minutes to go, UCLA tied at 54–all. But then the Bruins went four minutes without a field goal and Houston spurted ahead again. Alcindor, who had made only two field goals in the first half, was still no factor. Both teams were scrambling now, committing turnovers. UCLA tied at sixty-five and again at sixty-nine, but neither time could it get the critical basket to take the lead. With only twenty-eight seconds remaining, Hayes drove in for a short jumper and was fouled. His two free throws accounted for the final points in a 71–69 upset as his teammates carried him from the floor.

In this, his greatest game, Hayes scored thirty-nine points. For Alcindor it was the worst game of his college career. He made only four of eighteen shots from the floor for a total of fifteen points. "My eye didn't bother me, but I didn't feel physically good," he said after his first losing game since 1966. (For Lucius Allen, who had played on the same undefeated freshman team as Alcindor, it would be the first loss since 1963.) "We just got beaten by a better team," said Alcindor, and Wooden called the game "a great thing for college basketball." "My greatest victory," enthused Guy Lewis, the Houston coach.

A rubber match was still to be played, for once again the NCAA semifinals paired Houston and UCLA. This time Alcindor was in shape. The result was a one-sided 101–69 UCLA victory that the shaken Lewis called "the greatest exhibition of basketball I've ever seen." The finals were almost an anticlimax as UCLA became the first team ever to win back-to-back titles on two different occasions.

There was a symbolic note to Alcindor's final season. The 1969 schedule opened with the Bruins defeating Purdue, Wooden's alma mater, 94–82, and it ended with them beating the same team in the NCAA finals, 92–72. Now Wooden had to ponder the future without his great star. "It will be interesting," he said. "It's been a great strain these past few years with Lewis playing *not to lose*. Now we will have to go out to play to win again."

John Wooden's past had prepared him to coach to win. As a star high school player in Martinsville, Indiana, and through his Hall of Fame playing career at Purdue, Wooden had been a defensive standout. His teams would always reflect that heritage. A five-foot-ten guard, he played with such determination that he was dubbed by a sports writer the "India Rubber Man" for the way he kept hitting the floor and bouncing up again. As a dribbler he would often conduct a one-man freeze to protect a victory.

Having grown up in the Midwest, Wooden reflected all the virtues ascribed to that area. He didn't smoke, drink, or curse, except for an occasional "goodness gracious." He lived his religion and still serves as a deacon for the First Christian Church of Santa Monica, California. His credo is a self-devised "Pyramid of Success," a chart he developed that lists such building blocks as industriousness, loyalty, team spirit, resourcefulness, and patience. In a coaching career that began in 1932 and was interrupted only by navy service in World War II, he never had a losing season.

With Alcindor gone Wooden was able to discard the low post and return to his favorite style of a more fluid offense. Two forwards, Curtis Rowe and Sidney Wicks, and a junior college transfer guard, John Vallely, had performed well on the last Alcindor team and they returned for another year. Henry Bibby, a sharpshooting guard, came off the freshman team, and Steve Patterson came off the bench to replace Alcindor. With their new look the Bruins won their first twenty-one games of the 1970 season, lost two of their final five and then swept into the NCAA finals with three straight tournament victories.

The Bruins' title-round opponent that year was Jacksonville, a newcomer in college basketball—not too many seasons before, Jacksonville had been a two-year school. The Dolphins were coached by brash Joe Williams, a mod opposite of the staid Wooden. Wooden's full set of rules included dress, bedtime, and when to throw a cross-court pass. At times the Dolphin players seemed to be free-lancing on and off the court. "We have no curfew," Williams proclaimed, but he also pointed out that his players had been indoctrinated into a discipline-from-within concept and their free-wheeling offense was not as spontaneous as it looked.

Artis Gilmore, a goateed seven feet two, and speedy six-foot-five Rex Morgan were the Dolphin stars in a 23–1 season. Jacksonville averaged over a hundred points a game during its regular schedule and in the tournament scored over a hundred each game in defeating Western Kentucky, Iowa, and highly regarded Kentucky. In the national semifinals UCLA routed New Mexico State while the Dolphins were eliminating St. Bonaventure, which had lost its outstanding six-foot-eleven center, Bob Lanier, in the regionals to a knee injury.

The final was billed as a confrontation between two generations of basketball, and at first it appeared as if this was the day for the new look. The Dolphins swept out in front by as many as nine points midway in the first half. The Bruins called time, Wooden made some adjustments, and slowly, inexorably, UCLA fought its way back. Glowering Sidney Wicks, six feet eight, began playing eye-to-eye with the taller Gilmore. He blocked five of the Jacksonville giant's shots, outrebounded him, and forced Wicks into miss after miss. The Bruins led at half time, 41–36, and won it all going away, 80–69.

With only Vallely graduating, UCLA began the 1971 season where it had left off, as if Walt Hazzard and Lew Alcindor had never left. The Bruins won their first thirteen games, then added a fourteenth against Loyola in Chicago on a Friday night. The next afternoon they were scheduled at Notre Dame. The team arrived late in South Bend, Indiana, tired from the bus trip. The Fighting Irish, led by a great All-America shooter, Austin Carr, and with some fine supporting talent, were lying in wait. They won, 89–82, the only loss suffered by UCLA all year even though Wooden called his Bruins "the worst offensive team we've had in some time."

UCLA's closest call in the NCAA Tournament came in the finals of the Far West Regional against Long Beach State. Hitting less than 23 per cent of their shots in the first half, the Bruins trailed by eleven points at 44–33 with only fourteen minutes to play. But the Bruins had known tournament pressure before, and with Wicks making the free throws, they pulled out a 57–55 victory. Kansas and Villanova fell in the national finals, and UCLA and Wooden had captured another championship.

The 1971 victory made it five national championships in a row and seven in the last eight years for UCLA, a dynasty unmatched and unapproached in college basketball since James Naismith had posted his thirteen rules eighty years before. A case could be made for this to be the greatest coaching achievement of all time, surpassing even Red Auerbach's eight straight and eleven out of thirteen NBA championships with the Celtics. Wooden had to keep his streak going with a continuously changing cast: no player could remain more than three seasons. With small teams, big teams, shooting teams, defensive teams, Wooden kept on winning.

UCLA was the dominant college team as basketball completed its eightieth season, but it takes five men to make up an All-America unit and there was no shortage of individual stars to team with the Alcindors, the Big E's, the Sidney Wickses. Three, in fact, came along all at once, as if they'd been lining up alphabetically—Maravich, Mount, and Murphy. Each could shoot as if he were homing in on radar and each played the game with color and dash.

Pistol Pete Maravich, six feet five, began playing basketball when he was six years old and turned to the sport naturally. His father, Press Maravich, was a coach, and later he coached his son at LSU. On Pete's sixth birthday Press gave him a basketball and set up a goal, but the youngster ignored the gifts. Then, one day, the father went out and took some shots. Young Pete watched for a while, figured it was pretty easy stuff, and took a shot himself. He missed and he got angry. "I knew I had him then," his father recalls with a grin.

Pete grew up into an outstanding college player whose floppy hair and floppy socks were his trademarks. Playing for an ordinary LSU team, he did all the shooting, all the scoring, and most of the ball handling. Much of the time his teammates had trouble handling his tricky passes. But the crowds loved him. "The fans want you to win, sure; but they want to be entertained, too. Why not try both?" he asked.

As a sophomore he broke Frank Selvy's single-season record by averaging 43.8 points a game; as a junior

LSU's Pistol Pete Maravich.

he averaged 44.2; and as a senior he improved to 44.5. Scoring over a thousand points each year he broke Oscar Robertson's career scoring record by 194 points (3,067 to 2,973). And twenty-eight times in his eighty-three college games he scored fifty or more points. Matching Robertson's achievement he led the nation in scoring three times, and three times he made All-America.

Rick Mount at Purdue and Calvin Murphy at Niagara were instant stars, too, but they didn't win All-America honors until they were juniors. Mount's father had been an All-State basketball player in Indiana, and he started his son playing quite early, nailing a tomato can to the kitchen door so Rick could shoot tennis balls at it. Later he would shovel snow off the driveway so they could practice in the winter, with gloves on. No wonder the frail six-foot-four Hoosier became what his coach, George King, called "the best shooter I've ever seen" as he averaged over thirty points a game during his college career.

Murphy, who stood only five feet ten, was even more amazing. Who would think that such a little man could still dominate a basketball court? But Murphy, from Norwalk, Connecticut, did just that. He would entertain the crowd with a Harlem Globetrotter–type dribbling display during pregame warmups, then amaze them during the contest with an unbelievable display of distance shooting. (He could have provided the half-time show, too. During the football season, he gave baton-twirling exhibitions at

Niagara's Calvin Murphy proved that there remained a place on the floor for the little man among the giants.

games played by the professional Buffalo Bills.) Unlike Maravich and Mount, Murphy's scoring average went down in each of his varsity seasons, but there was a reason. Niagara was improving every year, and there was less and less reason for him to do all the shooting. Still, his senior average of 29.4 suffered only in comparison to the 38.2 points a game he had scored as a sophomore.

There were also other great stars during this period—Wes Unseld of Louisville, Bob Lanier of St. Bonaventure, Jim McMillian of Columbia, Jimmy Walker of Providence. The parade of talent showed no sign of diminishing. John Wooden put it best. "Lew Alcindor is the greatest basketball player of all time," he declared. "But someone will come along who is better than that man, too." Little did Wooden or the basketball world suspect that a new superplayer would be coming along so quickly and that he would enroll at UCLA. A shy six-foot-eleven giant with a shock of curly red hair, his name was Bill Walton.

Wooden sounded the call on Walton early. As he was savoring his fifth straight national championship in a posttournament press conference, Wooden warned the writers that UCLA would be a contender again the next season, partly because of this freshman named Walton "who throws the outlet pass [for the fast break] better than any player I've ever had." Leave it to Wooden to choose such an esoteric phase of the game for mention.

Walton, from La Mesa, California, near San Diego, had played on an undefeated team as a high school senior, and his UCLA freshman team

didn't lose a game, either. Surrounded, as Alcindor had been, by a perfectly complementary cast, Walton and UCLA continued that perfect pattern of success when he moved up to the varsity.

Almost mechanically the Bruins swept through their thirty-game schedule undefeated. Into the NCAA Tournament they went, and again it was as if the result was preordained. With guard Henry Bibby also playing a major role, the Walton Gang, as UCLA was being dubbed, brushed aside Florida State in a final that was not as close as the 81–76 score might indicate and made it six championships in a row, and eight in the last nine years. Walton, only a sophomore, was the tournament's Most Valuable Player and made all the "all" teams.

Who could succeed Lew Alcindor at UCLA? Bill Walton, who played the game passionately and who, until his senior year at UCLA, never played on a team that lost a game.

1963–64
Front (*left to right*): manager Dennis Minishian, Gail Goodrich, Jack Hirsch, Rich Levin, Walt Hazzard, Kent Graham, Mike Huggins, Chuck Darrow. Rear: trainer Elvin (Ducky) Drake, assistant coach Jerry Norman, Steve Brucker, Fred Slaughter, Doug McIntosh, Keith Erickson, Kim Stewart, head coach John Wooden.

1964–65
Front (*left to right*): assistant coach Jerry Norman, Gail Goodrich, John Lyons, John Galbraith, Mike Serafin, Brice Chambers, Larry McCollister, Freddie Goss. Rear: head coach John Wooden, trainer Elvin (Ducky) Drake, Rich Levin, Edgar Lacey, Doug McIntosh, Vaughn Hoffman, Bill Winkelholz, Mike Lynn, Keith Erickson, Kenny Washington, Bill Ureda.

1966–67
Front (*left to right*): Don Saffer, Lucius Allen, Dick Lynn, Gene Sutherland, Mike Warren. Rear: head coach John Wooden, assistant coach Jerry Norman, Joe Chrisman, Lynn Shackelford, Neville Saner, Lew Alcindor, Jim Nielsen, Ken Heitz, Bill Sweek, manager Ted Henry, trainer Elvin (Ducky) Drake.

1967–68
(*Left to right*): head coach John Wooden, assistant coach Jerry Norman, Ken Heitz, Lynn Shackelford, Mike Warren, Jim Nielsen, Gene Sutherland, Lew Alcindor (*behind Sutherland*), Mike Lynn, Lucius Allen, Neville Saner, Bill Sweek, trainer Elvin (Ducky) Drake, manager Frank Adler.

1968–69

Front (*left to right*): trainer Elvin (Ducky) Drake, assistant coach Denny Crum, head coach John Wooden, assistant coach Gary Cunningham, manager Bob Marcucci. Center: George Farmer, Bill Sweek, Ken Heitz, John Vallely, Terry Schofield. Rear: Lynn Shackelford (53), Curtis Rowe, Steve Patterson, Lew Alcindor, Sidney Wicks, John Ecker, Bill Seibert.

1969–70

Front (*left to right*): Henry Bibby, Terry Schofield, Andy Hill. Center: manager George Morgan, assistant coach Gary Cunningham, head coach John Wooden, assistant coach Denny Crum, trainer Elvin (Ducky) Drake. Rear: Kenny Booker, Rick Betchley, John Ecker, Sidney Wicks, Steve Patterson, Jon Chapman, Curtis Rowe, Bill Seibert, John Vallely.

1970–71

Front (*left to right*): Andy Hill, Henry Bibby. Center: manager George Morgan, assistant coach Denny Crum, head coach John Wooden, assistant coach Gary Cunningham, trainer Elvin (Ducky) Drake. Rear: Larry Hollyfield, Larry Farmer, John Ecker, Curtis Rowe, Steve Patterson, Sidney Wicks, Jon Chapman, Kenny Booker, Rick Betchley, Terry Schofield.

1971–72

Front: manager Les Friedman. Center (*left to right*): head coach John Wooden, trainer Elvin (Ducky) Drake, assistant coach Gary Cunningham. Rear: Tommy Curtis, Greg Lee, Larry Hollyfield, Jon Chapman, Keith Wilkes, Bill Walton, Swen Nater, Vince Carson, Larry Farmer, Gary Franklin, Andy Hill, Henry Bibby.

1972–73

Front (*left to right*): Bob Webb, Tommy Curtis, Gary Franklin, Casey Corliss. Center: Larry Hollyfield, manager Les Friedman, head coach John Wooden, assistant coach Gary Cunningham, trainer Elvin (Ducky) Drake, Greg Lee. Rear: Larry Farmer, Keith Wilkes, Dave Meyers, Bill Walton, Ralph Drollinger, Swen Nater, Vince Carson, Pete Trgovich.

Notre Dame's Austin Carr.

Except for Bibby, most of the Bruins would be returning for the following season as UCLA sought to extend its forty-five-game winning streak to record heights. And during this period the full personality of Bill Walton began to be revealed. He appeared to be as complex as his predecessor, Lew Alcindor, who was now known among the professionals by his new Muslim name, Kareem Abdul-Jabbar.

Walton ducked personal publicity even more assiduously than Abdul-Jabbar had done, but proved to be much more outspoken in the field of human rights. During that summer he was arrested, fined, and put on probation for his role in a peace demonstration. At this time, as he refused the first of many pro offers to leave school, it also became public knowledge that Walton had to overcome a major physical problem to keep playing, chronic tendonitis in both knees. But with his practice schedule carefully arranged so he could be nursed through the season, he showed few bad effects from this difficulty once the games in his junior year began.

The key number this season was "60," standing for San Francisco's record winning-streak established almost two decades earlier. The Dons were staging a basketball revival and had a place on UCLA's schedule for game number fifty-eight in January. Everybody knew the once-beaten San Francisco would be going all out to try to protect its record, but the Bruins responded with their best game of the season so far and won, 92–64.

Providence and then Loyola of Chicago fell before the UCLA juggernaut as the Bruins tied USF's record of sixty. And then came the most ironic moment of all in the quest for game sixty-one. The opponent was Notre Dame, the site was South Bend, Indiana, on the very floor where UCLA last had lost a game two years earlier. But this time it was not a sleepy bunch of Bruins who took the court. This was a team ready to meet its destiny. Play was rough. The Fighting Irish did not want to passively accept the role of parties of the second part in the setting of this record. But in the end it was UCLA again, 82–63. As usual the Bruin players accepted the victory and the record almost stoically, except for Larry Farmer and Larry Hollyfield, the only ones remaining from the team that had lost to Notre Dame.

Overjoyed, Wooden tried to put the victory into perspective. "This isn't the greatest thing that happened on this day," he told a national television audience. "It is my grand-daughter's birthday, too. But the most important thing is that this was cease-fire day in Vietnam. That's much more important than this." Bill Walton, who once said nobody over thirty-five should be allowed to be president, couldn't have put it better.

With Walton continuing as the dominant figure on both ends of the court, the Bruins refused to let down after their record achievement. They swept through the remainder of their schedule to become the first team to mesh two perfect seasons. Then came an 87–66 victory over Memphis State in the NCAA tournament finals. That ran UCLA's record streak to seventy-five victories and made it seven championships in a row.

Walton, again spurning multimillion-dollar pro offers, would be back for another year. And rival coaches weren't willing to bet that when the superplayer who would eclipse *his* records showed up, he wouldn't be wearing a UCLA uniform, too.

11

THE NBA

To the romantic, the phrase "Golden Age of Sports" conjures up memories of Jack Dempsey, Bobby Jones, Babe Ruth, and other larger-than-life glamour figures of the distant past. But to sports promoters, who look upon gold in a more literal sense, the golden days were those immediately following World War II. The war was over, the American public was ready to be entertained, and every sports enterprise in the nation set attendance records. Even minor league baseball flourished.

By 1946 professional basketball had settled into two general areas. There was the American League on the East Coast with teams like the Philadelphia SPHAs, the New York City Gothams, and the Paterson, New Jersey, Crescents. And there was the National League in the Midwest, with franchises ranging from Chicago to Sheboygan and Cleveland to Oshkosh.

Many of these teams were sponsored by industry. Farther west, industrial leagues, playing under the auspices of the AAU, provided opportunity for college stars when their eligibility was completed. But none of this was really big league. Not yet. Pro basketball still had not escaped its barnstorming, dance hall legacy.

As the war ended, owners of the big indoor sports arenas began to seek new attractions to keep their buildings busy. Ice hockey had developed over the years into a fine "arena" sport and most professional hockey teams were owned and operated by the management of the buildings in which they played. College basketball, too, was a fine attraction, especially in New York. Nonetheless, arena operators had nightmares at the thought of dark nights in their expensive buildings.

The idea of a new big league, a big city professional basketball circuit,

155

was first suggested by Max Kase, sports editor of the New York *Journal-American,* one of the promotion-minded Hearst-chain newspapers. Through contacts on the Hearst paper in Boston, Kase had gotten to know Walter Brown, president of the Boston Garden and owner of the National Hockey League Bruins. He told Brown of his basketball plan, and Brown liked it.

Brown then proceeded to contact his friends in the arena business and they agreed to join the enterprise. Al Sutphin of Cleveland was especially enthusiastic. Brown also talked to Ned Irish, representing Madison Square Garden. His college program prospering, Irish had little interest in a professional league, but he emphatically did not want an outsider promoting any kind of basketball in his building. So, claiming that the Arena Managers Association of America had agreed some time earlier to go into pro basketball on an all or none basis, and brandishing his control of the biggest city's biggest arena like a bludgeon, he muscled Kase out of the picture.

In June, 1946, the arena owners met in New York to organize a professional basketball league. They called it the Basketball Association of America and named Maurice Podoloff, a New Haven lawyer and president of the American Hockey League, to be their first commissioner. Podoloff, only five feet tall, may have looked out of place when dealing with his towering subjects, yet he, more than any man, is credited with keeping the league alive during its struggling infancy.

The BAA's charter teams were the Washington Capitols, Philadelphia

Maurice Podoloff, the first commissioner of the Basketball Association of America, later the National Basketball Association.

Warriors, New York Knickerbockers, Providence Steamrollers, Toronto Huskies, Boston Celtics, Chicago Stags, St. Louis Bombers, Cleveland Rebels, Detroit Falcons, and Pittsburgh Ironmen. Most of the owners had a strictly arena or hockey background. Eddie Gottlieb, who had run the Philadelphia SPHAs, was one of the few with a basketball background. Irish was another, and at first his fellow owners listened when the aloof entrepreneur spoke. Later, however, this changed and Ned eventually became isolated, ignored, and outvoted in league councils.

The length of the games provided one of the new league's first major problems. A college game of two twenty-minute halves did not provide a full evening of entertainment for fans, which is why Irish had invented the doubleheader format. BAA schedule makers, however, found the doubleheader plan unworkable on a regular basis although many twin bills would be scheduled. The American

League had solved this short-evening problem by playing three fifteen-minute periods, which not only provided a full two-hour "show" but also two intermissions during which the fans could patronize the concession stands. Gottlieb proposed this for the new BAA, but was outvoted. His partners thought it would be better business to have one long half-time break and, to stretch out the games, to play four twelve-minute quarters. The zone defense was outlawed during that first session.

One thing the new league did not have to worry about was players. The end of the war had made a flood of veterans available and eager to resume athletic careers. Some were already pros, others, returning to college, would soon be ready to play for money. The BAA got additional players from the American League, which still had been paying on a per-game basis. Oddly, there was little raiding between the BAA and the National League. For one thing, both sides knew such a war would be financially disastrous. For another, the BAA was less interested in old pros than in fresh college names. (In the beginning, the BAA's biggest competition for players just out of school was with the AAU industrial teams, which could offer young men like Bob Kurland a life-long future.)

The establishment of the BAA wrecked the ABL, but the National League, with a solid roster of proven professionals, was still a formidable competitor. Going into 1947, the first season of head-to-head competition, the NBL consisted of teams in Chicago, Detroit, Rochester, Fort Wayne, Syracuse, Toledo, Indianapolis, Oshkosh, Sheboygan, Anderson, Moline, and Youngstown.

Almost a franchise, even a league unto himself, was George Mikan, playing for the NBL's Chicago Gears. Mikan had refused $5,000 from the Gears to turn pro a year earlier, but when his eligibility at DePaul was up, he signed a five-year contract worth a then unheard of $60,000. In his first pro game after joining the Gears late in the season, Mikan had four of his teeth knocked out by the Oshkosh center. Welcome to pro basketball. But soon the Mikan elbows themselves were to become the most feared weapons in pro basketball. Once Mikan arrived, he averaged 16.5 points a game and led Chicago to the NBL title. He was unanimously named the league's Most Valuable Player.

The BAA, meanwhile, quickly developed some personalities of its own. Down at Washington a young naval officer with some high school coaching experience persuaded the operators of the Capitols that he could provide them with a pretty good team of former servicemen if they named him as their coach. Since his lack of coaching experience meant he couldn't insist on a big salary for himself, and since the ex-servicemen would come cheap, too, Arnold (Red) Auerbach was given the job. He immediately established himself and his team as the classiest in the new leagues.

Bob Feerick, whom Auerbach had known in the navy, was recruited to be the hub of the new team, and he responded with the second-best scoring average in the league. An unathletic-looking friend of Feerick's from the West Coast, Freddie Scolari, also became a regular, along with Bones

Joe Fulks of the Philadelphia Warriors drives in for a layup during a game against the St. Louis Bombers in 1947. Later in the contest Fulks set a season's scoring record of 1,406 points.

McKinney of North Carolina and former LIU star, Irv Torgoff. Feerick and McKinney made the BAA's first All-Star team as the Caps ran off a seventeen-game winning streak and easily won the Eastern Division championship.

The BAA's first playoff plan was a farce. The first-place finishers in each division would play a best-of-seven series to qualify for the finals. Meanwhile, the two second-place teams and two third-place teams would each play a best-of-three series with those survivors also going two-out-of-three for the right to challenge that first-place playoff winner for the title. This setup insured two things: one, no teams would be sitting around idle (and on the payroll) waiting for another series to conclude; two, one of the two best teams in the league had to be knocked out of the playoffs in the first round.

Chicago, which had qualified for the first-round first-place series by beating St. Louis in a one-game playoff for the Western Division title, eliminated Washington in six games. The Stags eventually lost in five games to Philadelphia for the BAA's first official championship.

Philadelphia's star player was Joe Fulks, a skinny six-foot-five Kentuckian who had enlisted in the Marine Corps right out of Murray State College. Fulks had served on Guam and Iwo Jima and had also participated in some fast-service basketball competition against big-name stars. "You've probably never heard of him, but I believe he has the potentialities of a great scorer," Gottlieb told the press when he announced the signing of Fulks.

Before the BAA's inaugural season was over, Fulks had established himself as the league's first star and scoring champion. Shooting an unstoppable jumper from off his ear, the gangly Fulks averaged an incredible 23.2 points a game. This was almost 7 points a game better than Feerick, the runner-up! Until they saw him, fans couldn't believe that any basketball player could score consistently at such a rate. His average over a sixty-game season was an even more incredible feat than the record forty-one points he scored in one game or the sixty-three points he scored against Indianapolis in 1949. Critics of Fulks point out that he was slow, not much on defense and, certainly, seldom passed off. But Honey Russell, the coach of the Boston Celtics, insisted, "I'd still build my team around him."

Fulks scored thirty-seven points, twenty-nine of them in the second half, to start Philadelphia to its playoff romp over Chicago in the finals, which earned the 190-pound Kentuckian and his teammates a grand prize of $2,000 a man. Since player salaries averaged only a little more than twice that amount—the league had a $55,000 team salary limit—it was a pretty good bonus for a fine season. Fulks was twenty-seven years old when he turned pro, so he had been able to persuade the Warriors to pay him the then magnificent salary of $8,000 for his rookie season. "I just came along twenty years too soon," he complained later, but if it had not been for Joe Fulks in the beginning, perhaps today's salaries would not be so high.

Money was quite important to the league's owners in those days; not that things have really changed. That first year the BAA had played a sixty-game schedule and some owners felt this was too much. If they played fewer games, they reasoned, they might still draw the same total crowds and they could justify lower salaries to the players. So for the 1948 season they dropped back to forty-eight games. Not only did revenue drop with the loss of the dozen dates (this especially hit hard at teams that were drawing well, like Philadelphia, since the home club kept all the receipts), but the players refused to accept any pay cuts. In 1949 the schedule was moved back up to sixty games, and all the players demanded raises because of the extra work.

Both leagues went through a major shakedown before the 1948 season, the second of their competition. The BAA lost its franchises in Toronto, Cleveland, Pittsburgh, and Detroit, then had to add the Baltimore Bullets of the skeleton American League to fill out an eight-team lineup. The Bullets proceeded to embarrass their new partners by winning the league championship.

Out in the NBL some complicated maneuverings were taking place. After a dispute with the league, Morris R. White of the Chicago Gears left the NBL to set up his own circuit, which never got off the ground. Meanwhile the NBL's failing Detroit franchise, which had won only four of forty-four games the year before, moved to Minneapolis taking the name of Lakers. In the draft of the newly available players from the Gears, the Lakers snatched Mikan, plus a forward named Jim Pollard. Both made the NBL All-Star team as Minneapolis won the league championship and Mikan the scoring title (he was also named MVP).

Two decades later competition between the leagues for college talent would become anathema to the professionals, especially to the young BAA, which depended so much on signing fresh new faces. Starting with Mikan, the greatest pro of all, the NBL had an edge in recognizable names. However, the BAA had the big cities and the arenas to go with them and its cities *sounded* big league. Maurice Podoloff spent the off-season playing this ace, probing for weakness in the NBL lineup of franchise holders. Before the 1949 season, he found that weakness. Indianapolis and Fort Wayne, eager to join the big-city wheel, agreed to jump.

Once these two had broken ranks, Podoloff went to work again on Minneapolis. At first the Lakers were hesitant because of their dominant position in the NBL. Apparently they had forgotten what the Celtics had once done to a league they had similarly dominated. But with Indianapolis and Fort Wayne already gone, Max Winter, who ran the Lakers, realized the BAA was the league of the future. He agreed to jump and that finished the NBL as a major factor. (Ironically, less than a dozen years later, Winter would pull virtually the same stunt in football. He was the leader of a Minneapolis group that held a charter membership in the American Football League, just getting ready to play its first season, when he was offered a franchise in the more prestigious National Football League; he grabbed it. That blow almost killed the AFL before it started.)

When the BAA had originally been formed, the owners of the Rochester Royals wanted to jump from the NBL right then, but they were turned down because they didn't qualify as

arena operators. Now, however, they tried again, and this time, after much pleading, the Royals—second in strength only to the Lakers—were allowed to join the younger league.

Podoloff's daring had wrecked the NBL, although it took the older league a year to die. With four of its top clubs jumping to the BAA, and with Toledo and Flint folding, the NBL added Denver, Dayton, Hammond, and Waterloo to its roster. But the name of the latter franchise was to prove prophetic. In 1950, with Oshkosh, Hammond, and Dayton left behind as financial casualties, the NBL survivors agreed to merge with the BAA. The new league would be known as the National Basketball Association, but Podoloff remained as commissioner, a short but vivid reminder of just who had won this war.

Mikan, of course, had been the big prize. "We weren't much better off than the NBL until he came along. It's no exaggeration to say he saved the league," one NBA official pointed out. And with Mikan came the rest of the Lakers, plus stars like Bob Davies of Rochester. Just as important among the new recruits were dynamic club owners like Ben Kerner of Tri-Cities, Danny Biasone of Syracuse, and the Harrison brothers of Rochester. Without the backing of big arenas these men had learned to survive in pro basketball the hard way.

Dropping back to 1949, the four original NBL jumpers had all been placed in the BAA's Western Division where Rochester and Minneapolis finished one-two in the standings only a game apart. In the playoffs the Lakers swept the Royals in the semifinals and went on to beat Washington in the title round, four games to two. In ten playoff games, Mikan, who had led the league with a 28.3 average in regular season, scored 303 points. Mikan, Pollard, and Davies all made the BAA All-Star team, showing just how strong the NBL had been.

The new seventeen-team NBA lineup for 1950 was unwieldy, its resemblance to "big league" strictly coincidental. Presumably the only reason the NBA invited in all those marginal NBL franchises was to prevent possible antitrust law suits. The new NBA's Eastern Division had some semblance of class, however. BAA holdovers New York, Washington, Philadelphia, Boston, and Baltimore were joined by Syracuse, which took over the position of the newly defunct Providence franchise. The Central Division, which was not exactly unimpressive, contained Minneapolis, Rochester, Fort Wayne, Chicago, and St. Louis. But the Western Division was a laughingstock. The Indianapolis Jets, who had jumped to the BAA with the first wave, had folded, their place being taken by the Indianapolis Olympians, who featured the stars of Kentucky's Fabulous Five, just back from their Olympic triumphs as players and owners. Others in the West were Anderson, Tri-Cities, Sheboygan, Waterloo, and Denver. Waterloo and Denver had actually failed the year before as NBL franchises, but were allowed back in as charter members of the new circuit.

Nobody could say the NBA wasn't giving everyone a chance to play. All they had to provide was a ball. Nobody questioned whether the ball was paid for. Within a year, though, some sanity was restored. Chicago, St. Louis, Anderson, Waterloo, Sheboygan, and Denver all dropped out before the

1951 season began. Washington, which had already lost its great coach and founding spirit, Red Auerbach, folded during the season. The NBA finished 1951 with a ten-team framework and the following season Tri-Cities (actually Moline, Illinois) moved to Milwaukee. The league schedule began to look less like a small-time vaudeville circuit wheel.

Mikan, Pollard, Davies, and Max Zaslofsky of Chicago repeated as All-Stars in the first year of the NBA and were joined by former Kentucky star Alex Groza, a rookie. Another first-year player, Ed Macauley, also impressed a lot of people, but, as usual, Mikan and his Lakers won the play-offs after finishing in a tie for the Central Division title with Rochester.

The 1951 season was the most important in the history of the NBA, on several counts, some of them interrelated. Red Auerbach joined the Boston Celtics as coach, and his second draft choice for this season was a forward from Duquesne named Chuck Cooper. Tri-Cities drafted Bob Cousy of Holy Cross. The League felt feisty enough to stage its first All-Star game. And, in the Manhattan district attorney's office, the façade of college basketball came tumbling down, leaving the stage to the often-maligned but clean professionals.

The All-Star game was a sign that the league was gaining stature and maturity as it continued to sort itself out after the merger. The college scandals, as much as they damaged the good name of all basketball, aided the pros. At one time college ball had so dominated the metropolitan scene that the Knicks, though owned by Madison Square Garden, played only a handful of their games there. The remainder

Chuck Cooper, the first black to be drafted by the NBA.

were farmed out to a local armory. But after the scandals, college basketball never recovered its appeal. The pros moved into the vacuum, and Podoloff, to his credit, handled the few hints of scandal without compromise. Kentucky fix figures like Groza, Beard, and Spivey were summarily barred from current or future competition. So was Jack Molinas when it was learned that the Fort Wayne rookie was betting on games. It didn't hurt either when Sol Levy, an NBA official, admitted taking $3,000 to fix three games but then got "cold feet" and only went through the motions. Levy, who emerged as a tragicomic figure, was also banned.

In retrospect, the most important action was the drafting of Chuck Cooper by the Celtics. When the NBA celebrated its silver anniversary in 1970, the All-Star team that year consisted of Billy Cunningham, Walt Frazier, Connie Hawkins, Willis Reed, and Jerry West. The second five consisted of Lew Alcindor, Bill Bridges,

John Havlicek, Lou Hudson, and Oscar Robertson. Seven of the ten are black. Chuck Cooper was the first black athlete to be drafted by any team in professional basketball. Auerbach, who was to become so closely identified with Boston's success, was the man who drafted him. The same year, the Knicks purchased Nat (Sweetwater) Clifton from the Globetrotters and together he and Cooper broke the color line.

In the draft before the 1951 season, in the spring of 1950, Auerbach had created a gale of criticism in Boston by overlooking Cousy, a local hero out of Holy Cross, in favor of six-foot-eleven Charley Share of Bowling Green. Cousy was drafted, to his horror, by Tri-Cities, a place he had never heard of and that in reality did not exist. However, before Cousy had a chance to lace on his sneakers, he was traded to Chicago. Then, three weeks before the season was to open, Chicago's franchise folded and it was decided to apportion the players to

Arnie Risen of the Rochester Royals shoots over the Knicks' Sweetwater Clifton. Clifton, purchased from the Globetrotters in Cooper's rookie year, was the first black to play in an NBA game. (*Right*) The Warriors' Andy Phillip applies some blanket coverage to the Lakers' Slater Martin.

other members of the league.

All went well until there were only three players left—and three teams were bidding for one of them: Max Zaslofsky, a four-time All-Star. New York, Philadelphia, and Boston all wanted him, but they probably would have settled not too unhappily for the second leftover, experienced Andy Phillip, the former Whiz Kid. The third player was Cousy.

Podoloff, the great conciliator, finally solved the dilemma with utmost simplicity. He put the names of the three players in a hat and invited the club presidents to draw. Ned Irish, picking first for the Knicks, was overjoyed to nab Zaslofsky. Eddie Gottlieb of Philadelphia drew Phillip. The Celtics were left with Cousy, the hometown hero they had overlooked —and the player who later would be credited by Walter Brown with saving his struggling franchise.

Ironically, the man Boston had drafted instead of Cousy, Charley Share, never played for the Celtics.

When St. Louis folded after the 1950 season, the Celts were able to grab off Macauley, who fulfilled their need for a big man. Although it would take the addition of other players to make the Celtics into champions, Macauley and Cousy at least made the team competitive as the club built for better days.

The Rochester Royals, led by Arnie Risen, Bob Davies, Bobby Wanzer, Jack Coleman, and Arne Johnson, finally halted the Lakers' string of two straight championships by eliminating Minneapolis in a four-game semifinal and then edging the Knicks in seven games in the finals. But the 1952 season saw the Lakers right back on top, and before Mikan retired after the 1954 season, they won three championships in succession to make it five out of six in the new league.

The Minneapolis-Mikan team must rank as one of the greatest in the history of professional basketball, right up there with both Celtic teams, the Originals of yesteryear and the

Rochester's Bob Davies cuts around teammate Arnie Risen and starts to sprint with the Knicks' Carl Braun (19).

later Bostonian variety. Mikan, of course, was the big man in many ways, a tremendous factor in every game even though the rule makers tried to curtail him before the 1952 season by widening the free-throw lane from six to twelve feet to keep him from planting his huge bulk so close to the basket.

Mikan weighed 245 pounds and he would simply bull his way to the basket, forearms first, overmatching such classy but slender opponents as Arnie Risen. But he took his punishment, too. Over his career, he sustained a total of 166 stitches for various combat wounds, two broken legs, a broken foot, broken wrist, broken nose, and three broken fingers. Once, when he heard in the dressing room that an opposing team had accused him of "getting away with murder"

under the boards, he ripped off his shirt and exposed a mass of fresh black and blue welts. "Ask them what they think these are, birth marks?" he demanded.

Mikan was not a one-man team, even though the Madison Square Garden marquee once proclaimed:

Tonight
George Mikan
vs.
Knicks

The Lakers also had two outstanding cornermen who combined with Mikan to provide a fabulous frontcourt. They comprised six-foot-three Jim Pollard and six-foot-seven Vern Mikkelsen. "A basketball player's basketball player," a rival once said of Pollard, who majored in finesse while Mikkelsen

George Mikan displays a left-handed hook against Sweetwater Clifton.

Paul Arizin of the Warriors shoots his characteristic jump shot between Knicks defenders Ray Felix (*left*) and Ken Sears.

was the power man. The guards were Herman Schaefer and five-foot-nine Slater Martin. The bench was impressive.

Before Mikan's retirement, first Paul Arizin and then Neil Johnston, both of the Warriors, had stolen his scoring laurels, but he continued until the end (excluding a brief comeback two years later to try to help his old team at the gate) to be the dominant player of his age. When he did retire, his coach, John Kundla, philosophized, "Well, at least this should even up the league."

By 1954 the Indianapolis Olympians, tarred by the college scandal two years earlier, had dropped from the NBA, and early the following sea-

son Baltimore disbanded with a 3–11 record. These defections left the NBA with a workable eight-team format. Only now was it generally agreed that pro basketball had made it.

Kundla's prediction that Mikan's retirement would even up the league came true. The year after he quit, Syracuse emerged as the NBA champion, defeating Fort Wayne in a "small-town" final round. Because a bowling tournament had preempted its coliseum, Fort Wayne's "home" games had to be played in Indianapolis. Syracuse won with a fine, well-balanced team led by Dolph Schayes and including Red Rocha, Paul Seymour, George King, Johnny Kerr, and Billy Kenville. Schayes, a six-foot-eight forward, had scored more points than any NBA player before him when he finally retired in 1964 after a sixteen-year career. He was probably as good an all-round player as ever performed professionally.

Schayes's career was marked by one of sport's great what-might-have-been questions. A product of New York high schools, Schayes attended NYU, where he became known as a good, hard-working college player. Although he put in long hours to improve himself, there were many people, including his own coach, who doubted that he had the physique to make it as a pro. The two basketball leagues had not yet merged when Schayes finished college, and he was drafted both by the Knicks of the BAA and by Tri-Cities of the NBL. Tri-Cities traded his rights to Syracuse, which was closer to home.

At this time the BAA had a first-year salary limit of $6,000 and that is what Ned Irish of the Knicks offered Schayes. Syracuse went $1,000 higher, but Irish would not match the Nationals' offer. BAA salary limits had been regularly violated, but this time Irish would not budge. Was he too cheap to go the extra thousand? Did the Knick president, by then already unpopular with his colleagues, fear they would blow the whistle at the least provocation? (Time after time on being voted down, 7-to-1, Irish would storm from NBA meetings yelling to his colleagues, "You can take my franchise." Podoloff would have to scurry out and calm him down.) Or did Irish just feel, in common with many, that Schayes wasn't worth the extra thousand? Whatever his reasons, he would not pay. Schayes went to Syracuse, an action that would have a

Dolph Schayes drives to the basket against Boston.

profound effect not only on the Nats, but on the Knicks, who would spend the next decade searching for a big man to make them a contender while having to compete against Schayes in their own division.

Fort Wayne, the Syracuse challenger, wasn't exactly a weak team itself. Larry Foust, a burly six feet nine, was the center, and George Yardley and Mel Hutchins were at forward. The guards, coincidentally, were Max Zaslofsky and Andy Phillip, two of the players involved in that Cousy out-of-the-hat affair. A reserve was Frank Brian, who happened to be the player for whom rookie Cousy had been traded when he went from Tri-Cities to Chicago in the first place.

These Pistons also made it to the playoff finals in 1956, but there they ran into Philadelphia, which featured the greatest one-two scoring punch in pro history in Paul Arizin and Neil Johnston. The two Warriors had finished second and third this year behind sophomore pro Bob Pettit, but between them they represented four straight titles, the last three by Johnston.

Arizin had been a late bloomer in basketball; in fact, he had never even made the varsity in high school and had enrolled, on his own without a scholarship, at Villanova in a suburb of his home town of Philadelphia. However, he loved the game and developed an uncanny jump shot while playing in neighborhood leagues almost every night. That's where Villanova coach Al Severance spotted him and was shocked to learn this hot prospect was already enrolled on his campus. The Warriors made Arizin a territorial draft pick while he was still in college. Although he stood only six feet four, taller opponents were never able to stop his jump shot. Arizin, who played despite a sinus condition that made him gasp for air as he raced up and down the court, broke in with one great scorer, Joe Fulks, and then finished his career playing with another, Neil Johnston.

Johnston, six feet eight, came out of Ohio State and excelled in scoring, with a pretty good one-hander and a deft hook shot from close in, as well as in rebounding. A knee injury ended his career prematurely but he and Arizin, at the height of their game in 1956, swept aside the Pistons in five games to win the NBA championship. Joe Graboski at forward and rookie

Tom Gola and Jack George in the backcourt were the other starters. With Philadelphia's victory, the NBA completed its first ten years as a major league and sealed the end of the Mikan Era.

Earlier, off the court, rule changes already assured that the fledgling league would be heading in new and better directions. From the beginning, BAA owners had realized that movement and scoring would be the key to the success of their league. Stagnant play had killed earlier pro leagues and so they early outlawed the zone defense. What they couldn't outlaw—or at least lacked the foresight to ban— was the rough style of play that had always seemed to separate the amateur from the professional.

As the BAA evolved into the NBA, rough play and fouling became a major tactic, and not just to beat down or intimidate an opponent or to provoke an opposition star into a disqualifying fist fight with a substitute, although this did happen. No, what did occur was that a team with a lead would hold on to the ball; and the only way the trailing team could catch up was to foul deliberately, thus giving up one point for a chance to make two. The leading team would then simply foul right back, certain it would remain in front until the final buzzer on this one-for-one swap. This trading of fouls turned the game into a travesty as giants in undershorts walked from one end of the court to the other in interminable foul-shooting contests. Occasionally, the foul trading would get too rough and fights would develop. A 1949 playoff game between the Knicks and Baltimore—an overtime yawner—saw a total of a hundred

Neil Johnston shows the style that made him top scorer in the NBA. The Hawks here are a Milwaukee franchise, later moved to St. Louis.

personal fouls called and three fist fights. (With personal fouls becoming so important, intimidation of officials also became a highly developed art. And the officials got little help from Podoloff and the league office because shortsighted owners wanted a "free" let-'em-play game.)

Early in the 1950–51 campaign, Fort Wayne was scheduled for a regular-season game at Minneapolis, where the Lakers played on a smaller-than-standard floor that made their physical bulk so much more of a factor and also compensated for their slowness afoot. Piston coach Murray Mendenhall was determined to end the Lakers' string of twenty-nine straight home-court victories and also to publicize his complaint that Minneapolis used an illegal zone defense. Committed to making the huge Lakers leave their set defensive positions under the basket, Mendenhall had his team pass the ball back and forth near midcourt in an old-fashioned stall. The Lakers refused to budge and the Pistons led, 8–7, after the first quarter. At half time, Minneapolis was on top, 13–11.

By this time Laker fans were showering Mendenhall and his Pistons with abuse and debris in equal amounts, and were hitting their target with both more frequently than the stalling Fort Wayne players were hitting the basket. They screamed they were being cheated and many demanded their money back. Going into the final period the Lakers led, 17–16. In the first eight minutes of the fourth quarter each team made only a single free throw, and Fort Wayne, with possession of the ball but trailing by a point, elected to play for a final shot. This meant a four-minute freeze,

which the Pistons pulled off. With only ten seconds remaining Larry Foust put home a hook shot. The Lakers had time to retaliate, but Slater Martin's long shot bounced off the rim and Fort Wayne had scored a most controversial 19–18 victory.

Although Podoloff agreed with the Lakers' complaints, Fort Wayne had violated no rule and so there was nothing he could do to void their victory. But the word was sent out to all the owners. This sort of thing would not be allowed to happen again.

But it did. Later that same season, Indianapolis beat Rochester in a game that took six overtime periods. Under normal circumstances each team might have been expected to score perhaps 150 points. The final score in this game was 75–73. In each overtime period, the team that won the center jump tried to hold the ball for a final shot.

In 1953 Bob Cousy scored fifty points as the Celtics beat the Nationals, 111–105, in four overtimes in an important playoff game. It sounds as if this was one of the NBA's most exciting moments. It wasn't. The game started with Bob Brannum, a lesser Celtic, provoking Syracuse star Dolph Schayes into a fight—both were thrown out. By the merciful final buzzer, a total of 107 fouls had been called and 130 foul shots attempted. Eleven players on the two teams fouled out. Cousy was able to break Mikan's one-year-old playoff scoring record by three points because he converted thirty of thirty-two free throws.

The next year the end of an NBA game on national television was never seen by the outside audience because it had lasted over three hours and the network ran out of time. At this point the league's Board of Governors (a fancy title for directors) knew something had to be done. Ten days after the playoffs came to an end, they tried to put aside their petty differences in a league meeting called to discuss saving their threatened game. Danny Biasone, owner of the Syracuse club, had a suggestion. Why not a time limit on how long a team could hold the ball? He had done some research: twenty-four seconds seemed like time enough for any team to get off a shot.

Twenty-four seconds it was.

Along with the time limit the governors put in a new set of rules to take some of the advantage from deliberate fouling. Foul trading was ended. The game was revived by these innovations. Mikan was retiring anyway, so nobody would ever know whether the lumbering giant could have adapted to the twenty-four-second speedup. But it didn't really matter. When pro basketball needed a star, bespectacled George Mikan was there. He had saved the game for future refinement.

LOWEST SCORING GAME IN NBA HISTORY
November 22, 1950, at Minneapolis

FORT WAYNE (19)

Player	FGA	FGM	FTA	FTM	Reb.	Ast.	PF	Pts.
Fred Schaus	1	0	3	3	0	1	0	3
Jack Kerris	1	0	4	2	2	0	5	2
Larry Foust	2	1	1	1	1	0	3	3
Bob Harris	0	0	1	0	1	0	1	0
John Hargis	1	1	0	0	0	1	0	2
Ralph Johnson	1	0	0	0	0	1	1	0
John Oldham	5	1	4	3	4	0	2	5
Paul Armstrong	2	1	2	2	0	0	1	4
Total	13	4	15	11	8	3	13	19

MINNEAPOLIS LAKERS (18)

Player	FGA	FGM	FTA	FTM	Reb.	Ast.	PF	Pts.
Jim Pollard	1	0	1	1	1	1	2	1
Bud Grant	0	0	0	0	0	1	1	0
Vern Mikkelsen	2	0	0	0	3	0	2	0
Joe Hutton	0	0	0	0	0	0	0	0
George Mikan	11	4	11	7	4	0	1	15
Slater Martin	2	0	3	0	1	2	2	0
Bob Harrison	2	0	2	2	0	0	3	2
Arnie Ferrin	0	0	0	0	0	0	0	0
Total	18	4	17	10	9	4	11	18

Score by Periods

	1st	2nd	3rd	4th	Total
Fort Wayne Pistons	8	3	5	3	19
Minneapolis Lakers	7	6	4	1	18

Referees—Jocko Collins and Stan Stutz. Attendance—7,021.

SOURCE: *NBA Guide*

12
DYNASTY

THE BOSTON CELTICS, charter members of the NBA, had never lived up to the great heritage of their proud name, but Walter Brown, their owner, believed strongly in the future of the pro game and in his team. When his fellow Boston Garden directors voted to discard the Celtics as an unprofitable venture, he took over the team himself and backed it with his personal fortune. A scrupulously honorable man, Brown gained new friends through basketball almost as fast as he lost his money.

In their first four years, the Celtics' highest finish was third in the Eastern Division. Twice they wound up sixth and last. However, before the 1951 season, the Celtics had turned into a respectable team, thanks to the genius of Red Auerbach as coach and general manager and to Bob Cousy as an unparalleled floor general. Brown gave Auerbach full control, even when

it hurt, as occurred when Red passed up the chance to draft Cousy, a Boston hero and personal friend of Brown's. ("What am I supposed to do, satisfy the local yokels, or win?" Auerbach had demanded at the NBA draft when Cousy's name came up and Brown had been forced to mutter glumly, "Just win.")

However, Cousy did eventually end up a Celtic and as Auerbach put his stamp on the Boston team, their fortunes improved. In the next six seasons they finished second in the Eastern Division four times and never lower than third. Each year they made the playoffs. Attendance improved. The Celtics of this era were a flashy high-scoring outfit with stars like Ed Macauley and Bill Sharman, both of whom had come to Boston in the same season as Cousy. But something was missing. They could not turn the corner from respectability to dominance

Walter Brown, owner of the Boston Celtics.

A rookie joined the Celtics after the Olympics in 1956 and quickly proved his value. Here Bill Russell soars over Minneapolis' Larry Foust.

without a big man.

As he began to formulate his plans long in advance of the 1956 draft, Auerbach believed he had found the man who could change the also-ran Celtics into champions—Bill Russell, six feet nine and playing devastating defense for the University of San Francisco. Auerbach elected to gamble on drafting Russell and the gamble was two-fold. The Olympic games were scheduled for Melbourne, Australia, in 1956, and Russell had let it be known that he intended to represent the United States. This meant that he would not be available to the Celtics until two months of the NBA season had elapsed. The second gamble was that Boston could outbid the Harlem Globetrotters, still a force in such things, who were also interested in Russell.

Auerbach decided to go after Russell anyway. But the Celtics would be picking sixth in the draft and it was impossible that all five teams ahead of them would pass up Russell. The lead-off position was held by Rochester, whose management, Auerbach knew, did not have the resources to back Russell's expected salary demands. Besides, they had Maurice Stokes, only six feet seven, but already established at center after an outstanding rookie season. The St. Louis Hawks were second on the list and Auerbach decided to make his pitch to the Hawks' owner, Ben Kerner. There is some doubt that Kerner would have selected Russell—he already had Bob Pettit—but Auerbach could not take the chance. He offered the Hawks Ed Macauley, who had been a big star at St. Louis U., for their first draft pick. Macauley would be a tremendous box office attraction for the Hawks, but

Kerner sensed Auerbach's eagerness. He demanded a little sweetener, forward Cliff Hagan, who was just coming out of service. Auerbach acceded. He wanted Russell badly. The deal was made.

In that same draft, the Celtics also made a territorial pick, six-foot-seven Tom Heinsohn of Holy Cross. Coming out of service after one season of pro play was Hagan's old Kentucky teammate, Frank Ramsey (Auerbach had pulled an earlier coup by drafting Ramsey and Hagan for future use even though they faced service tours.) Jim Loscutoff, a bruising rebounder, had been enrolled as a rookie the year before. Looking back, this roll call of Celtic recruits should have sounded an ominous note for Boston's NBA colleagues (especially when one adds Sam Jones the following season and K. C. Jones the year after that). At this time, though, any thoughts of perpetual championships for the Celtics existed only in Auerbach's whirling brain.

The key, of course, was Russell. It was essential to Auerbach's master plan to have a center who excelled in rebounding and on defense. With Russell under the basket, bending the NBA's rule against zone defenses, the other four Celtics could guard their men recklessly, going for the steal and the interception. The center would always be in position to pick up their mistakes. And with Russell there to snatch the defensive rebounds, his teammates could start up court on a fast break as soon as the opposition put the ball into the air. Russell's shot blocking was a bonus.

Heinsohn played center for the Celtics as the 1956–57 season began, but moved to forward once Rus-

Bob Cousy floats in for a two-handed layup against the Syracuse Nats.

sell completed his Olympic appearance and joined the team. Loscutoff, the muscle man, played the other forward. Cousy and Bill Sharman (a fantastic shooter), the guards, complemented each other perfectly. Cousy, taking those outlet passes from Russell to start the fast break, was the quarterback, Sharman the shooting guard. Up front Heinsohn was the shooter, Loscutoff the rebounder. Ramsey was the perfect sixth man, capable of playing up front or in the backcourt as ably as most starters on other teams.

He, too, reported late from the service, but as soon as he and Russell got into stride, the Celtics rushed to the Eastern Division championship, winning their first title by six games over Syracuse. Because of their divisional championship, the Celtics drew a bye into the playoff semifinals, where they polished off Syracuse in three straight games to make the final round.

Meanwhile, in the Western Division, St. Louis, Minneapolis, and Fort Wayne, all with losing records, tied for the regular season championship, and the Hawks won a series of playoffs to gain the title round against Boston. The Hawks, heavy underdogs, had Pettit, the league's premier cornerman and an intense competitor, at one forward and Macauley at the other. The center was Charley Share, the man Auerbach had once drafted ahead of Cousy. The guards were Slater Martin, obtained from the Lakers to be a Cousy-type quarterback, and Jack McMahon. Cliff Hagan filled the same sixth-man role with St. Louis as capably as his old Kentucky teammate, Ramsey, did with Boston.

The series started in Boston. If Celtic fans were distressed when St. Louis won the first game, 125–123, in double overtime, they soon got over it when the Celtics evened the series with a one-sided 119–99 decision. The competition then moved to St. Louis for the next two games (Auerbach and Kerner got into a brief fist fight before the third game). The third game—like the first—was decided in the final minute. A key basket by Pettit boosted the Hawks to a 106–98 victory. Again the Celtics had to bounce back, and again they did, winning the fourth game and then the fifth. Victory in the sixth game would

Boston's Russell and Heinsohn, the latter the winner of the Rookie of the Year award in 1957, climb over Bob Pettit in the championship finals.

have given them the championship, but they fell just short. Hagan put in a rebound as the final buzzer sounded and St. Louis won, 96–94, to tie the series at three games apiece. The decisive contest would be played in Boston.

This seventh game provided one of the classic finishes in NBA history. With six seconds left in regulation

Boston and St. Louis met in the NBA finals for the second straight year in 1957. Cousy shows some of his magic in the second game.

Cliff Hagan (6) of the Hawks and Andy Phillip claw for a rebound in the sixth game.

time, Pettit, playing with a cast on his wrist because of a broken bone, converted two free throws for a 103–103 tie that put the game in overtime. In the frenzied first overtime the Celtics pulled ahead. Then, with nine seconds left, Jack Coleman hit a jump shot for the Hawks to produce a tie at 113 and force still another overtime period.

The two teams battled back and forth, trading fouls and committing turnovers as the tension mounted for the thousands of screaming fans in Boston Garden. With two seconds left, Boston was on top, 125–123, after a Jim Loscutoff free throw. A safe lead at this point? Hardly. The clock which had been stopped for the foul, would start again when some player touched the ball *in bounds*. Alex Hannum, the Hawks' playing coach, was

Tom Heinsohn heads for two in the last game of the 1957 series. Bill Sharman (21) trails the play.

in the game by then and he recalled an old stratagem from a similar game played somewhere in his distant past. He stationed Pettit under the Celtic basket, then heaved the ball at the backboard from the other end of the court. The Hawks' only chance was for Pettit to get the rebound, at which point the clock would start, and then make the shot. Pettit, battling Bill Russell, got the rebound, shoved it toward the basket . . . and it fell away. The Celtics were champions at last.

When the season was over, Heinsohn, dubbed Ack-Ack because of his free-shooting talents, was named the NBA's Rookie of the Year over Russell. After all, he had been on hand all season and had averaged more than sixteen points a game. Cousy, goaded to greatness as he sought to earn Auerbach's grudging approval, was named the league's Most Valuable Player. He had also been named outstanding player in the league All-Star game in which Sharman had made a seventy-foot shot, and the two Celtic backcourt stars were named all-NBA at the end of the season. But Sharman, Cousy, and Heinsohn all knew, as did everyone in basketball, that it was Bill Russell who had turned Boston into a winner. That fact would be vividly demonstrated the following year when Boston and St. Louis met again in the playoff finals.

That 1958 season was marked by transition and tragedy. Fort Wayne's franchise moved to Detroit, and Rochester transferred its Royals to Cincinnati. Both shifts bolstered the NBA's big-league image. (Only Syracuse among the eight league members still carried small-town status in the sports world.) In addition to seeking a larger audience, the Royals' owners knew that two years hence a young man from the University of Cincinnati would be eligible for the professional draft. They would sit tight those two years to make Oscar Robertson a territorial selection.

The tragic note also involved the Royals. To provide support for Robertson, until he arrived to be their backcourt star, the Royals had been counting on the shooting skills of Jack Twyman and the rugged rebounding of Maurice Stokes. Stokes had led the league in that department in 1957 and his future appeared limitless. But during the season he was stricken with encephalitis, a brain disease. Completely paralyzed, he was doomed to many years of hospitalization and therapy before he could lead anything even approaching a normal life. The expenses involved in his care and treatment were staggering. Jack Twyman had himself declared Stokes's legal guardian so he could fully supervise his teammate's treatment, a task that ended only with Stokes's death many years later.

Wilt Chamberlain (*left*), the late Maurice Stokes (*center*), and Jack Twyman.

The instant an epoch began: Boston's 125–123 victory in the seventh game of the 1957 NBA title series. In the next twelve years the Celtics would win ten more championships.

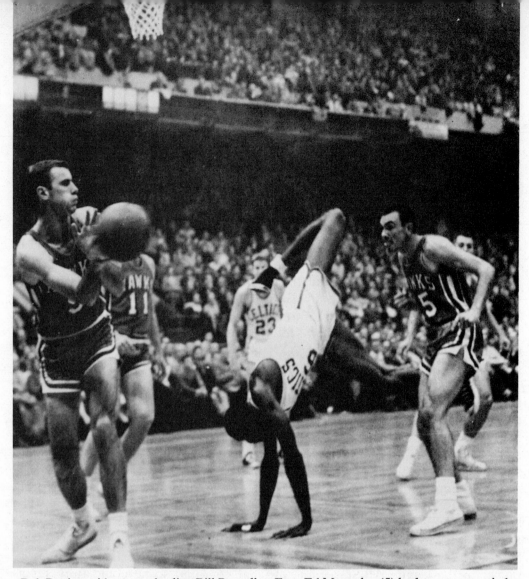

Bob Pettit avoids a cartwheeling Bill Russell as Easy Ed Macauley (5) looks on tongue-tied.

At the end of the 1958 season Boston and St. Louis again ended up in the playoff finals with virtually the same players who had starred the previous season. The exceptions were Loscutoff, who had been out most of the season with an injury (Ramsey replaced him), and Hannum, by now strictly a bench coach. Once again St. Louis, the underdog, won the first game in Boston, 104–102. And like the previous year the Celtics won game two with St. Louis taking game three back on its home court.

In that third game Russell had suffered a painful ankle injury. The Celtics won the fourth game without him, 109–98, but they couldn't recapture their old pattern with the big center not around to control the backboards and plug their defense. The Hawks won the fifth game in Boston, 102–100, and moved into position to clinch the championship in the sixth game on their home floor.

Russell tried to play in the sixth game, but he couldn't make it, and his absence was felt. The Hawks had led most of the way, the Celtics rallied to tie, and then Bob Pettit began to dominate the game. He had scored thirty-one points by the end of the third quarter and with the championship in reach he suddenly became unstoppable. Shot after shot fell in for the slender but tireless southerner, as

Jack McMahon sails by Arnie Risen (19) during a 1958 playoff game at Boston garden. The Hawks won the title.

Bill Sharman (21) challenges St. Louis's Len Wilkins.

Bob Cousy splits the Knicks' Ken Sears (12) and Richie Guerin.

he poured in nineteen of his team's final twenty-one points. Breaking George Mikan's playoff record of forty-two, Pettit scored fifty points in leading the Hawks to a 110–109 victory and the world's championship. The season before, the Celtics had shown what a team could do with the dominant big man. Their loss without him underscored Bill Russell's importance.

Russell was back in good health the following season, however, and it was almost no contest for Boston from start to finish. The Celtics won the Eastern Division by twelve games and then beat the Lakers in the play-

off finals four straight. This was the first title-round sweep in NBA history. The following season, Boston repeated as champion, the first NBA team since the Lakers to win back-to-back titles, and a year later they equaled the Minneapolis record of three in a row.

The Boston dynasty was rolling. Each season Auerbach replaced his older players and collected substitutes for every contingency with a genius that verged on the supernatural. But even as Boston continued winning and the Celtics' rivals gnashed their teeth in envy and frustration, new forces were entering the NBA.

In 1959 the hot rookie was Elgin

Vern Mikkelsen passes Bob Pettit on his way to the basket.

After Wilt Chamberlain joined the Philadelphia Warriors, he rewrote the record books, but despite his efforts, The Dipper and his teams could not wrest the NBA title from Bill Russell and the Celtics.

Baylor, a six-foot-five forward from Seattle University who became only the third first-year player in league history to make the All-Star team. Baylor, the complete ballplayer, was noticeable for his distinctive head twitch as he drove for basket after basket. He scored fifty-five points in one game en route to a rookie scoring average of almost twenty-five points. His second season he broke Joe Fulks's eleven-year-old record of sixty-three by scoring sixty-four—against the Celtics, no less.

However, the next season, even Baylor's emergence as a star was overshadowed. Wilt Chamberlain was

coming to town, and Eddie Gottlieb, known in NBA circles as The Mogul, had him with the Warriors. This was no more an accident than Boston's drafting of Bill Russell. Chamberlain had been an outstanding athlete at Philadelphia's Overbrook High, where he had also starred for the track team. As he grew in skill as well as in height, an army of college scouts surrounded him virtually everywhere he went, on or off the court. As a high school senior, he stood six feet eleven, and even the pro scouts knew about him.

While Chamberlain was selecting the University of Kansas out of the hundreds of schools wishing to provide him with a college education—and other emoluments—Gottlieb moved to assure himself of first shot at Chamberlain's professional services. He sought, and obtained, a ruling that the territorial draft could be extended to high school students on a future basis. The choice was immediately applied to Chamberlain. After the year touring with the Globetrotters, Chamberlain became eligible to play in the NBA, and he returned home to Philadelphia with the Warriors. But not before extracting what was believed to be the highest salary being paid to any NBA player, rookie or veteran.

Until Chamberlain, the season scoring record in the NBA had been 29.2 points a game, set by Bob Pettit in 1959. The next year Jack Twyman averaged 31.2—but finished second to Chamberlain, who averaged an implausible 37.6. Fans flocked to arenas all over the nation to see the muscular Philly pheenom, listed as a fraction over seven feet tall, but probably exceeding that figure by some inches. Included in the book of records set by The Dipper (a nickname he prefers to Wilt the Stilt), were new agate lines for most points, highest scoring average, most field goals attempted, most field goals scored, most rebounds, highest rebound average, and five games with fifty or more points.

Chamberlain was an awesome figure. His height was only one of his many weapons. He was an athlete who could have starred in other sports; he never fouled out of games; and he played the full forty-eight minutes just about every night out. The customers, and Gottlieb, got their money's worth.

When the 1960 season came to an end, the Celtics still were on top. They had won the Eastern Division by ten games over the Warriors with a record fifty-nine victories in an expanded schedule and then they had eliminated Philadelphia in the playoff semifinals, four games to two. Chamberlain, named not only the league's top rookie but also its Most Valuable Player, announced he was quitting the game. He said he felt he had proved himself a basketball player. He said he didn't like the beating he had been forced to take night after night. After saying this, he changed his mind.

The following season, as the Celtics were winning their third straight championship, the Lakers moved from Minneapolis to Los Angeles, and the NBA became a truly national basketball league. Also, two more amazing rookies came into the circuit, Jerry West with the Lakers and Oscar Robertson with the Royals. Robertson became an instant star, but it took West part of his rookie season to get over the awe in which he held the veteran NBA players who had been his idols.

Robertson, as a rookie, scored over thirty points a game, third best in the NBA, and supplanted Cousy as the league leader in assists. But the Royals still finished last in their division; the Lakers, even with Baylor and West, lost in the playoff semifinals; Philadelphia, with Chamberlain, lost in the first round of the playoffs; and the Celtics won another championship.

During this season the Knicks lost to Syracuse, 162–100, on Christmas Day, the largest margin of defeat in league history. The Knicks had been charter members of the NBA and in their early years had been one of the league's strongest teams even though they had never won a championship. They finished on top in the Eastern Di-

Laker Jerry West battles Bill Russell.

Dolph Schayes of the Syracuse Nationals tosses in the 19,000th point of his pro career.

Irish, the fan. His player judgments were what forced Joe Lapchick, the Knicks' highly respected and successful coach, to return to St. John's University. At one time, the Knicks' general manager, Vince Boryla, a former star player, ran the team from his home in Denver. The situation was incredible.

Irish, once so respected, had also managed to make himself almost unanimously disliked by his fellow NBA owners because of the arrogance with which he flaunted Madison Square Garden's vast resources. The year after that humiliating loss to Syracuse, the Knicks, with the worst losing record in the NBA, were entitled to the first draft choice.

The standout college senior in 1962 was six-foot-eleven Walt Bellamy of Indiana University. Bellamy was no Chamberlain or Russell, but he was the best big man available, and a big man was what the Knicks needed to rescue themselves from oblivion. A strong New York franchise would have been good for the league, but the NBA owners acted vindictively and against their own best interests. Chicago was coming into the league with a new franchise called the Packers. Spiting the Knicks (and Irish) the owners voted to allow the new team to take the leadoff position in the draft, an unprecedented procedure. Naturally, the Packers chose Bellamy. The Knicks had to settle for Tom Stith, a six-foot-five forward from St. Bonaventure, who contracted tuberculosis and did not play that year, or effectively ever again.

The Knicks reached a new low in futility one cold night in March, 1962, in Hershey, Pennsylvania. The NBA,

vision in 1953 and 1954 and between 1951 and 1953 they made the finals of the playoffs three straight years, twice carrying the winner to seven games. But now they had fallen into disrepair, finishing last six out of seven years. Between 1956 and 1966 they would make the playoffs only once. The fault had to be laid at the executive desk of Ned Irish, their guiding spirit. Irish, the businessman, had forgotten his basic precepts and become then much more so than now, followed a policy of farming out games. If their own arenas were not available, or if a profitable gate could be assured at some way station, they thought nothing of transferring home games hundreds of miles away. The "home" team in this case was Philadelphia; and Wilt Chamberlain, now in his third year, was enjoying his finest professional season. Earlier in the year Chamberlain and Baylor had engaged in a classic head-to-head scoring duel through three overtime periods. When it was over, Baylor had scored sixty-three points, one short of his record, while Chamberlain had seventy-eight. Later, Chamberlain had broken the regulation game record with seventy-three points against the Packers and his coach, Frank McGuire, predicted, "someday he'll get 100."

WILT CHAMBERLAIN'S 100-POINT GAME
March 2, 1962, at Hershey, Pennsylvania

PHILADELPHIA (169)

Player	Min.	FGA	FGM	FTA	FTM	Reb.	Ast.	PF	Pts.
Arizin	31	18	7	2	2	5	4	0	16
Conlin	14	4	0	0	0	4	1	1	0
Ruklik	8	1	0	2	0	2	1	2	0
Meschery	40	12	7	2	2	7	3	4	16
Luckenbill	3	0	0	0	0	1	0	2	0
Chamberlain	48	63	36	32	28	25	2	2	100
Rodgers	48	4	1	12	9	7	20	5	11
Attles	34	8	8	1	1	5	6	4	17
Larese	14	5	4	1	1	1	2	5	9
Total	240	115	63	52	43	60	39	25	169

NEW YORK (147)

Player	Min.	FGA	FGM	FTA	FTM	Reb.	Ast.	PF	Pts.
Naulls	43	22	9	15	13	7	2	5	31
Green	21	7	3	0	0	7	1	5	6
Buckner	33	26	16	1	1	8	0	4	33
Imhoff	20	7	3	1	1	6	0	6	7
Budd	27	8	6	1	1	10	1	1	13
Guerin	46	29	13	17	13	8	6	5	39
Butler	32	13	4	0	0	7	3	1	8
Butcher	18	6	3	6	4	3	4	5	10
Total	240	118	57	41	33	60	17	32	147

Score by Periods

	1st	2nd	3rd	4th	Total
Philadelphia	42	37	46	44	169
New York	26	42	38	41	147

CHAMBERLAIN'S SCORING BY PERIODS

Quarter	Min.	FGA	FG	FTA	FTM	Reb.	Ast.	PF	Pts.
First quarter	12	14	7	9	9	10	0	0	23
Second quarter	12	12	7	5	4	4	1	1	18
Third quarter	12	16	10	8	8	6	1	0	28
Fourth quarter	12	21	12	10	7	5	0	1	31
Total	48	63	36	32	28	25	2	2	100

Referees—Willie Smith and David D'Ambrosio.   SOURCE: *NBA Guide*

Darrall Imhoff, one of the parade of centers the Knicks had been using to fill the role they had envisioned for Bellamy, was opposite Chamberlain. It was a mismatch from the beginning. Chamberlain had twenty-three points in the first quarter and forty-one by the end of the half. Always a poor foul shooter—incredibly bad was more like it—Wilt was making his free throws as well as his fall-away jumper. By the end of the third period his scoring total had soared to sixty-nine. As the fourth quarter began, Wilt scored three fast baskets and broke his regulation game record with seventy-five points. After four minutes of the quarter, he had seventy-nine, breaking all the records.

The Warriors now started feeding Chamberlain in earnest, while the Knicks tried holding the ball for each of their twenty-four-second allotments. But the Dipper couldn't be stopped. When the Knicks tried deliberately fouling other members of the Philly team so Wilt would not have a chance to score, McGuire retaliated. He had his subs deliberately foul the Knicks to get the ball back. For more than two minutes Chamberlain did not score a point. Then he started again, ninety-four . . . ninety-six . . . ninety-eight . . . and, with forty-six seconds left, he took a high pass near the basket and stuffed it through with both hands. He had scored a hundred points. The final score of Philadelphia's victory, 169–147, a two-team record, was incidental. Chamberlain had hit on thirty-six of sixty-three field goal attempts and made twenty-eight of thirty-two free throws. He was basketball's ultimate weapon. For the season he averaged 50.4 points a game and scored sixty or more points fifteen times.

Boston dominated the Eastern Division during the regular season, winning by eleven games over the Warriors, but the Celtics had to suffer through a couple of close calls in the playoffs. The semifinal series against Philadelphia went a full seven games, with Sam Jones, who had replaced the retiring Bill Sharman, scoring the winning basket with only two seconds to play. Then, in the finals against Los Angeles, another seven-game series, the Celtics won the deciding game in overtime, 110–107, as Bob Cousy killed the clock with a dribbling solo. (Frank Selvy had missed a short jump shot with only seconds to play, which would have won the game and the title for the Lakers in regulation time.) The 1962 championship marked an unprecedented four in a row for Boston and set a pattern of frustration that would last for years for the Lakers and their two premier stars, Baylor and West.

Before the 1963 season the Lakers would get some company out West. Eddie Gottlieb sold his Warriors for $850,000 and the franchise was moved to San Francisco. At first Chamberlain did not want to make the move, but he was persuaded to go along out of loyalty to Gottlieb, who convinced him that the deal would fall through unless he was part of the package. Philadelphia, the birthplace of professional basketball, was summarily left without a team.

But nothing really changed. The Celtics won again—their fifth straight championship—in what Cousy had announced would be his final year. Some schmaltz was added to the sea-

Champions once again—the sixth time in a row. Tommy Heinsohn (*left*) and Bill Russell (*right*) celebrate with coach Red Auerbach, who smokes his traditional victory cigar.

son with sentimental outpourings at every stop as Cousy made his final swing around the league. The next year Cousy retired as promised and so did Commissioner Maurice Podoloff, the rotund little lawyer who had proved to be indispensable to the NBA's survival. Walter Kennedy, originally the publicity director for the NBA—he had branched out into other endeavors, including service as the mayor of Stamford, Connecticut— succeeded Podoloff as commissioner. The Chicago Packers moved to Baltimore, where they resurrected the old name of Bullets, and the Syracuse franchise shifted to Philadelphia, filling an inexcusable void and finally completing the NBA's big-city lineup. The players threatened to strike the All-Star game to get a hearing for their demands for a pension, and Bob Short sold his Lakers to Jack Kent Cooke for the staggering figure of $5 million.

But where it counted nothing changed. The Celtics won another championship. There was something special about this one, though. It was their sixth in a row. No team in major league sports history had ever won so many championships in succession. The baseball Yankees had won five World Series titles; in hockey the Montreal Canadiens had won the Stanley Cup five straight times. But by winning six in a row (and seven of eight), the Celtics had established themselves as the dynasty of dynasties.

To win that sixth championship the Celtics had to defeat a "new" defense-minded Chamberlain. With Alex Hannum as his strong-willed coach after the team moved to San Francisco, Chamberlain was scoring less but setting up his teammates more. And he got help with the rebounding from a six-foot-eleven rookie named Nate Thurmond. The presence of Thurmond on the San Francisco roster would have a far-reaching effect on the balance of power in the NBA the following season of 1965. Chamberlain was seriously ill during the months

The Warriors' Nate Thurmond (42) comes up short against the Celtics' Russell in the 1964 NBA playoffs.

preceding that season with what doctors eventually diagnosed as pancreitis. It took him a while to play himself back into shape after the season began, and the Warriors reflected his difficulties. The team had never been greeted with open arms and open pocketbooks by San Francisco fans, and now attendance sagged in direct proportion to its fading fortunes on the court.

In mid-January the NBA family gathered in St. Louis for the annual All-Star game. It was a thrilling game won by the East 124–123. Oscar Robertson scored twenty-eight points for the East, and his new Cincinnati teammate, Jerry Lucas, scored twenty-

five and was named the outstanding player for his fine rebounding.

As players, press, coaches, and owners gathered for the postgame party in Stan Musial's restaurant, rumors began to circulate. Something big was happening. Where was Frank Meulli, youthful owner of the Warriors? What about Ike Richman and Irv Kosloff, owners of the "new" Philadelphia 76-ers? Two and two were soon put together, and they came out seven feet one—Chamberlain back to Philadelphia. The idea seemed so logical it couldn't possibly be true. But it was. Rather than hold back the announcement until morning and risk a news leak, the principals decided to wipe their own All-Star game off the sports pages and tell the world with a post-midnight announcement; the Warriors were trading Wilt Chamberlain back to Philadelphia for three players, whose only claim to fame would be that they were parties to this deal.

In one stroke the struggling Warriors had unloaded Chamberlain's huge paycheck (estimated by one source as comprising a dollar out of every three in revenue the Warriors took in); opened the way for a younger Thurmond to play his natural position of center; provided Philadelphia with a great gate attraction (Wilt would be greeted as a homecoming hero); and provided the Celtics with a tenacious opponent in their division. An attempt by the NBA owners to hamper Chamberlain by widening the foul lane from twelve to sixteen feet had significantly affected neither his drawing nor his scoring power.

During the season there were two significant coaching changes in the Western Division. After the Pistons had lost nine of their first eleven

Detroit Piston player-coach Dave DeBusschere finesses 76er Wilt Chamberlain.

St. Louis owner Ben Kerner congratulates
Bob Pettit after the Hawks center scores his
20,001th point.

games under Charley Wolf, Fred Zoll-
ner, the club's owner and a wealthy
manufacturer of pistons (what else?),
replaced Wolf with Dave DeBusschere, a player. Only twenty-four years
old, DeBusschere was developing into
an outstanding forward and also
showed some promise as a major
league baseball pitcher. When he was
named the youngest coach in league
history he dropped baseball to concentrate on the winter sport. And in St.
Louis, Ben Kerner continued to play
his game of change the coaches. After
a 17–16 start under Harry Gallatin,
who had done well to hold on to his
post into a third season, Kerner
dropped him and named Richie Guerin, a tough guard out of New York,
as playing coach. Guerin thus became
the sixteenth coach in the sixteen-year
history of the Hawk franchise, and
that counts Fuzzy Levane only once
even though he had held the position

on two separate occasions. Guerin,
however, managed to hang on for
three more full seasons under Kerner
and eventually accompanied the team
to Atlanta when the franchise was
sold.

The firing of Gallatin would eventually influence the fortunes of still another team, the New York Knicks.
When Gallatin became available, Eddie Donovan, who had been handling
both jobs, hired the former Knick rebounding star to be his coach and
moved into the front office exclusively as general manager. The
Knicks' outstanding player draft that
season included Willis Reed as Rookie
of the Year. With Donovan taking
over the reins as a full-time, in-resi-
dence general manager, the Knicks at
last had a major league operation.

Before the 1965 season began,
Walter Brown, who had meant so
much to the NBA and his beloved

Celtics, passed away. The players wore a mourning band on their uniforms in his memory and then proceeded to break their own record, winning sixty-two games in regular season. By now Frank Ramsey was gone, but John Havlicek had developed into an established star. His former Ohio State teammate, Larry Siegfried, and Tom Sanders filled the important reserve posts.

In the playoff semifinals the Celtics had to battle the full seven games with the 76ers of Philadelphia, their one-point victory in the decisive game saved only by a critical deflection by Havlicek in the final seconds. But in the final they swept Los Angeles aside in five games despite a fantastic series by Jerry West, who averaged forty points a game.

The Celtics' string of championships stood at seven in a row. People were saying that some day the end had to come. Perhaps 1966 would be the year, they reasoned, as the NBA celebrated its twentieth anniversary. Heinsohn had retired and those great Celtics who remained were indeed no longer young. K. C. Jones was thirty-three, Sam Jones was thirty-two. So was Russell. During the regular season, it appeared that the critics might finally be correct. Led by Chamberlain, now making over $100,000 a year (Russell had insisted on a paycheck of $100,001 from the Celtics), the 76ers supplanted the Celtics as Eastern Division champions for the first time in ten years. It wasn't exactly a runaway, for Philly's final margin was only a single game; still, it seemed significant.

The playoffs continued to be the thing, though, and for the first time in years the Celtics, as division runners-up, had to engage in a first-round elimination. Losing two of the first three games, Boston rallied to win the last two and eliminated Cincinnati in a best-of-five series. Meanwhile, the 76ers spent those two full weeks resting on their championship. When the semifinal round began, Philadelphia appeared to have lost its competitive edge. The 76ers were sluggish and the Celtics swept them aside in five games.

Out in the West, the Lakers had won their championship easily and gained the finals by eliminating St. Louis in seven games. This looked like a good year for the Lakers to crack the Celtics' dominance.

The series opened in Boston where the Lakers survived a late Celtic rally to win in overtime. The Celts had lost their home-court advantage, but they hadn't lost the wiles of Red Auerbach, not just yet, anyway. For some time Auerbach had let it be known that this was his last season as coach. He would remain with the Celtics as general manager—an announcement greeted with glee by Chinese restaurants in Boston that depended on Auerbach for regular patronage—but he would turn the bench job over to someone else. As early as the Philadelphia series, Auerbach knew who that man would be, but he kept silent. He would await the proper moment for public announcement.

The morning after the Celtics lost that critical opening game at home against Los Angeles, Auerbach called in the press. Boston's new coach would be a player-coach. His name: Bill Russell.

It was a master stroke. Russell, like Auerbach, was getting weary. The schedule never seemed to end, the road trips ran one into the other in an endless succession of airports and hotel rooms. Russell was thinking of quitting, too, so Auerbach decided to give his aging star a new incentive. Many times Bill had handled the team in workouts when Auerbach's duties as general manager had prevented him from being present. He had also served as coach in games when Auerbach was banished from the floor by officials. Auerbach knew Russell as an astute basketball mind and, more important, as the acknowledged team leader. Auerbach, who had drafted the first black player into the NBA, tried to minimize the fact that Russell would be the first black man to serve as head coach of a major league team.

The Celtics responded as Auerbach had expected they would: they swept the next three games. But then the Lakers pulled themselves together and won the next two, sending the series back to Boston for the seventh-game showdown. Before the game, Auerbach took note of the emotion surrounding his last game as Celtic coach, but, typically, his approach was ultraprofessional. He reminded his players of the monetary difference between winning and losing. "I want you to win this one for you, not for me," he told them.

The Celtics roared onto the court to do just that. They scored the first ten points of the game against the stunned Lakers and led by as many as nineteen points in the opening minutes of the second half. Going into the final quarter, the score was 76–60, but the Lakers hadn't gotten as far as they had by quitting. With four minutes left the Boston lead was down to thirteen points, then to seven. The Celtics led by eight into the final minute, then Russell scored to make it ten. On-

ly sixteen seconds remained when Jerry West hit a jump shot to cut the margin to eight again; but now Auerbach knew there was an insurmountable ally on his side—the clock.

For years, Auerbach had enjoyed the habit of lighting up a "victory cigar" on the bench whenever another Celtic triumph was assured. The gesture infuriated his opponents, which was the general idea. The league office didn't like it, either, which was even better. And so, with sixteen seconds to go, Auerbach stuck the long cigar in his mouth and John Volpe, the governor of Massachusetts—which shows how far basketball had come—gave him a light.

Although the Lakers managed to close to two points at the buzzer, Auerbach didn't miss a puff. A score of 95–93 was plenty good enough. He even had a point to spare. For the fourth time the Lakers had faced the Celtics in the final round of the playoffs, and for the second time they had taken them to seven games, but they still didn't have a championship. All the championships belonged to Boston, and Boston belonged to Red Auerbach.

Eight straight championships, nine in ten years. Who could match such an achievement? Of course, the players on the court had won the championship games, but Red Auerbach was the man who had brought them together and welded them into a team. The Celtics carried his indelible stamp. This was his team and always would be. He had a right to his pride. The few puffs he managed on that final victory cigar before the crowd surged around him and crushed it to the floor must have tasted mighty good.

⑬
SILVER YEARS

SOME INTERESTING THINGS HAPPENED in the 1967 season. The NBA elected to again try a team in Chicago, a city that should logically have been able to support pro basketball all along. This enabled Baltimore to be shifted back to the Eastern Division, where it logically belonged. The change proved significant to the struggling New York Knicks, because they now had a team in their division that they figured they could beat.

Out in the West the San Francisco Warriors, who had dropped Alex Hannum as coach two years after unloading Chamberlain, climaxed their rebuilding program. With Nate Thurmond developing into a first-rate center capable of challenging the league's top big men, and with Rick Barry leading the league in scoring as a sophomore pro, the Warriors won their division. Bill Sharman, the old Celtic star, was their coach.

The dropping of Hannum had repercussions in the East. Dolph Schayes had been coaching the 76ers since they moved from Syracuse, but, although he brought his team home first in the Eastern Division in 1966, his owners were unhappy about the humiliating playoff loss to Boston. Schayes was fired and the newly available Hannum was brought in to take his place.

While in San Francisco, Hannum had been the only coach ever to get Chamberlain to subordinate himself to his team. In his early days in Philadelphia it had been necessary for Wilt to do all the scoring. Under Hannum he agreed to go along with the defensive tactics his new coach felt were needed to be successful, and they worked. Chamberlain had faith in Hannum, and so did the rest of his Philadelphia teammates because, after all, these were basically the transplanted Syr-

acuse Nationals and Hannum had been their coach before the switch.

Hannum was able to surround Chamberlain with a perfectly matched supporting cast, and it was the first time Wilt had ever enjoyed such a luxury. Up front were six-foot-six Chet Walker and six-foot-nine Luke Jackson, who had been playing center before Chamberlain arrived. Billy Cunningham, not yet blossomed as a scoring star, was a super-sub in the Ramsey-Havlicek mold. In the backcourt were veteran Hal Greer, a consistent twenty-point scorer, and Wally Jones, a local boy out of Villanova just beginning to find himself. Larry Costello, another veteran guard who had played for Hannum in Syracuse, was lured out of a year's retirement to add stability to the backcourt. Another sub was rookie Matt Guokas, whose father had played for Philadelphia's charter entry in the first NBA playoffs of 1947.

Twenty years later young Matt would have the same experience. With Chamberlain concentrating on rebounding, defense, and passing off, the 76ers, under Hannum's driving direction, won forty-five of their first forty-nine games and ran away with the Eastern Division race. Their sixty-eight victories were a league record. For the first time in his pro career Chamberlain did not lead the league in scoring, but he was third in assists and led in rebounds and shooting percentage.

The 76ers won the Eastern Division title by eight games over Boston, but the playoffs still were the heart and crown of the season. Dolph Schayes had learned that lesson the hard way, Hannum would not make the same mistake.

The 76ers were awesome in the playoffs. They required only four games, one over the minimum, to win their best-of-five first-round series, and then needed only five more, again one more than the minimum, to brush aside the hated Celtics in the semifinals. Chamberlain had set the tone in the opening game when he outrebounded Russell, 32–15, and added thirteen assists, quite high for a center. Drained by their emotional victory over Boston just three days earlier, the 76ers were carried into overtime before winning their opening game in the finals against San Francisco. Then they turned on the power again and in six games whipped the team that had deserted Philadelphia five years earlier.

About the time the 76ers were cracking the Celtic dynasty, a new professional league, the American Basketball Association, announced that it planned to go into competition with the NBA the following season. Spurred by this threat, the NBA scheduled immediate expansion into Seattle and San Diego for the 1968 season and promised additional new teams for Phoenix and Milwaukee the year after. In addition, after the season, the St. Louis Hawks were sold to an Atlanta group by Ben Kerner. Among other things this meant that there would be few areas in the nation outside radio-television range of NBA games.

The demise of the Celtics appeared certain when they finished second to Philadelphia in the Eastern Division by eight games for the second straight year. But, once again, the 76ers had to prove themselves head-to-head in the semifinals of the playoffs. If the 76ers had thought repeating as

The Lakers' Pat Riley pursues an elusive Rick Barry.

champions would be easy, the Celtics disabused them by taking the series opener in Philadelphia. But then the 76ers' power began to tell. Even though they had lost Billy Cunningham to a broken arm during the first-round series against New York, they won the next three games. No NBA team had ever lost in any round of the playoffs after taking a 3–1 lead. But Boston refused to accept this historical fact as binding. The Celtics won the next two games, sent the series into a decisive seventh, and came up with a historical fact of their own. No Celtic team had ever lost the final of a seven-game series. But then no Celtic team had ever had to play the seventh game on the road, either.

The decisive game was close all the way. The weary Celtics used all their guile on offense and saved their muscle for defense. In the lowest scoring game of the series, they eliminated Philadelphia, 100–96. The "new" Chamberlain had played his role to the kind of tragic conclusion only the Greeks and Shakespeare seem to enjoy. Even though his teammates were very much off the mark, Chamberlain refused to shoot in the second half: as the 76ers crumbled around him, only one year after winning the championship, Wilt Chamberlain took only two shots. And the Celtics' six-game victory over Los Angeles in the final round was virtually anticlimactic.

The next season Wilt Chamberlain left his old home town once again for the West Coast, this time traded to Los Angeles for three players. Jack Kent Cooke, the Canadian multimillionaire who owned the team, felt he had insured the moody giant's happiness with a four-year contract reportedly worth a round million dollars. At the same time, Hannum, really a West Coaster, left the 76ers for a piece of the action with an ABA team. But it was Cooke's Chamberlain coup that stirred the imagination of pro basketball fans.

The Lakers had Jerry West, superstar. They had Elgin Baylor, superstar. Now they also had Wilt Chamberlain, super-duper star. They would be unbeatable. And in the Western Division, during the regular season, they were, finishing seven games ahead of the Hawks, newly resident in Atlanta. Meanwhile, in the East, the defending champion Celtics staggered home fourth, nine games out of first place. K. C. Jones had retired to take a college job. Bill Russell, still the playing coach, was hampered by injury. The Celtic lineup could best be described as old, older, oldest. John Havlicek and Larry Siegfried, the youngest starters, were approaching thirty. Bailey Howell, one of Red Auerbach's most brilliant pickups three years earlier, was thirty-two. Both Sam Jones and Russell were thirty-five.

Still, fourth place meant a spot in the playoffs, and the Celtics were thankful for that. In the short second season, their professional pride, savvy, and poise would carry them to heights their aged legs might not have been able to scale over an eighty-two-game schedule. Playing Philadelphia without Chamberlain in the first round of the playoffs was a breeze. The Celtics romped through five games. In the semifinals it took only six games to drop the rambunctious New York Knicks. Los Angeles, with its awesome Big Three, had advanced to the finals

Bill Russell meets an obstacle as the Lakers' Elgin Baylor uses the goal as a screen for an over-the-head shot in the 1969 playoffs.

just as easily. So here it was again—the Lakers against the Celtics in the final round. Chamberlain against Russell.

Los Angeles took a 2–0 lead on its home court as Jerry West scored ninety-four points in the two games, but then the Celtics won twice on their court and the home team held service in each of the next two games at alternate sites to set up a seventh-game showdown.

The Celtics broke fast from the gate that night in Los Angeles, as if they feared time would suddenly turn their aging legs to rubber. They hit eight of their first twelve shots and led by 24–12. But the Lakers, with Jerry West leading the way while still limping from a fifth-game injury, pulled within three points. During the third quarter they tied the score at 60–all,

but then for five and a half minutes the Lakers failed to score a single point. During this stretch the Celtics scored eleven straight and they went into the final period with a 71–62 lead. With six minutes to play the Celtics were still on top by nine, when Wilt Chamberlain, the indomitable super-human Dipper, came down hard with a rebound, grimacing with pain. He had injured his leg, but play continued even though he was unable to make his way up court.

When the Lakers did manage to call time out, Wilt hobbled to the bench. Butch Van Breda Kolff, the excitable, strong-willed Laker coach, who had sparred with Chamberlain throughout a troubled season, sent in his speed boys and probably mumbled a little prayer. Surprisingly the Lakers started to do better with Chamberlain

Bill Russell battles the Lakers' Wilt Chamberlain during the 1968 playoffs.

on the bench, scoring eight straight points to trail by only one with less than three minutes to go. Now, if he could make it at all, was the time for Chamberlain to return and crush the fading and weary Celtics.

The next moments are muddied with controversy. Chamberlain later insisted he had motioned to Van Breda Kolff that he was ready to go back in. Van Breda Kolff insisted just as vehemently that he received no such message. In any event, Wilt Chamberlain remained on the bench. The Celtics were there for the taking, but without Wilt the Lakers didn't have the reach. Don Nelson made a basket to

increase Boston's lead to three. Siegfried added two free throws and the seconds ticked away on a 108–106 Celtic victory.

Another championship for Boston, this one achieved by a fourth-place team under the most crushing handicaps, the Celtics' eleventh championship in thirteen seasons. For Russell this was the ultimate achievement; his body had been warning him through the season that it was no longer up to the rigors of NBA play. Financially secure, could he find a better time to quit? Although Auerbach would try to dissuade him until opening day of the following season, Russell made his decision to retire as player and coach. He had been part of every one of the Celtics' eleven championships, but he would not have a hand in any more.

Meanwhile Van Breda Kolff and Chamberlain continued to argue publicly about whether Wilt was, bluntly, a quitter. (Russell fueled the controversy by charging that Wilt should not have left the game with anything less than a broken leg.) In any case, it was predictable who would be the loser in an argument between a coach and a player who combined Wilt's talent with his binding long-term contract. Van Breda Kolff departed and Joe Mullaney, a former college teammate of Cousy's, was hired away from Providence College to replace him.

The departure of old stars always opens the way for new heroes to enter center stage. Even in Russell's final year, new players were making their mark in the NBA. From the University of Houston, San Diego presented Elvin Hayes, the Big E, averaging over twenty-eight points a game, the best in the league. Hayes, six feet nine

Westley Unseld on the move.

and a half, was the kind of player to build a franchise on. And when San Diego failed three years later, the club was moved to Houston, not coincidentally the city where Hayes had gained his greatest fame.

But as great as Hayes's debut had been, it was still only the second best in the NBA. Down at Baltimore, a young man named Westley (Wes)

Unseld from the University of Louisville was turning a franchise around. Unseld, only six feet eight, was a first-round draft choice of the Bullets, who envisioned him as a strong corner man opposite the tough and steady Gus Johnson. But after a month they moved him into the pivot, and Unseld and the Bullets took off from there. The season before Unseld enrolled as

Baltimore's Earl Monroe looks for a way around, or through, future Knick teammate Walt Frazier (*center*).

a pro, Baltimore had finished sixth and last in the Eastern Division despite the scoring heroics of a slithery dervish of a rookie named Earl (The Pearl) Monroe. Monroe quickly established himself as the greatest one-on-one player in the NBA, and perhaps of all time.

Now, with Unseld in to complete their lineup, the Bullets surged to first place in their division, the first time any NBA team had ever completed such a turnabout. Unseld, despite his lack of height, used speed and strength to maneuver under the boards and finished second in the league to Wilt

Chamberlain in rebounding. Rookie of the Year and picked for the All-Star team, Unseld also became the first rookie since Oscar Robertson to be named the league's Most Valuable Player. The Bullets were blitzed out of the playoffs in the first round by New York, but that didn't dim Unseld's achievement . . . or his promise.

The 1970 season saw an even more outstanding rookie explode on the NBA. Lew Alcindor was his name —at least until he legally changed it to Kareem Abdul-Jabbar a couple of years later—and he had dominated college basketball to an extent far greater than any player in the past, including Russell and Chamberlain. The year seven-foot-two Alcindor became eligible for the pro draft, Milwaukee won a coin toss with Phoenix for the first choice and the right to select him.

The American Basketball Association, meanwhile, was reported to have called on all its members to chip in to provide a package big enough to lure Alcindor to play for any team of his choice, presumably his home-town New York Nets. But Wes Pavalon, the Milwaukee owner, was too persuasive. He prepared a deal worth $1.4 million for Alcindor, and he won out in what the UCLA star had insisted would be a one-bid battle for his services.

Alcindor more than lived up to his advance notices, just as he had in college. He averaged almost twenty-nine points a game (second best to Jerry West, who was winning a scoring title for the first time in his distinguished career) and was second to Hayes in rebounds. Unanimously chosen as Rookie of the Year, he also made the second All-Star team as he carried the Bucks from seventh, and last, in the Eastern Division to a closing second behind the Knicks. For the last third of the season, as Alcindor found himself in the pros, the Bucks had a better record than the Knicks, but this was the season when New York was not to be denied.

New York fans had waited twenty-four years for this season. Charter members of the NBA, they had yet to win a championship, and for too many seasons they had been classed as buffoons. But with Eddie Donovan as general manager, they began building their way back to respectability. The method was really quite simple. Donovan had some theories about basketball, and he stressed movement and defense. Red Holzman agreed with him, and before he became coach of the Knicks, he served several years as head scout, finding the players to fit Donovan's theories.

The tipoff on how the Knicks improved so dramatically could be found in the 1964 Olympic Trials, six years earlier. At that time there were forty-eight college players among those seeking berths. These were presumed to be the forty-eight best college players in the land. At one time or another seven of them would wear Knick uniforms. Those who weren't around for the championship year would be used as trade material. From this sterling group of forty-eight, the Knicks would eventually be represented by Jim Barnes of Texas Western, Bill Bradley of Princeton, Howard Komives of Bowling Green, Barry Kramer of NYU, Willis Reed of Grambling, Cazzie Russell of Michigan, and Dave

Boston's John Havlicek parries the hand-checking of the Knicks' Dick Barnett.

Stallworth of Wichita State.

That Olympic-year draft would prove the cornerstone of the Knicks' future championship. Jim Barnes and Willis Reed were the Knicks' first two choices on a list that also included Komives and Emmette Bryant. As these youngsters were learning their way, the Knicks continued to be last in the East, but their won-lost percentage improved by over a hundred points. At last they had some players and could make some trades. The following year Dick Barnett, a slick guard, was obtained in one deal, and then Barnes and two veterans were traded off to Baltimore for Walt Bellamy. Bellamy, who should have been playing for the Knicks all along,

would be their center. Willis Reed, who had been New York's first-ever Rookie of the Year, would shift to forward. Although the Knicks would again finish last during Bellamy's first season in New York, he provided the size and muscle that finally got them into the playoffs the following year.

More blue-chip recruits were added for the 1966 season. Bill Bradley, the Princeton star, was taken in the first round even though it was known that he planned to study at Oxford for two years as a Rhodes Scholar and might not want to play pro ball when he returned. Dick Van Arsdale, who would contribute to the Knicks' finally making the playoffs the next year, was also drafted with Bradley's class, as was Dave Stallworth. Stallworth's career would be interrupted by a heart attack, but he staged a remarkable recovery in time to assist in 1970. Two more prize rookies were enrolled in the next year, first Cazzie Russell, who signed with them for a $250,000 contract package, then Walt Frazier, a guard out of Southern Illinois, who had caught the Knicks' eye when he led the Salukis to the NIT championship.

For years, the Knicks had been futile in the draft, but now wise selections had provided virtually all the parts for a championship team. It remained only to put them all together and to add one more player to make it all work. With the 1969 season begun, the Knicks made their move.

For many years Donovan had coveted Detroit's Dave DeBusschere, a hard-working complete pro whose greatest tribute as a man was not that he had been chosen so young to be the Pistons' playing coach, but that he had been retained as a player on that same club after being relieved of his coaching assignment. Due to a combination of circumstances, the Knicks felt DeBusschere was finally going to be available, and so they bid for him. The price—Bellamy and Komives—proved a bargain for the Knicks. With DeBusschere's arrival and Bellamy's departure, Willis Reed could shift back to his natural position at center, strengthening two positions.

Injuries near the end of the season wrecked the Knicks' hopes in 1969, but they opened the 1970 season like a team that knew its destiny. With DeBusschere and the equally hard-working Bradley at forward, Reed at center, and Barnett and Frazier at guard, the Knicks won their first five games, lost a game, and then reeled off a record eighteen-game winning streak. Suddenly the race in the East was over. (The Celtics, without Russell, settled to sixth. Detroit, with Bellamy, finished behind the Celtics.)

In the West, Atlanta finished two games ahead of the Lakers, who had lost Wilt Chamberlain early in the season with a knee injury that required surgery. Chamberlain vowed he would return for the playoffs, and when he did make it back, ahead of even his own optimistic schedule, he found that his courageous effort had finally earned him the cheers of the crowd. For the first time since he had grown taller than the rest of the world, Chamberlain was a sympathetic character.

The Knicks were extended to seven games by the Bullets in the first round of the playoffs, but they prevailed and then swept aside Milwaukee in five games as Reed gave Alcindor a painful—physically and psychologically—demonstration of pivot play.

Out in the West, the Lakers awoke from their lethargy one game short of elimination, just in time to beat Phoenix three in a row. Then they swept Atlanta in four straight to gain the finals. For the seventh time in the nine years since the franchise had moved to Los Angeles, the often-frustrated Lakers found themselves in the championship finals.

Reed's knee had been bothering him during the latter part of the season as well as through the playoffs, but he was primed with medication and ready to go for the big prize. But the Knicks had known frustration for years, too.

In the first four games each team won once at home and once on the road, and the two games in Los Angeles were decided in overtime. An astonishing fifty-five-foot shot by Jerry West at the buzzer forced the extra period in the first game in Los Angeles. As West's shot dropped in, DeBusschere went into a mock swoon under the basket, and Chamberlain actually started to leave the court, thinking the Lakers had won.

Back in New York for the fifth game, the Lakers had raced to a 25–15 lead in the first eight minutes when Willis Reed, dribbling uncontested to the basket, suddenly collapsed on the floor, his face contorted with pain. He had torn the large muscle in his right thigh. He was through for the night, or longer.

The Knicks should have been through, too, but, incredibly, Reed's teammates rallied and prevented Los Angeles from increasing its lead for the remainder of the half. During the intermission they were able to regroup. Bill Bradley recalled an old offensive pattern the Knicks had once used to keep the middle open without the use of a real center. On defense, Dave DeBusschere, giving up almost a foot in height, was assigned to try to guard Chamberlain. Red Holzman told his players "to go out and create a little havoc," and that's what the darting, driving Knicks did.

With Reed listening in the dressing room in disbelief to a play-by-play account of the game relayed over the telephone by public address announc-

er John F. X. Condon, the Knicks rallied for an incredible victory—107–100. They had outplayed and outscored the mighty Lakers by twenty-two points after Reed's injury. The victory was especially significant because the Knicks now had a one-game cushion in the best-of-seven series. They could give up the sixth game in Los Angeles without Reed and have two additional days to try to get their star center healthy for the climactic contest back in New York.

And that's the the way it worked. Day and night Reed took medication and treatment for his torn muscle. Finally, the afternoon of the seventh game, doctors told him he would risk no permanent injury if he tried to play. Late that afternoon, he walked stolidly onto the Garden floor to try a few tentative shots. Wilt Chamberlain watched silently from one of the runways. Reed gave no hint of pain to his opponent, but safely behind the dressing room door, he told a friend, "It's killing me."

As game time approached, Reed was still undergoing treatment. His own teammates, as well as the Lakers, wondered if he would be able to play. The same question was on the minds of 19,500 spectators in the jampacked Garden. "Can Willis make it?" The teams were already on the floor and DeBusschere, acting as captain, was conferring with the officials before the center jump when Reed walked out, in uniform. The ovation he received was overwhelming, almost frightening. He took a few shots, then moved into his starting position.

As the game began, Reed made a basket on a short one-hander. Then he made another. He would score no more, but he had established his presence both as an offensive threat and as an inspiration to his teammates. On defense, dragging his damaged leg behind him as he moved from one end of the court to the other, Reed used his wiles and his physical presence to anticipate Chamberlain's moves and then deny him the place on the floor he wanted. Handicapped, perhaps, by his own recent surgery, but still infinitely more mobile than the hobbled Reed, Chamberlain simply refused to try any movement, even from side to side, that would give him the advantage. He was outplayed, negated, nullified by a one-legged man.

Inspired by Reed's courage, the Knicks played for glory. They won the game, 113–99, and for the first time a championship pennant would fly in Madison Square Garden. Overenthusiastic fans hailed the Knicks' victory as the start of a dynasty. Evidently the Celtics' recent success had given them ideas, or at least added to their vocabulary. But as usual the still-proud Red Auerbach had the last word. "How many championships have they won?" he asked bitingly.

Besides, if anyone wanted to form a dynasty, the line was forming in Milwaukee. When Wes Pavalon paid $2 million to enter the NBA as operator of the expansion Milwaukee franchise, he had told his people that he expected a championship team in three years. If he was to make it in this, his third year, he would have to thank two extraordinary turns of luck.

The first, of course, was the flip of the coin that brought him the rights to Lew Alcindor. (Signing the UCLA star, of course, involved not luck but gifted salesmanship and business acumen.) The second fortunate circumstance was a clause in Oscar Robertson's contract with the Cincinnati Royals that allowed him the right of approval on any trade in which he was involved. The Big O, whose shrewdness was attested by his election to president of the NBA Players Association, wanted some say over where he would display his ample talents if he ever left Cincinnati. Since the Royals were not a wealthy franchise, Robertson realized early that as his salary increased so did the chance of his being unloaded.

When Bob Cousy retired from the Celtics, he became the coach at Boston College, but he soon wearied of the collegiate scene and returned to the pros as coach of the Royals. In Cousy's debut season of 1970 the Royals finished fifth in the Eastern Division for the third straight year, and the former Celtic star formulated a plan to rebuild the team into a contender. Youth and movement would be the ingredients. First he traded Jerry Lucas, a six-year All-Star whose play had been affected by outside business failures, to the Warriors. Then he attempted to deal Robertson to the Baltimore Bullets, only to have the Big O pull out the fine print in his contract and demur. After the season the Royals renewed their efforts to trade Robertson, and with his permission dealt him to the Bucks.

As has been proven time and again, even the biggest man needs a qualified supporting cast. Alcindor would not have dominated in college if John Wooden had not recruited players to complement him, and now the Bucks had done the same by "recruiting" Robertson. To many the

Robertson deal promised to be even more effective than the trade that had sent Chamberlain to Los Angeles. In Chamberlain, West, and Baylor, the Lakers had three players with clashing styles. Baylor and West needed the ball and room to drive. But Chamberlain needed the ball, too, to hand off, and he was used to parking himself near the basket, which clogged up the lane for his super teammates. It was his refusal to move away from the offensive boards that led to much of his friction with Van Breda Kolff. Robertson, on the other hand, was a more versatile ballplayer. As a shooter he could take defensive pressure off Alcindor; as a ball handler he could get the ball to him. Few doubted that he would adjust to the role of supporting player after being a primary star for so many years. Robertson had never played on a championship team; with the end of his career in view, he would make any sacrifice.

The experts were quickly proved right. The Bucks won all ten of their exhibition games. And then, in a new four-division alignment established to accommodate still more new teams in Portland, Cleveland, and Buffalo, Milwaukee made a ruin of the Midwest Division. Finishing just two games short of the all-time mark, the Bucks compiled an amazing 66–16 season record, and they broke the Knicks' one-year-old record by running off a twenty-game winning streak. They also produced victory strings of sixteen and ten games and outscored their opponents by an average of 12.2 points a game, seven points better than the league runner-up. Alcindor, playing with new confidence in his second season as a pro, led the NBA

Larry Costello, coach of the Milwaukee Bucks.

by scoring 31.7 points a game.

The defending-champion Knicks, despite the knee ailment of Willis Reed, easily won the Atlantic Division, while Baltimore triumphed in the Central by a wide margin despite the physical miseries of Gus Johnson and Earl Monroe. Los Angeles was an easy victor in the Pacific quartet. The top two finishers in each division qualified for the playoffs.

In the first round of the playoffs the Knicks and Bucks won easily in five games, but the Lakers and Bullets had to struggle the full seven to gain the semifinals. The Knicks thought that the long series would take too much out of their old rivals, the Bullets, but, instead, it was the Knicks who succumbed in seven games. Meanwhile the Bucks breezed past the Lakers in five games and awaited their opponent out of the Eastern Conference.

By the time the battered Bullets

Though one man can "turn a franchise around," winning the NBA title requires a team. Oscar Robertson (*left*), an NBA standout for a decade with the Cincinnati Royals, never played for a championship team—until he was traded to Milwaukee and paired with second-year star Kareem Abdul-Jabbar (*right*). The result: in its third year of existence as a club, the Bucks won their first NBA championship.

staggered into the finals, they were physically and emotionally spent from fourteen playoff games. But it probably wouldn't have mattered if they had been in perfect condition. Earlier in the season the Bucks had demonstrated their superiority over Baltimore in a crushing 151–99 victory, and now the Bucks were honed to a fine edge.

Alcindor, of course, was the jewel in this fine Milwaukee team, and Robertson provided a starry, if secondary, glow. Bob Dandridge and Greg Smith were the forwards and Jon McGlocklin was the other guard. All five finished in the top ten in the league in shooting percentage as the Bucks produced a record team average of .509. Alcindor was second in the league at .577; McGlocklin, an outside shooter, was fourth at .535.

Against this array the Bullets had little chance. Milwaukee controlled the tempo of every game, playing for a four-game sweep. Not since 1959, when Boston had started its run of eight straight championships by ousting Minneapolis in such swift order, had any team won the final series in four straight games. No team had ever matched Milwaukee's 12–2 playoff record for one season, either. The only dispute was whether the playoff MVP trophy, which went to Alcindor, should have gone to Robertson instead. The Big O, enjoying his first championship after eleven years in the league, couldn't have cared less.

Thus, with a blazing finish, awesome enough in its one-sidedness to make up for the lack of competition, the NBA completed its first quarter-century. But even before the next season began, there were indications that the second twenty-five years might be just as eventful. Merger arrangements, completed between the new American Basketball Association and the older league, were stalled when the leagues

Two former stars of the ABA—Connie Hawkins and Spencer Haywood—renew the contest in the NBA.

sought congressional approval, a far cry from the painless absorption of the NBL many years earlier. A year earlier Seattle had signed Spencer Haywood, who was jumping from the ABA, a year before his college class was to graduate, and the ensuing law suits jeopardized the complete structure of the basketball draft. The reserve clause was being threatened in court and in negotiations with the militant players association. The failing San Diego team moved to Houston. And Frank Mieuli gave up his frustrating campaign to win fans in San Francisco and jumped across the bay to Oakland.

New York and Boston were the NBA's only surviving charter members, and just three executives remained from that initial struggling year: Ned Irish, still running the Knicks for Madison Square Garden; Eddie Gottlieb, Philadelphia's first coach and now a league "consultant" whose major responsibility was to deliver a workable schedule each year (computers tried to accomplish this task and failed); and Walter Kennedy, the first press agent and now the commissioner with a new mandate from the owners granting him more power than Maurice Podoloff had ever had. These men would face challenges that twenty-five years ago they had never dreamed of. But try as they might to overshadow their own sport with front-office bickering, the story of pro basketball continued to be told on the court, not in court.

Pro basketball's twenty-sixth season became the year of the Lakers. After all the years of frustration, the juggernaut Jack Kent Cooke thought

Injuries play a role: Dave DeBusschere plows into Laker Happy Hairston during the second game of the 1972 playoff finals and reinjures a bruised hip.

he had assembled years before finally came alive. But when it did, there was one ringing irony. Elgin Baylor, who had meant so much to the franchise, was no longer a part of the team. Hobbled by damaged knees, Baylor elected to retire after playing in only nine games. The move was hastened by the emergence of still another potential Laker star, young Jim McMillian. McMillian deserved not only to play but to start. The once-great Elgin Baylor had to move aside.

With McMillian providing more movement and with Jerry West taking more and more the role of playmaker as well as scorer (he would win his first league title for assists), the Lakers proved unbeatable, at least for the two months during which they unreeled an NBA record of thirty-three straight victories. As a measure of this

achievement, consider that the old record, held by Milwaukee for only a year, was *twenty*.

The Lakers practically rewrote the NBA records during the 1972 season, starting with their all-time high of sixty-nine victories during a season, and West and Chamberlain were the individual winners in three of five major statistical categories. Bill Sharman, the Lakers' new coach (he had coached in the ABA), lost his voice as he drove his team down the stretch, but he was amply rewarded by his overwhelming selection as Coach of the Year.

The playoffs, though, remain the story. Seven times since the Lakers had moved to Los Angeles in 1962 they had been beaten in the finals. Could they shake that hoodoo this time? The first round was no problem,

A determined Wilt Chamberlain, playing with an injured hand, did his thing, and the Lakers won their first NBA championship for Los Angeles.

a 4–0 sweep over Chicago, but then came the Western Conference final against Milwaukee, the defending champions whose Kareem Abdul-Jabbar had just been named the league's most valuable player after winning his second straight scoring title. Again the Lakers won easily, this time in six.

Over in the East the New York Knicks had been the league's most surprising team. Willis Reed, the leader of their championship drive two years before, had been forced to miss virtually the entire season because of a damaged knee. Yet Jerry Lucas, obtained in a trade for Cazzie Russell as a substitute forward, moved into the pivot and performed brilliantly. With an offense revamped to make use of Lucas's particular talents, the Knicks finished second in their division to Boston, but then beat the Celtics in five games in the playoffs to gain the finals against LA.

Hitting 53.8 per cent of their shots in an amazing exhibition, the Knicks won the first game of this dramatic final, 114–92, but then their long-range marksmen cooled, Dave DeBusschere suffered a hip injury, and the Lakers won the next three. Going into the potential clincher in Los Angeles, however, the Lakers had a major problem. Wilt Chamberlain was hurting. He had been playing with a broken bone in one hand, and in the fourth game he had hurt the other hand. So close—would the Lakers be denied again?

This time, however, Wilt Chamberlain left no doubt of his courage. He scored twenty-four points, pulled down twenty-nine rebounds, and played all but one minute in the decisive 114–100 victory. The Lakers were champions at last, and when Wilt

Chamberlain showed up to receive his award as the final's Most Valuable Player, the new cast on what had proved to be a broken right hand finally gave the lie to all those "gutless" charges.

There was another major franchise shift as the 1972–73 season prepared to get under way. The Royals finally gave up on trying to succeed in Cincinnati after almost two decades and moved further west, splitting their home games between Kansas City and Omaha. They became known as the Kansas City–Omaha Kings, although some suggested that Gypsies might be a more appropriate title.

No matter what their home base, the Kings brought their franchise with them in the form of a swift and clever six-footer named Nate (Tiny) Archibald. Archibald, a New Yorker who had starred at Texas–El Paso, was only in his third season as a pro but already he had made an impact on the NBA. He overcame the defensive weaknesses caused by his height by being such a dominant offensive figure that opposing teams had to worry most about stopping rather than taking advantage of him. He soon noted that "now every team has to have a small man to keep up with the other team's small man."

The Kings, still coached by Bob Cousy, were far from a competitive success, but without Archibald they would have been a disaster. When the season ended the scorers tallied up his figures and discovered that Archibald had become the first NBA player ever to lead the league in both scoring and assists. No player had ever been credited with more assists, 910, and no guard had ever scored better

Little Nate Archibald of the Kansas City-Omaha Kings drives on Chicago's Bob Weiss.

than Archibald's thirty-four points a game. He also led the league in minutes played. Yet, despite his super-season and new-found fame, when the campaign ended Archibald returned home, to the Bronx apartment where he had been raised. He has never forgotten the ghetto and each summer he conducts clinics and coaches teams of youngsters, hoping to save them from poverty as he himself was saved. It is one of the NBA's most striking stories.

While Archibald was conducting his individual heroics, back on the

Boston's Dave Cowens.

JoJo White on the drive.

East Coast an old familiar specter was rising again—the storied Boston Celtics. As Bill Russell had led their earlier dominance, so another center was now leading the way, red-haired Dave Cowens. Cowens had been originally drafted out of Florida State as a forward, but in his first training camp Red Auerbach could tell that the fiery six-foot-nine competitor could make it at center. With his ability to shoot and move, he would add a new dimension to the position.

Tom Heinsohn, with no previous coaching experience, had taken over the Celtics when Bill Russell retired after the 1969 season. The former Celtic star's first two seasons were difficult, and the team failed to make the playoffs. But with Cowens coming of age, and aided by another young star, JoJo White, Boston showed signs of regaining its past glory. In 1973 the Celtics set a club record with sixty-eight victories, one short of the Lakers' league mark, and Heinsohn was honored as Coach of the Year.

The Celtics were confident as they

Nate Thurmond sails to the hoop watched by Warrior teammate Cazzie Russell.

entered the playoffs, but they had forgotten how other teams had been able to win the championship in post-season play even though their records during the regular schedule had not been the best. Boston had done it before, and now New York was to remind the Celtics of what can happen.

After eliminating Atlanta in the first round, they bowed in a seven-game semifinal to the New York Knicks, as John Havlicek tried desperately to play despite an injured shoulder.

Walt Frazier shows the body control needed by agile guards when driving against a tough defense. Dave Cowans (*left*) and Don Chaney try to stop the shot.

Meanwhile, out in the West, the Lakers had swept aside the Golden State Warriors, as the Oakland team was called, in five games, and they waited impatiently for the Eastern title to be decided. To a man they publicly rooted for the Knicks, for they felt Boston would provide much tougher opposition.

The Knicks finally eliminated Boston on a Sunday, flew out to Los Angeles on Monday, and, despite their requests for a delay, were forced to open the finals on Tuesday night without a single day's practice. They showed it, too, bowing in the opener,

115–112, as a last-quarter rally fell short. Given a day off before game two, the Knicks were able to readjust their thinking from "Boston" to "Los Angeles." They worked out, they studied films—and they swept the next four games, to take their second championship in four years.

Two men embodied the Knicks' playoff triumph. In the early games it was Walt Frazier, who by this time was acknowledged as the best guard playing in the NBA. West and Robertson were aging and Frazier was playing about as well as they had in their golden years. In the finals Los

Dave DeBusschere seems to sweep circus paraphernalia from the roof of Madison Square Garden in the 1973 NBA finals against Los Angeles. The Knicks' Bill Bradley (*left*), Laker Jim McMillian, and Walt Frazier await the landing.

Angeles set its entire defense to stop Frazier, and so the other Knicks, including subs, took turns in leading the attack. However, through the finals there was one consistently dominant figure, Knick center Willis Reed. Reed had undergone knee surgery two years earlier, and when the operation failed to take he was forced to sit out almost an entire season. There were many who believed his career was over.

Reed had had his doubts, too, but he was determined to come back. The 1972–73 season was an ordeal. Every time he seemed to be on his way to recovery, a minor injury would slow

his progress, although none of these hurts involved the critical knee. There were also the public doubts and criticism, but Reed and coach Red Holzman never lost faith. When it counted, Willis Reed discovered that he had, indeed, recaptured his skills. The Lakers learned that, too. For the second time in four years Reed was named the championship round's Most Valuable Player.

Willis Reed and Nate Archibald —a big man and a little man—both won their battles on and off the court. These were the real stories of basketball.

⑭
COMPETITION

PRO FOOTBALL, PRO BASKETBALL, and Madison Avenue, where "merchandising" is an everyday verb, all came together in the winter of 1966, and before they were done the NBA learned painfully that it would no longer be alone, or the same.

Professional football figured in only an inspirational sense. Half a dozen years earlier the American Football League had been organized to challenge the established National League. Fighting immeasurable odds the newcomers had survived to become partners in a full-scale merger, and the first fruits of that union were soon scheduled to blossom in Los Angeles. They called it the Super Bowl.

If mavericks could succeed in football, why not in basketball? After all, the overhead for a basketball team is much lower. The squads are smaller, in number if not in stature, and a whole basketball team can be outfit-ted for what it costs to put a single football player on the field. By now financially stable and assured of regular exposure on national television, the NBA offered quite a model for the sincerest form of flattery.

The thought of a new basketball league originated independently with two separate groups. Dennis Murphy, a retired public relations executive and former mayor of Buena Vista, California, is credited with putting the ball in play on the West Coast. For years he had watched the Lakers on television and felt sad that so many large cities around the country were denied that pleasure because they had no NBA team. By 1966 he had determined to fill the void with the help of friends like Gary Davidson, a lawyer, and John McShane. (Davidson was a real basketball nut. He showed up at one of the new league's organizational meetings with his arm in a cast. He

Gary Davidson, organizer of the American Basketball Association.

had broken it playing basketball.)

Meanwhile, in New York, the same idea occurred to a promoter named Constantine Seredin, president of a company called Professional Sports Management. Seredin, perhaps drawing inspiration from the highly successful merchandising of NFL Properties, Inc., in pro football, envisioned a new basketball league in which one progressive firm (his, of course) would handle all public relations, television sales, and merchandising.

Seredin and Murphy eventually got together, sounded out potential franchise owners, and in December of 1966 held their first organizational meeting. Six weeks later, the league was in business—more or less.

At a meeting in New York's posh St. Regis Hotel on February 2, 1967, formation of the American Basketball Association was announced with the following charter cities: New York, Anaheim, Pittsburgh, Houston, Kansas City, New Orleans, Minneapolis, Dallas, Oakland, and Indianapolis. While this announcement was being made, frantic negotiations were continuing in the back room between the league owners and the man they wanted to be their first commissioner, George Mikan. Mikan, by now a successful Minneapolis attorney, had the prestige the new league needed, and he knew it. The owners agreed to his terms and his appointment was announced.

The new league would open play for the 1967–68 season, Mikan promised, but even before the ABA commenced operations, there were franchise changes. Rightly aware that a team in Louisville would definitely be successful, the ABA found backers in the city, and an eleventh franchise, the Kentucky Colonels, was added to the league's lineup. However, on the debit side, the New York team could not find a suitable arena in its home city, and so, much to the ABA's chagrin, moved to a tacky armory in Teaneck, New Jersey. The Kansas City team, faced with a similar arena problem, moved to Denver. Denver proved a solid franchise, but the move to Jersey was a disaster. Without a "big league" New York identification, the ABA was unable to even give away its television rights for many years.

By June the league was ready to go. It had by-laws, a schedule, officials, and a basketball—a basketball such as had never been seen before—colored red, white, and blue. The idea was Mikan's. Before the critical June kickoff meeting he had obtained a regulation basketball and had it painted in three colors to display to the owners. Despite opposition from all sides, especially players and coaches, he held firm. "The only place a ball like that belongs is on the nose of a seal," one coach complained, and some players insisted on practicing with the old brown ball before games until Mikan put his substantial foot down. Wherever the ABA appeared in public, its players would be bouncing a red, white, and blue ball.

The ball quickly became the ABA's trademark, its most recognizable feature. Just as important, it also became a tremendous moneymaker. Each year the ABA collects a royalty on close to half a million red, white, and blue basketballs purchased by the public. (Unfortunately for Seredin, his outfit did not share in this marketing bonanza, the kind of thing for which it had been invented. He was frozen out in the beginning even though most of the West Coast founders ended up with a piece of various franchises.)

That summer the ABA formulated its playing rules with two major differences from the NBA. The time limit for getting off a shot would be thirty seconds rather than twenty-four, and all baskets shot from outside a twenty-five-foot circle would count three points instead of two. The three-point basket stirred memories, for this was the one surviving reminder of an enterprise called the American Basketball League, which several years before had mounted a futile and costly challenge against the NBA.

The genius behind the ill-starred ABL had been diminutive Abe Saperstein, founder and promoter of the Harlem Globetrotters. Saperstein had organized this team of all black players in Chicago in 1926, and took them on the road to become the most popular and financially successful barnstorming team in history. Comedy soon became their forte, although in the years the NBA was closed to black players the Globies were more than a match for any team and won several national titles. When more and more top teams refused to play them, the Globies had to emphasize comedy

Abe Saperstein, founder of the Harlem Globetrotters.

even more as they toured with a picked team of stooges that was paid to lose to them. (For a while, this team included Bevo Francis of Rio Grande fame.)

Top comic stars of the Globetrotters over the years included Goose Tatum, Marques Haynes, and Meadowlark Lemon. As they toured the world the Globetrotters attracted huge crowds everywhere they went. They continued to lure customers in large numbers in this country, too, even after Tatum and Haynes left to form their own troupes. Often, to fill conflicting dates, Saperstein would be forced to split his squad and have "Globetrotters" performing in two or three places at the same time. Still the people came.

During its early years the struggling NBA was quite dependent on the Globetrotters. A full house was assured whenever the Globies came to town, and NBA teams often shared the bill with Saperstein's clowns on a doubleheader. Occasionally the Globetrotters would even play the featured second game. It may have been demeaning for pro basketball, but it was a financial lifesaver.

The NBA began to turn its back on Saperstein in 1950 by breaking the color line and going into competition

Reece (Goose) Tatum.

with the Globetrotters for black players. As pro basketball became more established there was less need for the Globetrotters as a gate attraction. Then in 1960 the league governors gave Bob Short permission to move his Lakers from Minneapolis to Los Angeles. This was the last straw. Saperstein had hoped to operate an NBA franchise in Los Angeles himself, but had been turned down in the past by the other owners. However, he had gotten the impression that if the NBA ever expanded to the West Coast, he would be allowed to operate in Los Angeles.

In a fit of pique Saperstein decided to form his own league, which commenced operations for the 1961–62 season with teams in Chicago, Hawaii, Los Angeles, Kansas City, San Francisco, Washington, and Cleveland. Since it was "his" league, Saperstein proclaimed himself commissioner, as well as operator of the Chicago team. This didn't do much to promote confidence in the league. Neither did the eventual disclosure that Saperstein actually had a financial interest in five of the eight teams and that there were

Meadowlark Lemon and the flying hook.

other interlocking ownerships.

It also didn't help that several players slightly tinged by the scandals, like Bill Spivey of Kentucky and Connie Hawkins, a former Iowa freshman, were allowed to play for Saperstein while still banned by the NBA. The tie-in with the Globetrotters and their choreographed competition didn't make the ABL any less suspect.

Naturally, the Globetrotters deserted the NBA arenas and devoted their crowd-pulling talents exclusively to the ABL. However, league prestige wasn't helped when after the Globetrotter exhibition fans often put on their coats and walked out before the featured ABL game.

A couple of recognizable NBA players jumped to the new league, the best of them being Dick Barnett, who left the Syracuse Nationals to play for the Cleveland Pipers and his old college coach at Tennessee State, John McLendon. McLendon technically preceded Bill Russell as the first black coach of a professional team; but since the ABL operated in almost complete obscurity—and there was much doubt about its major-league status—his appointment was not nearly as important in setting a precedent as was the naming of Russell by the Celtics five years later.

The ABL did survive its first season and Connie Hawkins of Pittsburgh, who had never played a college game, won the scoring championship. The next season, Hawaii, which had been impoverishing the league while enriching the airlines with unbelievable travel costs, Washington, and Cleveland folded. Los Angeles moved to nearby Long Beach and San Francisco to Oakland. But before the sea-

Marques Haynes, world's greatest dribbler.

son was half over, Saperstein, by then bankrolling almost the entire operation, had had enough. With losses estimated at two million, he folded the league on New Year's Eve.

All that remained was Saperstein's idea of the three-point basket, but the roly-poly entrepreneur was not around to see the ABA renew his challenge of the NBA. He died in 1966, and his heirs sold the Globetrotters for $3 million.

Like its predecessor, the new ABA also agreed to hire those who had been only indirectly involved in the scandals, fellows like Tony Jackson of St. John's, Doug Moe of North Carolina, and Roger Brown and Hawkins. It had never been proven that any of them had been asked to fix a game. Brown and Hawkins supposedly had been given "sweetening" money by Jack Molinas while still New York high school stars. The most important ABA recruit, though, was a nonplayer, at least temporarily. Rick Barry had been an instant star when he joined the San Francisco Warriors out of the University of Miami. Even though many scouts had doubted the spindly six-foot-seven forward's ability to survive a tough pro season, he averaged more than twenty-five points a game as one of only four players ever to score more than 2,000 points as an NBA rookie. His second year he led the league with a 35.6 average.

Then, along came the ABA with an Oakland franchise that included entertainer Pat Boone as one of its owners. Barry, bright-eyed, handsome, and articulate, had show-business ambitions and admitted that his greatest dream was to star in a movie. Boone was able to promise Barry entrée into the entertainment world, but that wasn't his only in with the slender shot maker. The coach of the Oakland Oaks was Bruce Hale, formerly of the University of Miami. Hale was not only Barry's former coach, he was also his father-in-law. (While in college Barry had married Hale's pretty daughter, Pam.) These pressures proved insurmountable. While Warrior owner Frank Mieuli was vacationing in Europe, Barry signed with the Oaks. It wasn't all that simple, though. When Mieuli returned home, he sued. The judge ruled that the Warriors still had an option on Barry's services for one more year, but that Barry did not actually have to play out the option. He could sit it out, and

that's what he did. Enjoined from playing for Oakland, Barry practiced his future career by broadcasting their games.

While Barry sat and waited, collecting a $25,000-a-year personal services contract with Boone and playing in charity games with a team of disc jockeys, the ABA completed its first season. Led by Connie Hawkins and given a late boost by the addition of Art Heyman, who inspired them to win fifteen straight, the Pittsburgh Pipers won the Eastern Division championship and then defeated Western titlist New Orleans in a seven-game final playoff. Hawkins was the league's Most Valuable Player and leading scorer. Vince Cazetta of Pittsburgh was named Coach of the Year. Mel Daniels, one of the new league's prized college selections out of New Mexico, led the ABA in rebounding for Minnesota and was named Rookie of the Year.

One oddity in that opening season was an eighty-eight-foot shot by Jerry Harkness with one second to play that gave Indiana a 119–118 victory over Dallas. Harkness had forgotten about the three-point rule and thought his basket had only forced the game into overtime.

The real dilemma of the league as the season ended concerned the futile New York area franchise. Now called the Jersey Americans, the team had tied with Kentucky for the fourth and final playoff spot in the Eastern Division. A one-game playoff was to break the deadlock, and the Americans, because they had won the season series over Kentucky, were given the home-court advantage. However, because the circus was booked into the Teaneck Armory, the Americans rescheduled the big playoff game for Commack, Long Island, many miles from New York City and even farther from their Jersey home. No basketball had been played in the dingy arena for years and nobody bothered to check the facilities. The night of the game the floor was ruled unplayable and Kentucky was given the playoff spot on a forfeit.

The ABA had confounded its critics by surviving this first season, but the second year would provide a truer test. Except for possibly Mieuli, NBA officials were still inclined to scoff at the ABA and its funny basketball. Both sides remembered that Saperstein's ABL had made it through one season only to fail in the next.

Although the league membership remained stable at eleven, there were several franchise moves before the second season. The Jersey Americans decided they needed a "New York" before their name and so they moved to Long Island and back into the Commack Arena, after making certain the floor was repaired. Arthur Brown, owner of a trucking company and president of the team, had heard that a plush new arena would soon be built to serve Long Island's growing population and he wanted to preserve his franchise rights until that time. (He didn't make it, but the team, under new ownership, did.) The Anaheim franchise also moved into Los Angeles proper.

The most complicated changes involved Pittsburgh and Minnesota. To start the game of musical franchises, the Minnesota Muskies shifted to Miami, moving into an arena that was still being prepared for basketball. (As fans purchased tickets on opening night, a runner would dash from the box office to inform the carpenters how many more bleacher seats to nail up.) Since Minneapolis was the home office of the commissioner, it was embarrassing to have that city without a franchise. Mikan wasn't about to move, so the champion Pittsburgh Pipers shifted to the north country, and volatile Jim Harding replaced Cazetta as coach.

In other coaching changes, two respected NBA names came into the league, Alex Hannum at Oakland and Bill Sharman at Los Angeles. Rookie standout Mel Daniels was traded from old Minnesota to Indiana.

Crippled by a knee injury, Barry played less than half the season for the Oaks, but his thirty-four-point scoring average was the best in the league and good enough to get his team off and winging in the Western Division. Scoring at least a hundred points in every game the Oaks finished up fourteen games ahead of New Orleans. Indiana, which scored 172 points in one victory over Los Angeles, beat out Miami in the East by one game. In the playoffs, with Rookie of the Year Warren Armstrong of Wichita State making up for Barry's absence, Oakland bested the Indiana Pacers four games to one in the playoff finals.

The ABA, which undertook the usual formality of a new league by suing the older for antitrust violations, suffered two damaging blows to its prestige in the 1969 season. The first was more comic than serious. Jim Harding, coach of the Pipers, and Gabe Rubin, the president of the Pipers, got into a fight during the All-Star game party in Louisville. Harding, who may or may not have won the fight, certainly lost the decision. He was relieved of his assignment of coaching one of the All-Star teams and then was fired as Piper coach. General manager Vern Mikkelsen, the old Laker, replaced him. Meanwhile the Houston Mavericks folded in midseason, but the league used its $100,000 forfeit fee to continue operating the club until it could be moved eastward to become the Carolina Cougars under new and aggressive ownership.

But, again, more significant than any of the byplay, the ABA had survived its critical second season with the membership still pegged at eleven teams. It had outlasted Saperstein's ABL. Quietly, tentatively, individual owners from each league began to hold conversations. The subject was merger. The cost of signing players out of college was skyrocketing. The war was even more bitter and expensive than the pro football hostilities because one superplayer in basketball can singlehandedly turn a franchise around.

In addition to Carolina taking over the defunct Houston franchise, the Pipers moved back to Pittsburgh and the Oakland team moved to Washington, D.C., much to the annoyance of Rick Barry, who signed future contracts to jump back to the NBA. The Pipers' move out of Minnesota signaled the resignation of George Mikan as commissioner. He was replaced by CBS executive Jack Dolph, who transferred the league office to New York and indicated that through his connections he would soon come up with that most important television contract.

But all this activity was unimportant compared to the failure of the new league to sign Lew Alcindor of UCLA plus the defection of its biggest star, Connie Hawkins, to the NBA. Alcin-

dor was by far the outstanding player to come out of college in years. His signing would have made the ABA. The New York Nets had just come under the new ownership of Roy Boe, a dynamic ladies' wear manufacturer, and if Alcindor played for any team in the ABA, it would be for the Nets in his old home town. But Boe did not match Milwaukee's offer and Alcindor went to the NBA.

Even more staggering was the loss of Hawkins, for his move seemed to stamp the ABA as inferior to the old league in the minds of the players. Hawkins was one of the few casualties of the second round of scandals who was able to come all the way back. He had never been convicted of anything, but his association with fixer Jack Molinas, who had done favors for many high school stars, had been enough to frighten off not only the University of Iowa, which revoked his scholarship ostensibly on scholastic grounds, but also the NBA, which banned him for life. For Hawkins, a shy product of the Brooklyn ghetto, basketball was life. When he returned from Iowa he spent days alone in his mother's apartment, staring at the walls, hoping the nightmare would end.

Eventually Hawkins got a chance to play for the Pittsburgh Rens of the ABL, and when that league folded he drifted to the Globetrotters, where he tried to play the game as straight as possible so his skills would not erode as he toured the world. In 1967 he quit the Globetrotters and brought suit against the NBA. His lawyers were asking $6 million in damages. What he really wanted was to have his name cleared so he could play in the NBA.

While the six-foot-eight-and-a-half Hawkins was waiting for a resolution of his suit, the ABA came into being and Connie was snatched up by the new Pittsburgh franchise. However, before he signed with the Pipers, Hawkins's lawyers insisted that the contract include a clause stating that he would be a free agent after two seasons. That was when they expected his suit to come to trial.

Pittsburgh fans remembered Hawkins's exploits with the ABL Rens, and he didn't disappoint them. Agile, a great shooter, rebounder, and ball handler, he was easily the best in the new league even though a knee injury hampered him at the end of his second season. At last he was earning the money and recognition his skills deserved, but still there was the dream of playing in the NBA against stars he had faced, and bested, so many times in high school and in the schoolyards of New York.

The 1969 season over, the time of legal decision drew near. Hawkins's lawyers had prepared well. Faced with the real prospect of an unfavorable decision—and not knowing how the judge's decision might affect their contractual control over players—the NBA capitulated. If Connie would accept a $1.5 million settlement to be spread over several years, and withdraw his suit, the NBA would clear his name and free him to sign with the Phoenix Suns. Thus the Suns, who had lost the coin toss for Alcindor, were provided with a potential superstar of their own.

The ABA owners were not exactly passive in the war between the leagues. One of the top college players was Spencer Haywood, a University of Detroit junior. Haywood, from a large and impoverished family in Mississippi, had become a high school basketball star in Detroit and then had enrolled at Trinidad Junior College in Colorado. In 1968 he starred for the United States Olympic team, and then transferred to the University of Detroit, where he enjoyed an outstanding sophomore season.

Haywood wasn't happy in college, though. He didn't like college ball and near the end of the season he was suspended for punching a referee. He wanted to turn pro right away, and the ABA accommodated him. Even though his college class had not yet graduated, he was signed by the Denver Rockets as a "hardship" case for a reported $250,000. Haywood blossomed into an instant star in the ABA, leading the league in scoring and rebounding and earning a Rookie of the Year–Most Valuable Player double. With Haywood as their leader, the Rockets won the Western Division championship, but bowed in the playoff semifinals to Los Angeles, which lost, in turn, to Indiana in the finals.

The Rockets had only a brief time to enjoy Spencer Haywood, though. During the 1971 season he jumped to the NBA, signing with Seattle over the protests not only of the ABA but of other teams in the NBA. Haywood was still not eligible for the NBA draft because his college class had not yet graduated. (This is why Chamberlain had been forced to spend a year with the Globetrotters.) But Seattle owner Sam Shulman took the case to court, and won. The judge ruled the NBA could not deprive Haywood, or anyone, of a chance to play just because his class had not yet graduated. The suit was expected to

Zelmo Beaty of the Utah Stars rises to the occasion against the Colonels' Dan Issel.

Mel Daniels on the rim.

have a far-reaching effect on all sports.

The war of the leagues was escalating. NBA players threatened to jump, and some even signed contracts with the ABA. But after wringing new concessions and higher salaries from their owners, most of them stayed put in the NBA, except for a couple of standouts like Zelmo Beaty and Joe Caldwell. Like Barry, these two had to sit out their options. As salaries increased with the competition, merger talks, broken off when the ABA had filed its suit, were quietly renewed.

The ABA moved more franchises going into the 1971 season, and continued to climb off the canvas each time the NBA thought it had landed a knockout blow. The Los Angeles team moved to Utah, and New Orleans to Memphis. Miami and Dallas joined the trend to a statewide base, and Washington's franchise was shifted across the district border to Virginia. The discontented Rick Barry was sold to New York, where presumably his off-court television talents would be better rewarded. (They were.)

The ABA also did better in the signing mart. Charlie Scott, a rookie from North Carolina, helped Virginia fans forget about the departure of Barry as he led the Squires to the Eastern Division championship before eventually jumping to the NBA himself. The Colonels, led by another first-year man, Dan Issel of Kentucky, who won the scoring championship, finished second but gained the playoff finals before losing to Utah in seven games.

By season's end most owners in both leagues were convinced that merger was the only answer to the increasingly bitter and costly war for talent. The infighting for college stars was especially nasty. For several years the ABA had conducted much-publicized "secret" drafts during the college season, and there were reports that its agents were approaching collegians while they were still playing. Villanova and Western Kentucky both had to forfeit high finishes in the NCAA Tournament when it was discovered that their stars had already signed pro contracts while the college season was under way. All order seemed to have disappeared. Questions of morality and loyalty were raised.

The merger, however, was favored only by the owners and the college coaches. The NBA Players Association, much more militant than its pro football equivalent, fought bitterly. They demanded a full hearing in Congress. And when club owners said that only a merger could provide such dubious benefits to the public as interleague competition, the players blithely promoted their own All-Star game in Houston.

The ABA made major progress in the signing wars for the 1971–72 season. Artis Gilmore of Jacksonville, signed by Kentucky, was a major prize. So were three youngsters who turned pro as hardship cases with college eligibility remaining—Julius Erving, George McGinnis, and John Neumann. Gilmore scored a double by winning Rookie of the Year and MVP awards, but his Colonels were upset in the playoffs by the New York Nets, who bowed in the finals to the powerful Indiana Pacers.

Attendance in the ABA showed a marked increase, but two more franchises fell by the wayside, Florida and

In an interleague exhibition Kareem Abdul-Jabbar scores over Zelmo Beaty.

Kentucky's Artis Gilmore happily eyes his handiwork.

The deft touch of Billy Cunningham (32).

Pittsburgh. Their players were apportioned to other teams in the league, but then a new franchise was added in San Diego to bring the roster to an even ten teams for 1973. These weren't the only changes. A court ordered that Rick Barry would have to honor a previously signed future contract with the NBA Warriors, and so the New York Nets were left bereft of his services. However, what the court taketh, the court also can give: Billy Cunningham of the NBA 76ers was awarded to the ABA Carolina Cougars.

What did not change was the dominance of the Indiana Pacers, who won their second championship in a row and their third in four years. It had to be more than coincidental that the Pacers were also one of the league's most stable franchises under long-time coach Bob Leonard.

During the 1973 season Julius Erving emerged as an ABA superstar and possibly the league's biggest attraction. Erving had been signed by the Virginia Squires after his junior year at the University of Massachusetts. Although he was a legend in New York's Harlem playgrounds, few thought Dr. J was ready for stardom, but he quickly became a standout pro. By his second season he was the ABA's leading scorer and a drawing card wherever he went because of his scintillating and unbelievable moves to the basket.

Stardom breeds desire, however, and as the season ended, NBA teams were casting jealous eyes at Dr. J. Acting to forestall a costly loss to the league, the Squires traded Erving to the New York Nets, who badly needed a star to replace the departed Barry. Happy to be back home, Erving

Julius Irving shows his "flying dunk."

talked no more of jumping leagues.

Then, with one of its best players in its biggest city, the ABA moved to aid its weakest franchise: league members chipped in to pay the $1.8 million salary that would bring Wilt Chamberlain to San Diego from the Lakers as part owner, coach, and player for the Conquistadors. Chamberlain had helped make the NBA. Perhaps he could do the same for this new league, which, as it entered its seventh season, had certainly proved it had more than a funny-colored basketball.

15

THE GLORY OF THE GAME

ONCE THE YMCAs relinquished supervision of the new sport of basketball to the Amateur Athletic Union, the AAU moved directly into the tournament business. The handoff of authority came in 1896, and the AAU instituted its first national tournament. That inaugural competition was held in New York under the auspices of the AAU's Metropolitan Association. The first winner was the 23rd Street YMCA, a team that subsequently won fame as the New York Wanderers.

No tournament was held in 1897, but competition was resumed the following year with the New York Knickerbocker YMCA emerging as champion in a round-robin playoff. When these original "New York Knicks" repeated as champions in 1899, the Spalding *Guide* related, "In contrast to the national championship last year, the team showed a decidedly sportsmanlike spirit and no men were

disqualified." Although the competing teams had paid a five-dollar entry fee, the AAU disclosed it lost $119 on the tournament. The organization felt this proved they were "not in it to make money, but desire to foster the game."

Fortunately for its treasury the AAU found a sponsor for its 1901 tournament, which was held in the Chicago Coliseum as part of the First Annual Exposition of the International Forest, Fish and Game Association. Eight teams competed, including the Universities of Minnesota and Nebraska, but the popular favorites were the Silent Five of New York, a deaf-mute team. The Ravenswood YMCA of Chicago won the tournament, but only after a disputed finish that saw two contenders disqualified because they refused to play after the schedule for the final games had been changed at the last minute.

The Buffalo Germans, winners of the Pan-American competition in 1902. (*Left to right, rear*) Maier, Burkhardt; (*middle*) Faust, Heerdt, Miller; (*front*) Redlein, Rohde.

Another big tournament was held later in that same year in conjunction with the Pan American Exposition in Buffalo. That competition was won easily by the Buffalo Germans. For one game, only three members of the Germans team were on hand for the opening tip-off, but play was started anyway. After about five minutes had elapsed a fourth German player showed up, stripping to his uniform as he ran toward the court. A few minutes later the fifth arrived, "divesting himself as he ran, first coat, then cuffs, then collar and necktie and strewing them all along the field." Despite this personnel problem the Germans managed to stall through a scoreless first half and then won in a rout after the intermission.

For the next two years there was no AAU tournament, but in 1904 competition was renewed as an adjunct of the Olympic Games in St. Louis. Again the Germans emerged victorious.

Between 1904 and 1913 only one formal AAU championship was held, but in between there were several match games and series in which the victor claimed the national amateur title. In 1905 the Germans were de-

throned by the Kansas City Athletic Club Blue Diamonds, a club team organized by a brash young man named Phog Allen. But the next year the Diamonds were beaten by Ed Wachter's team, then representing Company E of Schenectady, New York. The Wachter aggregation was subsequently declared professional, a problem that plagued the AAU for many years. (As far back as 1901 the Pastime AC of New York had been disqualified from second place in the Metropolitan Basketball Championship for using a professional. The following season one team was reprimanded for using a professional boxer under an assumed name.)

The first college team to win the AAU championship was the University of Utah in 1916. In 1920 NYU beat Rutgers in the first all-college final. As the colleges developed their own tournaments in the 1930s, the AAU became more an outlet for company-sponsored teams. The most successful of these was the Phillips 66ers, led for many years by seven-foot Bob Kurland. The Peoria Cats and Akron Goodyears were also numbered among the AAU powers and for a while in the late 1940s these teams competed in a formal National Industrial Basketball League. Until the NBA became established these industrial teams competed with the pros for talent, and especially in the Far West AAU ball was a major outlet for basketball players once they had completed their college eligibility. However, with the growth of the pros and the loss of college teams for their entry lists, the AAU Tournament has dwindled in importance.

The AAU, of course, also has a women's branch and a distaff national tournament has been a fixture since 1926. Girls' rules specify six players on a side and include other modifications. The greatest female basketball player of all time was Mildred (Babe) Didrickson, who scored 106 points in five games in leading the Golden Cyclones of Dallas, Texas, to the 1931 championship. (The Babe also starred in track and field and as a professional golfer. She was easily the outstanding woman athlete of all time.) Nashville (Tennessee) Business College has dominated women's basketball in recent years.

While AAU competition was thriving in the twenties the nation's college coaches began to mount a campaign to achieve international recognition for their sport as part of the Olympic Games. In 1928 Phog Allen—who could have been a better choice?—was named chairman of a committee on Olympic basketball by his fellow coaches and he immediately dispatched to Amsterdam where the games were being held that year. Allen's goal was to talk up the American sport and have it included on a demonstration basis when the Olympics next were held in Los Angeles in 1932.

Allen did well among the representatives of other nations, but his own countrymen sabotaged him. The local California committee ordered that an All-Star football game be placed on the schedule as the host country's choice for a demonstration sport. The reasons, Allen charged, were purely economic. A football game, despite its minimal international interest (especially when compared to basketball) figured to draw more

AAU competition was outstanding. Here Bob Kurland, who chose not to play professional ball, shows his form with the Phillips 66ers.

spectators in southern California.

Allen, however, was neither idle nor silent. He continued to buttonhole Olympic officials from other countries, and a Japanese committeeman promised that his nation would include basketball as a demonstration sport when the games were held in his nation eight years hence. The Germans, however, beat them to it. The 1936 Games were scheduled for Berlin and the host country included basketball on the official Olympic program. (This could have been because the Nazi regime was anxious for American support in its campaign to keep from being disqualified as host nation because of Hitler's repressive policies.)

Surprisingly, a representative total of twenty-two nations signed up to enter the 1936 Olympic basketball competition, although the Spanish team had to withdraw at the last minute. (The Spaniards were called home because of the outbreak of civil war in their nation.)

As the Olympic games approached, the National Association of Basketball Coaches realized how much it would mean to Dr. Naismith if he could be present for this international recognition of the game he had invented. The coaches thought it would be a nice gesture to send Dr. and Mrs. Naismith to Berlin as their guests. At their annual meeting, while ways of raising the necessary money were being discussed, Adolph Rupp was assigned to take his old teacher out of the room. Naismith, of course, knew nothing of what was going on and wondered why his usually serious former pupil kept prattling on and on for over an hour in the hotel lobby. The coaches were not debating wheth-

er to send the Naismiths, but how to raise the money, since as usual their treasury was bare. Finally they found a way, and the flustered Rupp was allowed to bring Dr. Naismith back into the room.

The opening game of Olympic basketball competition was between Japan and China, where American soldiers had introduced the sport during the Boxer Rebellion. Dr. Naismith threw up the first ball on this historic occasion. Despite the sport's international acceptance, Western Hemisphere teams dominated the competition. Mexico won the bronze medal for third place, and competition for the first-place gold ended up between Canada and the United States. The American team was made up mostly of players from the Universal Pictures and Globe Refining AAU teams selected in tryout competition. The games were staged on an outdoor court with a surface of brick dust on a hard-clay base. It wasn't a bad court, unless it rained, which it did the day of the finals. The typically rigid Germans refused to postpone the finals, so the Americans, who had had to contend throughout the tournament with a variety of different-sized official basketballs and inept international referees, had another problem, a quagmire of a court under an inch of water. One American player started to dribble down court on a fast break and the ball simply stuck in the mud. The Canadians took a 3–0 lead, but then the United States team rallied to win the championship, 19–8.

World War II intervened before the next Olympic games could be held, and competition was not resumed until 1948 in London with twenty-three teams in the field. The

American squad was a powerhouse, made up mostly of players from the Phillips 66ers and the University of Kentucky's Fabulous Five. Competition was rough, but the United States swept through the field with only one close call, a two-point victory over Argentina. In the finals the Yanks overwhelmed France, 65–21. Predictably, the stars of the American triumph were the giants, Alex Groza of Kentucky with seventy-six points in eight games, and Bob Kurland of the 66ers with sixty-five.

The 1952 games in Helsinki opened with a political storm. The Nationalist Chinese team withdrew from basketball competition because an entry from Red China had been accepted, but then the Communist Chinese arrived too late to compete. The big news, however, was the first appearance of the Russians in modern Olympic competition. The Russians had held off until they could field competitive teams in all sports, and basketball was no exception as they made it to the finals against another strong American team. The United States entry was stocked with players mostly from the Peoria Cats and the University of Kansas, and the Russians started out using an old capitalist technique of holding the ball against their more powerful opponents. After ten minutes the Americans led by only 4–3, but then they opened up for a 36–25 triumph. Clyde Lovellette led the United States with nine points, and Bob Kurland, by now a veteran of international competition, had eight.

Again American giants had proved the difference. But for the 1956 games in Melbourne, the Russians thought they had solved that problem when they produced a giant

of their own, seven-foot-two Ivan Krouminch. However, Krouminch, a mastodon who weighed 340 pounds, proved no match for the Americans. Slaughtering all opposition in eight straight games, the United States twice beat the Russians, 85–55 in the preliminary round and 89–55 in the finals. Krouminch, guarded by American star Bill Russell, did not score a field goal in the championship game. (Better men than he would know the same frustration in the NBA.) Russell was also high scorer with 113 points in the tournament.

The Russians didn't even make the finals in the 1960 Games in Rome. A superior American team led by Jerry Lucas, Oscar Robertson and Jerry West whipped them, 81–57, in a preliminary round and then went on to rout Brazil in the finals, 90–63. Four years later Bill Bradley of Princeton was the floor leader as the

U.S.A. Olympic basketball teams were often star-laden. Oscar Robertson and Jerry West wear the gold medals at the 1960 awards ceremony.

United States swept the field in Tokyo, winding up with another 73–59 triumph over the Russians.

Thus far the United States had never lost a single basketball game in Olympic competition, but the odds looked bad for a continuation of that streak as a call went out for candidates to try out for the 1968 Games in Mexico City. This was a time of social and racial unrest in the United States, much of it centered on the nation's college campuses. Black athletes threatened to boycott the Games entirely. Although a full-fledged black boycott of the Games never developed, many of the best black basketball players declined to try out for the team. Some claimed conscience, others claimed school work, many just went ahead and signed their professional contracts. Stars like Lew Alcindor, Elvin Hayes, and Wes Unseld were not available when Hank Iba, the defensive genius from Oklahoma State, started to put his team together.

Few big-name seniors were in the group Iba finally chose to weld into the highly disciplined unit that has always been his trademark. But Iba turned the absence of these stars into an asset. He kept reminding his players how the American people, and the world, were expecting them to be humiliated in Mexico City. He counted on the players' pride to make up for any physical limitations.

The American team opened with easy victories over Spain, Senegal, and the Philippines, but these proved nothing. The opposition was among the weakest in the tournament. However, when the Americans routed Yugoslavia, 73–58, in the fourth game, some of the doubters began to change their opinion of this so-called ragamuffin

For the 1968 Olympics the situation had changed, but the American "unknowns" still had the ability to win. Spencer Haywood, a college sophomore, dunks a shot.

United States team. Yugoslavia had been one of the pretournament favorites.

In their next game the Americans routed Senegal once again, and then were given their toughest test of the tournament by a stubborn Puerto Rican five. The Americans had to go all out to achieve a five-point victory in the last game of the opening round.

The semifinals confirmed that the United States victory over Yugoslavia had been an impressive achievement. While the Americans were routing Brazil, 74–63, Yugoslavia scored the tournament's outstanding upset by eliminating Russia, 63–62. Yugoslavia had been preparing for this moment since the previous Olympic Games. Every year since then Yugoslavia and Russia had engaged in a basketball game. Each time they met, the Yugoslav coach had withheld three of his best players from the game. Each time the Russians won easily. When the two teams finally met again in the Olympics the Russians were overconfident while the Yugoslavs were lying in wait, this time with all of their best players suited up.

Yugoslavia's victory set up a rematch with the United States in the finals for the gold medal. The Americans led by only 32–29 at the half, but then they came out with a full-court press and blew the Yugoslavs out of contention by running off seventeen straight points. Iba cleared his bench near the end, and the final score of 65–50 did not indicate the wide difference between the two teams.

Star of the United States team was the heretofore unsung Spencer Haywood of Trinidad Junior College with 145 points in nine games. JoJo White of Kansas scored 105 points and led the devastating Iba press. Other American standouts were burly Mike Silliman, an army officer who had played at West Point, and lithe Charlie Scott of the University of North Carolina. The sweep gave the United States a record of fifty-six victories without a loss in Olympic competition, but this game was truly American basketball's finest moment.

As the American team returned in glory, words of warning were posted by observers of international basketball. The foreign entries, they reported, were getting stronger, playing with greater savvy. If the United States was to continue its basketball dominance, it must pursue the sport internationally with greater dedication. Otherwise it was only a matter of time before the proud Olympic record would be shattered.

Instead, as the years went on, international basketball became less and less important in the States. More and more top stars declined to participate. In 1971 the United States fell to Cuba, of all teams, in the semifinals of the Pan-American games.

Again some of the leading American players declined to participate when it came time to choose a team for the 1972 Olympics to be held in Munich in the fall. The seniors were rushing to sign lucrative pro contracts as the ABA and NBA continued their bidding war, and there were no Bill Russells to tell the pros to wait awhile. Other top collegians wanted out for a variety of reasons: Bill Walton, for example, cited the need to rest his ailing knees. The American team that was finally put together in June averaged less than twenty-one years in age, and there was definitely a generation gap between these youngsters, brought up on run-and-shoot basketball, and their aging coach, Hank (Ball Control) Iba.

The Americans won their first three games with ease, capped by a 67–48 revenge victory over Cuba. But then in two of their last four preliminary games there were signs of trouble. The Americans trailed Brazil, the '71 Pan Am champion, by seven points with just under eleven minutes to play before rallying for a 61–54 victory, and they found themselves tied with a weak Spanish quintet with nine minutes left before pulling away, 72–56. Still, the Americans finished their preliminary play with a 7–0 record. Competing in a different group, the veteran Russian squad was also undefeated.

That set up another U.S.-Russia showdown in the finals, and the Americans trailed from the beginning. Twice, once in each half, the Russians led by as many as ten points, and with fifty-five seconds left the young Americans still trailed by 49–46. At this point Jim Forbes hit a jump shot to cut the gap to one. Then Doug Collins stole the ball, was fouled while driving for a lay-up, and crashed into the backboard supports. Although dazed from the impact, Collins hit both free throws to give the United States a 50–49 lead. The Munich arena was a bedlam.

As the Russians put the ball back in play, they managed to call time out with only one second showing on the clock. Then they protested that the clock was wrong, and somehow were able to persuade the timekeeper to set it back to three seconds. Again they put the ball in play, but their wild last shot failed. The Americans rushed onto the floor in glee, only to have their celebration abruptly halted. The referee ruled that the ball had not been properly put in play and that the Russians would be given another chance, with three seconds still to play.

The floor was cleared and again the Russians put the ball in play. The court-long pass went to six-foot-eight Aleksander Belov, double-teamed by Kevin Joyce and Forbes. But still the Russian got his shot off. The short jumper banked off the backboard and through the net as the horn sounded. As the Americans stood in shocked disbelief, the Russians wept with joy over their 51–50 gold-medal victory.

"I cannot fathom anything so incomprehensible," Iba rasped afterward as he vainly protested the Russian victory. "I've never seen anything like this in my entire life. The Russians were given three chances to win."

The United States Olympic delegation continued to protest the Russian victory in vain, and the American team ended up boycotting the presentation of medals. But even this

gesture—and the fact that an American team decisively beat the touring Russian Nationals later that year in the United States—did not obscure the fact that the losers had played badly throughout most of the final game. "We kept waiting for them to crack and they didn't," Iba said of the victorious Russians. Many observers agreed that if the U.S. team really had been that superior, it would not have placed itself in the position to be beaten by a last-second shot.

If the Olympics are the crown of amateur basketball, the roots are to be found in the nation's high schools where youngsters are steered not only toward stardom but also, hopefully, on the right road in life. The first high schools to take up basketball were Central High in Philadelphia and Holyoke (Massachusetts) High School. By 1897 Holyoke was playing a full schedule, and in 1900 the Massachusetts school defeated a field of eleven other teams in Boston to win the first recorded high school tournament. Holyoke eventually won eighty-two games in a row before being defeated by a team of sophomores from Dartmouth College. (In those days it was not unusual for high schools and colleges to play each other, and there were no age limits for high school competition as there are today.)

By 1903 the Public School Athletic League was holding its first tournament in New York City, and the next year, as part of the St. Louis Exposition, a national tournament was held with teams from New York, Chicago, San Francisco, and St. Louis. Flushing High of New York won. There were, of course, the usual eligibility problems. In 1903 the Spalding *Guide* indignantly reported that a manager had entered a team of ringers in one tournament for high school teams. When they were discovered, after winning the tournament, they had to forfeit their title and four players were asked to return their prizes. The manager kept the championship banner, however, and one player refused to surrender his medal. All involved were "suspended indefinitely," but from what it was hard to say.

Americans also carried the sport to schools abroad—the report of a 1903 intradepartment game at the Syrian Protestant school in Beirut is fascinating. The game, seven on a side, was played outdoors before 1,500 spectators, and for the second straight year the Preparatory Department beat the Collegiate Department, 2–0. According to a contemporary account, "Then ensued a scene of wild confusion. Captain and men were borne aloft and marched around to the triumphant shout of . . . 'Prep! Prep! Prep-a-rep! . . . Prep! a-re-a tory . . . Prep-pa-Prep-a-ra . . . Preparatory!' "

One of the few teams to surpass Holyoke's great record was coached by Professor Ernest A. Blood at Passaic (New Jersey) High School. Professor Blood was eventually elected to the basketball Hall of Fame on the basis of a lifetime coaching record of 1,296 victories against only 165 losses at various high schools. He enjoyed his greatest success at Passaic, where he developed a farm system among the city's twelve grammar schools so that players could start learning his system at an early age.

Called the Wonder Five, Passaic High put together a winning streak of 159 games over six seasons. The streak started with a 44–11 victory over Newark Junior College in December, 1919, and ended—the season after Professor Blood resigned—in February, 1925, with a 39–35 loss to nearby Hackensack. Star of the 1921 team, which won thirty-one straight, was Johnny Roosma, who went on to an outstanding career at West Point. Personnel on the team shifted, of course, and Blood considered his 1922 edition the best. This team had a 33–0 record and won eight games by a hundred or more points. Four of these came consecutively in an eleven-day period, including a 145–5 victory over Williams Prep of Stamford, Connecticut, in which the losers were outscored 80–0 in the second half. Bobby Thompson, scoring star of the 1922 Passaic team, tallied the unheard-of total of 1,000 points that season, including sixty-nine in the romp over Williams Prep.

The most one-sided high school game ever reported, though, was chalked up the following season when Kansas High of Kansas City beat an outfit called the Rainbows, 234–2. Although the caliber of opposition furnished by the Rainbows may be suspect, Kansas High didn't need any pushovers to fatten its record. Unbeaten in thirty-four games, Kansas High outscored its opposition 1,746 points to 615 en route to the national championship.

In those days an authentic national high school champion could be crowned, because in 1917 Amos Alonzo Stagg had persuaded the University of Chicago to sponsor such a competition. In 1923, the year of Kansas High's victory, forty schools representing thirty-one states were in the field.

PASSAIC HIGH SCHOOL TEAMS

1919–20
Bottom (*left to right*): Coach E. Blood, Karl Helfrick, A. Marks, A. D. Arnold. Center: William Kerr, Herbert Rumsey, John Roosma, Charles Lent, Milton Schneider, DeWitt Kealser, Leon Smith. Top: Paul Blood, Winfred Knothe, Raymond Gale, Harold Swenson.

1920–21
Bottom (*left to right*): DeWitt Keasler, Abe Rosman, John Grabies, Harold Swenson, Robert Saxer. Center: manager Edward Sullivan. Top: A. D. Arnold, Robert Thompson, Ira Vonk, John Roosma, Winifred Knothe, Paul Blood, Coach E. Blood, Zep the Bear.

1921–22
Bottom (*left to right*): Abe Rosman, Robert Thompson, Ira Vonk, Coach E. Blood and Zep the Bear, Paul Blood, Winifred Knothe. Center: Ralph Prescott, Robert Saxer, Michael Hamas, Henry Janowski, Chester Jermalowitz, Sam Blitzer, Charles Humphrey, Elmore Taylor, A. D. Arnold. Top: William Troast, Walter Margetts, Blase Zilenski, Edward Lucasko, Howard Soule, Allen Smith, John Freeswick.

1922–23

Bottom (*left to right*): Moyer Krakovitch, Michael Hamas, Fred Mersalis, DeWitt Keasler, Winifred Knothe. Center: Milton Pashman, John Pomorski, John Vanderheide, Harry Herman, Sam Blitzer. Top: A. A. Marks, Royald Drew, Coach E. Blood.

1923–24

Bottom (*left to right*): Coach E. Blood, Irving Berg, Moyer Krakovitch, Sam Blitzer, Milton Pashman, Edward Hanson, A. D. Arnold. Top: A. A. Marks, Al Gee, Phil Riskin, Stanley Adams, Nelson Rohrback, Albert Waczko, John Freeswick, Maurice Cantor, Robert Russell, Joe Gardner.

1924–25

Bottom (*left to right*): Phil Riskin, Robert Russell, John Harwood, John Pomorski, H. Rebele. Center: Moyer Krakovitch, Nelson Rohrback, Milton Pashman, Stanley Adams, S. Goldstein. Top: Ray Pickett, Richard Wall, A. D. Arnold, A. A. Marks, Steve Sattan, Irving Berg.

The first champion, in 1917, came from Evanston, Illinois, a Chicago suburb, winning out in a field of twenty-three schools representing eight states. After a lapse of two seasons because of World War I, the tournament was resumed and ran through 1930.

Probably the most colorful team to compete in Stagg's tournament was not a winner. In 1928 little Carr Creek High of Kentucky had startled everyone in that basketball hotbed by going all the way to the finals of the state tournament. Carr Creek had no post office and a population of 140. The high school enrollment was only fifteen pupils and eight of them, all related, were on the basketball team. Most games were played outdoors and the boys never had real uniforms until they went to the state tournament.

Carr Creek's opponent in the state finals was undefeated Ashland High, and the game went through four overtimes before highly favored Ashland finally won, 13–11. The victory earned Ashland an automatic bid to the national tournament in Chicago, but Carr Creek was invited along, too. Chicago fans had read about the colorful Kentuckians and took the Carr Creek lads to heart, cheering them to victories over three straight state champions. Carr Creek finally fell to Vienna, Georgia, in the quarterfinals, but Ashland salvaged the State of Kentucky's honor by edging the Georgians in the next round, 20–19. In the finals Ashland beat Canton, Illinois, 15–10, for the national title with a perfect 43–0 record.

Another tiny school, this one representing Athens, Texas, won the last two Chicago tournaments in 1929 and 1930, traveling up North in cars both years and stopping off en route to play other games. There is no Athens High today since the school building burned down some years ago and was never replaced, the students being transferred to a consolidated school. There is no more national tournament, either.

The tournament was finally killed by a combination of the newly formed National Federation of State High School Athletic Associations and the new president of the University of Chicago, Dr. Robert M. Hutchins. The Federation, formed in 1931, opposed national tournaments since many had become commercialized because of competition among sponsors. Although a rule banning such competition was not put into effect until 1934, Dr. Hutchins, an outspoken critic of overemphasis on sports, prevailed on Stagg to end his tournament after the 1930 renewal.

This does not mean that high school basketball is any less important than it was then, however. The opposite is true. Basketball remains the number one high school sports activity, the only differences being that competition is much more structured and there are few teams playing any more of those forty-three-game schedules and barnstorming the length of the land. High school powerhouses still exist, though, especially in large metropolitan areas where games involving such schools as Boys High in Brooklyn, DeMatha in Washington, and DeWitt Clinton in the Bronx still draw their share of college scouts. The same goes for basketball-happy areas that have state tournaments, like Indiana, Kentucky, and Illinois. The high school basketball court still opens the way for thousands of youngsters to a fuller life, and, for the lucky few, a college education, professional riches, and perhaps Olympic glory.

Over the years basketball has always been the sport of the inner city, and this has become even more true in recent times. For many in the ghetto, basketball provides the only way out. Some twenty years ago a man in Harlem named Holcombe Rucker realized this. Rucker worked for the Department of Parks as a recreation supervisor, and in the early 1950s he got the idea of forming a city-wide summer basketball league that would play its games in a local playground. Competition was held on all levels: grammar school, high school, college, and pro, and there also was a league for girls. Some days Rucker would referee as many as six games by himself.

The object, of course, was to keep the younger kids out of trouble during the long summer months, and by bringing in the pros Rucker gave these youngsters living and visible sports heroes to whom they could relate. The subliminal message was stay in school in order to be able to play college ball and then go on to the pros. (Rucker had never gone to college, but he realized the need for a degree to further his work, and so he got one through an arduous course in night school. A program of tutoring that he

subsequently set up is credited by many with being the foundation of some of the various antipoverty programs like the HARYOU-Act.)

The summer-league play was capped by an interborough tournament, which eventually outgrew the small playground. In 1965 Holcombe Rucker died of cancer at age thirty-eight, and the Rucker League is his monument. Eventually the league was split, with the new Harlem Professional League branching off. This league, as its name implies, is strictly for pros, but it helps fulfill one of Rucker's goals by keeping these professionals highly visible in the ghettos. Similar summer pro leagues now operate in places like Philadelphia, Los Angeles, Chicago, and Louisville.

But Rucker's dream of organized summer competition for youngsters also is spreading. It continues in New York, and Rucker's disciples have helped set up similar competition in cities like Philadelphia, Baltimore, Washington, and Los Angeles. In Philadelphia it's called the Bill Berry League, after a former black baseball contemporary of Satchel Paige and Josh Gibson, whose summertime team, named the Philadelphia Colts, sent young men like Wilt Chamberlain and Guy Rodgers on to college and the pros.

When the honor roll of basketball is written, names like Rucker and Berry must be included, too. These men may be closer in spirit to Dr. Naismith than many of the glamour coaches with their fancy records and national titles.

16

HALL OF FAME

ACCORDING TO THE TESTIMONY of close friends and relations, Dr. Naismith enjoyed no expensive vices, so it is not surprising that he and his wife returned from their junket to the 1936 Olympic Games in Berlin with money left over from the sum subscribed by the coach's association. Typically the good doctor provided an accounting and refused to keep the surplus. Instead he offered it to the coaches with the suggestion that perhaps they might want to use it "to start a Hall of Fame."

The coaches agreed that this was a grand idea, and they began the groundwork, in a very tentative way, until Dr. Naismith's death in 1939 inspired a formal resolution calling for a basketball Hall of Fame to be constructed on the campus of Springfield College.

In 1941, the fiftieth anniversary of the invention of basketball, Springfield College started an intensive campaign to raise funds for the basketball shrine, but all activity was halted with the attack on Pearl Harbor and American entrance into World War II. It wasn't until 1948 that the project was revived under the direction of Ed Hickox, a former Springfield coach and friend of Dr. Naismith's, who served as unpaid executive director of the foundation. But it took eleven more years before enough money was raised to even break ground. Two years later a cornerstone was laid, but then the project was once again allowed to languish.

In 1966, however, Lee Williams, dynamic former basketball coach at Colby College, took over as executive director, and the Basketball Hall of

The Honors Court in the National Basketball Hall of Fame.

Fame finally got off its foundation. In only one year Williams raised enough money so that construction could begin, and on February 18, 1968, the Naismith Memorial Basketball Hall of Fame was opened to the public.

The red brick building cost $650,-000. The feature, of course, is the Honors Court, a cathedral-like room in which portraits and deeds of the enshrinees are displayed on replicas of stained glass windows. The second floor includes a library, and downstairs there is a meeting and film room. The rest of the structure is crammed with basketball memorabilia (the main hall on the ground floor being a reproduction of the Armory Hill YMCA gym in which the first game was played, complete with peach basket and a running track on the balcony above).

The first class of enshrinees was named in March, 1959, by the thirteen-member Honors Committee. Then, as now, ten votes were necessary for election. The format provides that candidates may be honored for their roles as players, coaches, referees, or contributors to the growth of basketball. Great teams may also be inducted as a unit. Unlike many sports shrines, the basketball hall does not distinguish between amateurs and professionals. It is dedicated, simply, to basketball.

The charter inductees were Dr. Naismith, of course; Phog Allen, Ralph Morgan, and Oswald Tower as contributors; John Schommer, a four-time All-America from Chicago, as a player; and Naismith's original basketball team at Springfield, not only for first playing the game, but also for popularizing it through a series of exhibitions. Morgan, of Penn, had founded the intercollegiate rules committee and had helped organize the collegiate Eastern League. Tower was a longtime editor of the *Basketball Guide* and an important member of the rules committee.

The following September, coinciding with the ground breaking, eleven more candidates were enshrined in the Hall of Fame. Those selected as contributors were Dr. Naismith's mentor, Dr. Luther Gulick, Ed Hickox, Amos Alonzo Stagg, and Harold Olsen, a former coach at Ohio State and an influential member of the rules committee. Two others were selected strictly for achievements in coaching, Dr. Henry Carlson of Pitt and English-born Walter Meanwell, producer of eleven conference champions at Wisconsin and Missouri and developer of basketball equipment. The first players selected after Schommer were Chuck Hyatt of Pitt, who later starred in AAU competition; Hank Luisetti of Stanford, popularizer of the one-handed shot; and George Mikan, the giant from DePaul who helped change the face of both college and pro basketball. The second team to be honored was the Original Celtics, and the Honors Court also saw fit to select a referee, colorful Pat Kennedy. Each year the Honors Court meets, and each year new names are added to those of the great figures who are already enshrined.

Included in the exhibits at the Hall of Fame are the thirteen original rules for basketball as typed by Miss Lyons on the day Mr. Stebbins was sent searching for boxes or baskets that would serve as goals. They were the beginning.

BIBLIOGRAPHY

Books that proved the greatest assistance in this history were:

HOLLANDER, ZANDER, ed., *Modern Encyclopedia of Basketball* (rev. ed.). New York: Four Winds Press, 1973.

KOPPETT, LEONARD, *Twenty-four Seconds to Shoot*. New York: Macmillan, 1968.

MOKRAY, BILL, ed., *Ronald Encyclopedia of Basketball*. New York: Ronald Press, 1963.

NAISMITH, JAMES, *Basketball: Its Origin and Development*. New York: Association Press, 1941.

WEYAND, ALEXANDER, M., *The Cavalcade of Basketball*. New York: Macmillan, 1960.

Other sources included:

ALLEN, FORREST, C. (PHOG), *Basketball* (rev. ed.). New York: Sterling, 1968.

———, *My Basketball Bible* (7th ed.). Kansas City, Mo.: Smith Grieves Co., 1928.

COUSY, BOB, AND AL HIRSHBERG, *Basketball Is My Life*. Englewood Cliffs, N.J.: Prentice-Hall, 1958.

HIRSHBERG, AL, *Basketball's Greatest Stars*. New York: Putnam, 1963.

———, *Basketball's Greatest Teams*. New York: Putnam, 1966.

HOBSON, HOWARD A. *Scientific Basketball*. Englewood Cliffs, N.J.: Prentice-Hall, 1950.

HOLLANDER, ZANDER, *Basketball's Greatest Games*. Englewood Cliffs, N.J.: Prentice-Hall, 1970.

HOLMAN, NAT, *Holman on Basketball*. New York: Crown, 1950.

JULIAN, ALVIN (DOGGIE), *Bread and Butter Basketball*. Englewood Cliffs, N.J.: Prentice-Hall, 1960.

KOPPETT, LEONARD, *Championship NBA*. New York: Dial, 1970.

LAPCHICK, JOE, AND CLAIR BEE, *Fifty Years of Basketball*. Englewood Cliffs, N.J.: Prentice-Hall, 1968.

MIKAN, GEORGE, *Mr. Basketball*. New York: Greenberg, 1951.

NAISMITH, JAMES, *Basketball* (pamphlet). Springfield, Mass., 1892.

PADWE, SANDY, *Basketball's Hall of Fame*. Englewood Cliffs, N.J.: Prentice-Hall, 1970.

PEPE, PHIL, *Greatest Stars of the NBA*. Englewood Cliffs, N.J.: Prentice-Hall, 1970.

RUPP, ADOLPH, *Rupp's Championship Basketball* (2nd ed.). Englewood Cliffs, N.J.: Prentice-Hall, 1957.

STAGG, AMOS ALONZO, *Touchdown*. New York: Longmans, 1927.

SULLIVAN, GEORGE, *Wilt Chamberlain*. New York: Grosset, 1966.

WALTON, LUKE, *Basketball's Fabulous Five*. New York: Greenberg, 1950.

WOLF, DAVE, *Foul: The Connie Hawkins Story*. New York: Holt, Rinehart, 1971.

Periodical sources consulted included *Kansas Historical Quarterly, Psychological Review, American Physical Education Review,* various YMCA bulletins, Spalding guides, Converse yearbooks, college press brochures, the NCAA College Basketball All-Time Record Book, sports magazines, and Madison Square Garden's basketball scrapbooks.

INDEX

Numbers in italic refer to illustrative material.